Cyclone: My Story

Cyclone: My Story

Barry McGuigan

2 4 6 8 10 9 7 5 3

Published in 2011 by Virgin Books, an imprint of Ebury Publishing

A Random House Group Company

© Barry McGuigan 2011

Barry McGuigan has asserted his right under the Copyright, Designs and Patents Act 1988 to be identified as the author of this work.

The Random House Group Limited Reg. No. 954009

Addresses for companies within The Random House Group can be found at: www.randomhouse.co.uk

A CIP catalogue record for this book is available from the British Library

The Random House Group Limited supports The Forest Stewardship Council® (FSC®), the leading international forest certification organisation. All our titles that are printed on Greenpeace approved FSC® certified paper carry the FSC® logo. Our paper procurement policy can be found at www.randomhouse.co.uk/environment

Typeset by SX Composing DTP, Rayleigh, Essex
Printed in the UK by Clays Ltd, St Ives plc

Hardback ISBN 9780 7535 3994 1
Trade paperback ISBN 9780 7535 3995 8

This book is dedicated to Sandy for a lifetime of love and commitment, and to the memory of my father and my brother, who I miss every day.

Contents

Prologue

8 June 1985

I had never set foot in Loftus Road before the Pedroza fight. In fact, I never went back until 2005 when I was filming a programme for Sky Sports, to commemorate the twentieth anniversary of my winning the world title. I didn't recognise anything as we were driving in, until we got to the entrance and I saw this flash of blue on the outside of the building. Then it all came back to me. Suddenly I could remember it all as though it was yesterday: pulling up, walking straight through and down to where the dressing rooms were. I was in the home dressing room that night, Pedroza the away.

The fight was a 27,000-seat sell-out. By the time we got to Loftus Road that evening, driving from my central London hotel in the Team McGuigan bus, most of the fans were already inside. Earlier in the day, we'd used the bus as a decoy, driving to the weigh-in in a separate car to avoid the crush of fans. That evening, with fight time approaching, the streets were quieter, though I still recall seeing a fair few supporters milling about and making their way to the stadium. What I really remember about arriving was the noise: you could hear this buzz from inside the ground and that really pumped me up. As we waited in the dressing room it built and built and got louder and louder. Because the fight was on television, everyone knew exactly what time I would be coming out. The closer it got to my entrance time, the more the expectation and the atmosphere grew.

While all that was going on, Pedroza's people were still trying to pull their tricks. We'd sent my brother Dermot into Pedroza's dressing room to watch him bandage up, and Pedroza's manager, Santiago Del Rio, came in to watch me. Dermot didn't tell me until afterwards, but Pedroza played it cool in front of him. He looked huge, Dermot told me later: big muscular arms and completely relaxed. He was chatting away in Spanish and looking at my brother and smiling, confident as you like. Dermot watched the bandages being wrapped and told them that they were fine.

Del Rio came in to watch my hands being bandaged, and he was determined to do what he could to wind me up. What you do with the hands is you wrap your surgical bandage back and forth over your knuckles to build a pad. The knuckles are the first point of impact: it's where the energy and trauma are absorbed, and therefore you try to protect them by creating a pad with the bandage. Del Rio was watching all this carefully, same as we'd always done them, and said, 'What is this? Let me see that.' So we showed him and he shook his head: 'Too much, too much.' We took it all off and had to start again. He was still complaining and I lost it: I swore at him and said, 'For fuck's sake.' Del Rio looked at me and said, 'Mmm . . . OK, OK, right.' He left because he had achieved what he'd come to do: to get me going. Del Rio had succeeded in that, and didn't even stay to watch us do the other hand.

I was annoyed, really annoyed, but I'm not sure that his plan really worked. The incident just served to pump me up even more. Not that I needed it, I was already on a high, but after that I was really psyched. I gloved up and the noise outside was rising to a crescendo. All you could hear was this thump-thump-thump because the dressing room was right underneath the stand. Every time the door opened, this wave of sound from outside came crashing in.

I can't remember whether it was the floor manager or the fellow from the Boxing Board of Control, but someone with a set of headphones on came in and said, 'Right, let's go.' The idea was that because I was the challenger, I would be brought out first. We had the *Rocky* theme playing over the PA. Everyone has their music now but I swear, honest to God, that we were the first to do that. The noise was so loud, so deafening, however, that you could hardly hear the music above the crowd.

We came out and were supposed to turn left and walk along the side of the football pitch by these metal barriers. The idea was that we would walk across, thirty metres up and then turn and walk diagonally towards the ring. But they had no idea what my crowd were like: we were immediately submerged and the fans just poured in around me. Pandemonium. This was less than a fortnight after the Heysel football disaster, in which thirty-nine fans had been crushed to death at the European Cup Final between Liverpool and Juventus. All the police and security were aware of that, and were on edge about things getting out of control.

I was there in the middle of it, trying hard to keep my cool. The police were all a bit taken aback. We were saying to the fans and to the police, come on, guys. The last thing we wanted was anyone getting hurt or annoyed, anything getting out of hand. Then someone out front took the decision that rather than going on our original route, we weren't going to go left because there were all these people, thousands of them, standing in the way. There was no way we were going to move them all back without causing a scene. So we just got the barrier lifted up and out, and went straight for the ring. We had to move around some seats, saying

3

'Excuse me, excuse me' to people, and walked to the ring like that. All in all, it took us twelve minutes to get from the dressing room to the ring. It was so slow and took so long that the American TV station broadcasting the fight had to keep going to commercial breaks.

I could see how large the stadium was, and how big the crowd was too. Everyone was getting excited, they were all up and cheering, but I just kept my head down as well as I could. I didn't want to make a big fuss; I just wanted to get to the ring. I had this guy Vince McCormack, who used to walk with me through the crowd before the fight, with Sean McGivern, Barney Eastwood and all my team. We had this routine where we would recite a little prayer as we walked to the ring. It was called 'Angel of God': 'Ever this day be at my side, to light and guard, to rule and guide'. It was as much routine as anything; something to focus your mind with everything else going on. Such was the noise and the madness that night, you couldn't hear yourself think, let alone hear the words. So I just repeated them to myself, over and over, as we made our way towards the ring.

I climbed through the ropes to more cheers, and Pedroza came in. There was no interruption with him from the fans, he just walked straight through. I was in the ring and moving around and then within a few minutes, he got in on the other side of the ring. You couldn't make this up, but then a little guy dressed up as a leprechaun appeared. That was Barney Eastwood's idea: he'd heard and seen how Sean O'Grady in the States had a dwarf dressed up as a leprechaun in the ring before the fight, throwing his magic dust to bring good luck. Panamanians are meant to be superstitious and Barney thought it might spook Pedroza. As if. But he got this act in, had him skipping and tumbling about the ring. I wasn't looking at Pedroza, but glanced across the ring as this was going on, and remember catching sight of his hooded figure.

My father got up to sing 'Danny Boy'. That was a big deal for me, that he was there singing. Yet at the same time as he was singing and everyone was joining in, I had to separate myself from it, and make sure that I didn't get caught up in the emotion of it all. As much as I wanted to listen to him, I had to let it wash over me and focus on the fight. While Dad was singing, Dermot shouted that Pedroza was staring at me, giving me this dead-eyed stare. He was trying to psych me out but, actually, it was the perfect distraction from the song. I gave him the stare back, to let him know I was ready for him and meant business.

I was there to do a job. I had to have my head right for potentially fifteen flat-out rounds. I had to be ready to push Pedroza back and bully him, to take control and win the fight. That was my objective. Nothing could distract me from that, not even the sound of my father leading the 27,000 fans singing this emotionally charged song. I figured I could always listen to that later, and I did, many times. Especially after my dad had passed away, I would listen to him singing and it always made me cry. But all that was for later, much later. The ring was clearing, the noise was rising, the waiting was over. In front of 27,000 fight fans, twenty million watching at home and God knows how many abroad, there was just me, Pedroza and fifteen rounds to decide the featherweight championship of the world.

Chapter 1

Beginnings

I was born on 28 February 1961 in Monaghan Town, which is about thirteen or fourteen miles down the road from Clones, in the Republic of Ireland. I was the third of eight children, preceded by my elder sister Sharon and my brother Dermot. For the first year or so of my life, we lived in a placed called Millbrook, a little housing estate just outside Clones. Then my parents bought a grocery store on the Diamond in Clones. It used to be an old Lipton's tea mill, dating back to the nineteenth century. It had a long yard, plenty of room for us to live, and a decent ongoing grocery business. We sold briquettes and little bags of sticks for fire-lighting, but predominantly it was vegetables.

My mother ran the grocery business with her father, Johnny Rooney. They took the shop over in 1963, and my grandfather worked there right up to his death twenty years later. He was there every day when I was a kid. He would turn up every morning at half-past nine and would leave about half-four or five o'clock. Mum would have her mother or my father's mother in when they were particularly busy and they would cook the dinners. It was a great life, a very happy life.

About a year and a half after I was born, my sister Laura came along. Then a couple of years later, my identical twin sisters, Rachel and Rebecca, were born. After that came Catherine, and then my younger brother Daniel. Dermot and I shared a bedroom, the twins shared a bedroom, and Laura and Sharon had their own rooms upstairs. It was a big old lump of a house, and we had loads of room. Dermot and I shared because we preferred it: two boys together and only a year and a half's difference in age. That was the way it was. But despite there being so many of us, it was never crowded.

It was always busy, though, I remember that. Always loads of people around, even as a kid. I loved the fact that it was always busy and Mum would pull out the twin tub for doing the washing a couple of days during the week, and Granny was always there, either Granny McGuigan or Granny Rooney, or sometimes both of them together. Papa Rooney was always around, working the slicer at the back of the shop. There were always lots of family there.

It must have been such hard work for my mum, looking after all those children and running the shop. We were open all hours too: it was as if we never shut. I remember that every evening, I would help bring the vegetables from the front of the house round to the back. Next door was the office of the solicitor Baldwin Murphy: he had a wooden covered space where we'd store the vegetables. We'd stack them up in crates, and put a plastic cover over the top. Then each morning we would pull the cover off and I would take all the stuff round, and would present it at the front of the house. There were carrots, parsnips, turnips, sprouts, cauliflowers, cabbages, potatoes . . . everything really. I would put them out and try to make them look attractive. Even as a kid, I knew that if I packed them right and made the displays look full then they would sell. Presentation was really important and I used to take a lot of care in displaying them. I would take great pride in getting it right, so people would say, 'Doesn't that look wonderful?' and 'I'll have some of that'.

The fruit-and-veg man, McEntee, would come up from County Cavan, and I would go and pick out of his lorry what I thought were the best vegetables. I don't know what he made of that, he must have thought me a right little whippersnapper, but I'd stand there and tell him, 'No I don't want that one, can I have that one there, please?' He would say, 'OK, OK,' and I made sure we always got the best. That was the routine: every morning before going to school and every evening before I would go to bed. When I was eleven and started the boxing, I would come back from training pretty exhausted, but would still go out and bring all the stuff round and pull the plastic cover over the top. Every morning I would get up early and go for a run, come back and shower and put it all out again.

I would come home from school and if I saw my grandfather at the cash register, I knew that Mum and Dad were away to the cash-and-carry in Cavan or Monaghan or even down to Dublin. I would walk into the shop, see Papa Rooney, and ask, 'Have Mum and Dad gone to the cash-and-carry?' He would nod and I would then say, 'Don't tell me,' because I could smell from what was cooking which grandmother was there. I'd sniff, and go, 'Granny McGuigan is here.' Granny McGuigan would always make Irish stew and Granny Rooney would always make boiled bacon with parsley sauce and cabbage and mashed potato. I never got it wrong once, and Papa Rooney would ask, 'How do you know that?' It was great. I always loved his reaction.

It was Papa Rooney's grandfather who came over to County Monaghan: I would say he came over the border from the North to the South, but that was before there was a border. They came across many years ago. My great-grandfather on the Rooney side signed up and fought for the British Army in the First World War. He was captured and imprisoned as a prisoner of war for four years in Germany. He died of TB two years after he returned in 1919, leaving his wife and seven children. My great-grandmother became the first lady caretaker of the post office in Clones and she reared her seven children on her own.

My grandfather Johnny was one of a big family again: I think there were seven boys in his family. He married a girl called Josephine McCall who, would you believe, came from a family of twelve children. They lived in Scotshouse, which is about five miles outside of Clones. Johnny and Josephine married, and they had a big family too: seven or eight of them, of which my mum was the second eldest.

My mother's family, the Rooneys, originally came from Lisnaskea in County Fermanagh. They date back there to the 1800s. All the Rooneys came from South Fermanagh, from Lisnakea, Newtownbutler, Magheraveely and Roslea. It is from the Rooneys from Roslea, I believe, that the footballer Wayne Rooney is descended. If you traced our family histories far enough back, he and I are probably distantly related. Which is remarkable when you think about it.

My grandfather on my dad's side, now there is a story to tell. His name was James McGuigan, and he was a captain in the IRA. He was born in 1897, and came from a place called Mulnagore in County Tyrone. My grandfather was a young man during such historic events as the Easter Rising and the War of Independence. There was a sizeable Catholic minority in the area my grandfather lived in, and they would have been threatened and under pressure from the Protestant community: there were a number of sectarian attacks against the Catholics in the North as events in the South escalated. Consequently, people like my grandfather got involved.

We're talking right at the start of the 1920s here, and without getting too much into the history of it all, I should stress that being an IRA captain back then had somewhat different connotations than it does in more recent Irish history. I don't think my grandfather was ever involved in any sort of active service, but he was certainly part of the Republican movement at the time. I suspect he had his rank because he was bright and well educated: he was a porter on the railway, which I imagine would also have made him useful in reconnaissance terms.

He was imprisoned twice. The first time was in 1921, when he was taken to a prison camp at Ballykinlar in County Down, where he was held for nine months. The camp was notorious for its harsh treatment of prisoners, with appalling conditions and a brutal regime: minor infringements would be punished severely by guards, and no visits were allowed. In 1923, he was imprisoned again. This was part of a policy of internment, which involved the mass arrest of nationalist and Republican supporters: I think they put away about 500 people or so in this particular sweep alone.

My grandfather was not arrested on the night most of the arrests took place. I think he must have heard there was something happening and got out of the house. But they caught up with him a few days later. They turned up at six in the morning, broke the door down, ran up the stairs and dragged him outside. I remember my grandmother describing how they took him out, and there was an army lorry outside, a Crossley, I think it was. The soldier told him to get in the back, but the step was quite high, and my grandfather was only a little guy. He was cuffed and said, 'I can't get up, it is too high.' The Black and Tan hit him with the butt of a gun on the back of the head and it started bleeding. My grandmother started to cry and her sister Margaret, who was also there, said to her, 'What a cowardly thing to do. No proper man could do that to a fellow who is cuffed.' The soldier put the bayonet to her throat and said, 'Shut your fucking mouth or I will run this right through you.'

The Black and Tans was the name given to British soldiers who'd fought in the First World War and had now been brought over to Ireland to combat the IRA. But they were also notorious for their behaviour towards the Catholic community in general (it is fair to say the B Specials – police reservists – were no angels either). They would bully and threaten and ransack people's houses. That was why Margaret was there, because Granny didn't like being on her own in case anything happened. My grandmother lived next to a Protestant family who couldn't have been nicer. When word got out that the Black and Tans were on the loose, she would go and stay there. They would go in and ransack her house, because of who my grandfather was, but would leave next door alone and my grandmother would be safe.

My grandfather was interned as part of this round-up. He was sent to a workhouse in Cookstown, then Larne, and from there he was taken to HMS *Argenta*, which was a prison ship moored in Larne Harbour. He actually went on the *Argenta* at his own request: he'd been learning the Irish language in one of the workhouses, and his teacher had been transferred there, so my grandfather asked to follow him. He spent several months on that ship, and in his papers it has him listed as a 'scholar': my grandfather had actually left school at fourteen, but that was the name they gave anyone who could read and write. He was incarcerated on the boat and in the workhouse for about a year and a half, and then was taken back to Larne and given a choice. He could go back to his home, but he would live under curfew: he'd have to stay within a three-mile radius of his house, and check in at the police station every couple of days. Alternatively, he could leave Northern Ireland – which by now had split from the new Irish Republic to remain part of the United Kingdom – and never return.

My grandfather initially asked to go home. Before he'd been interned he had worked as a railway porter at Annaghmore and in Donaghmore. Even though he was in the Railway Union of Ireland, he was notified that his job had been given to someone else. So at that point, he started looking at the option of leaving the North. He put some feelers out and there was a job in Clones, which in those days was a big railway town. My grandfather was allowed to spend Christmas at home – I think he had three days, that was all – and then he left for Clones. His wife and children followed on. He only ever went back to the North once: it was to watch a Gaelic game at Aughnacloy, which is just over the border from Monaghan. The police stopped him and detained him for an hour or so. They ran tests on him and frightened the life out of him. He never went back again.

My grandfather worked on the railways in Clones until he retired. He was a 'shunter' at first, and then became a signalman: you had to be really strong for that, to pull the levers. These fellas would come in, big lumps of guys, to give it a go, but they could never manage it. My grandfather wasn't big, he was only five-seven, but he had big hands, disproportionately big. He was a similar build to me, and I was fortunate enough to inherit his strength and his hands, which is great if you want to be a boxer.

I never knew any of this stuff about my grandfather's past when I was growing up. I only found out about it all much later. He died when I was six, so my memories of him are far more straight-forward. I remember him as this wizened old man who sat in the corner: he was quiet and gentle and always lovely to me. He was soft and kind, with these huge hands: his hands, as we'd say in Clones, were like a bunch of bananas.

My dad was a musician and singer. He was a very, very good vocalist, one of the finest in the country. Him and a guy called Red Hurley, they were widely considered the best by all the other singers and musicians. My dad was a tenor, but he could hold low notes brilliantly. He could flip into falsetto without any break, and was fantastic at singing ballads. He was an all-round musician too:

Dad could play the tin whistle and the concert flute, saxophone, bass guitar, drums, piano, anything. Music was very much part of our house, growing up. Dad and his band would rehearse down the back – we had garages and sheds and that was where they would practise, try out new stuff. I always used to listen. I loved it, loved the music they made and was mesmerised by how good it sounded.

Before my dad became a musician, he followed his father onto the railways. He was a coaler, too, and would shovel the coal into the wagon that accompanied the steam engine. Dad was a tough little guy: he would go across to Belturbet every morning, he would cycle there, which is about fourteen miles away. He'd shovel coal until two o'clock in the afternoon, fill up the engines with coal, then cycle back to Clones, get washed and have his tea, and then go out with the band. My dad did that for a number of years before he decided to do the music full time. The band was beginning to pay him more than he was earning on the railway, so he thought, 'Sod this, no point in breaking my back.' He quit the railway and moved on to singing full time.

Dad started playing in the mid-fifties with a group called The Dave Dixon Big Band and Eddie Roy's Big Band. Big bands did good business back then. You'd have ten or twelve musicians and a guy out front who would sing various different ballads and swing songs, dressed well and would either be a tenor or a baritone. He would be the front guy and behind him you'd have the whole works: strings and horns or whatever. Dad started off doing that, and then it mutated as the pop scene came along. Show bands were coming in and they were basically playing the stuff that was in the charts. So Dad would do all that: play the dance halls and the ballrooms all over the country. It was a good little scene: Gloria Hunniford was a singer back then and on the circuit, as were Jean and Gerry Corr, whose children would have huge success as The Corrs.

By the mid-sixties, my dad had a little band called The Big Four. It was him, Mike McGeedy, Douggie Stewart and Bill Davidson. He did some work too with this guy John Kennedy, who was a songwriter from Dublin. It was with John's song that my dad entered the Irish Song Contest, and he came first. I remember watching on TV and the great excitement when he won. We had bonfires in the Diamond and we all ran out to the road to meet him. We didn't know whether it would be the Cavan Road or the Monaghan Road he'd be coming in on. So we kept watching both roads until finally he came down the Cavan Road. It was a really exciting moment. Having won the Irish Song Contest, my dad then went on to represent Ireland in the Eurovision Song Contest in 1968. The competition was held in the Royal Albert Hall that year, and Dad's entry, 'Chance of a Lifetime', finished fourth.

Dad's career really kicked on after that. He was a big name down in Dublin, and got gigs all over Europe on the back of Eurovision. He'd fly out to Budapest or Sofia, and sing out there. I remember him doing this one gig out in Malta, and his support act, just before he hit the big time, was David Bowie. Dad did his own shows and played with various show bands and offers kept coming in. He was offered the chance to be the lead singer of The Bachelors, but it would have meant a life on the road, so he didn't take it. He would not do it because he had responsibilities and a family to look after.

Dad would play gigs all over Ireland, but would always come back, even though the roads were terrible back then and it might take hours. Because we had loads of rooms, we'd always have lots of bandsmen coming through and staying at our house. The bandsmen who knew my father would often pop in, and even though Dad was not going to be there, they would ask, 'Do you mind if I stay at your place?' Dad always told us to say, 'Yes, no problem, I'll see you in the morning.' My mother or someone would let them in. They would arrive late at night and would stay over and we would see them in the morning. We would be sitting round having breakfast, and my mum would say, This is John from Enniskillen, or Cork or Galway, or wherever it was they were from.

That was cool, growing up, as you could imagine. There'd be all these great musicians in the house, and great music too. My dad would go over to America and come back with these wonderful records, fantastic stuff that nobody else had. He'd bring back Stevie Wonder or George Benson, Motown stuff when it was right in its prime. He'd play us Jerry Reed and Willie Nelson, John Lee Hooker and Johnny Cash, a fantastically eclectic collection of stuff. I've always had music around and it's always been part of me. Though I didn't pick up an instrument myself, my dad's talent has gone down to my kids: Shane's a handy drummer, Jake is an exceptional guitar player (although he does not practise) and Blain plays bass, piano, guitar and sings. He's in a band that is making a go of it, and they come over and practise at our house. It's a different kind of music, of course, but I stop and listen to them play, and it's like being back to when I was growing up all over again.

My mother must have had a terrible time with me when I was growing up. If I saw something that looked dangerous, I would do it. If I could get up something that nobody else could get up, I would want to climb it. When I was four, I climbed up this pole in the centre of the Diamond. It was about twenty feet up, and people were going into my mother's shop and saying, 'Katie, I don't want to alarm you but your child is on top of the pole in the Diamond.' And she'd be, 'Oh, don't worry about that, he does that all the time. I'll come out and shout at him.' Because that was me. I'd be climbing up, jumping up on the roofs and weaving across them. It was just general childish stuff but I was a bit of a tearaway, always full of energy.

My neighbours used to be annoyed by me because I was always climbing and walking across their roofs. Looking back, it was dangerous stuff I was doing. At the back of our house there was a wall about thirty-five feet up: that sort of drop is enough to kill a kid. I used to walk along the wall, then jump down on to the roof and then walk along the top from one house to the next. I would slide down anything that was galvanised, though invariably there would be a rusty bit that would stick in your backside!

The next-door neighbour on the other side was a guy called Cecil Chapman and he was a chemist. It was like a 1940s chemist with wooden shelves and all the old proper wooden side counters, and at the back was where he stored the bottles. One day, myself and a boy called Paul Newell decided we would jump down on the roof. I jumped too near the centre and my legs went through the roof. I grabbed the top, so I was OK, but I was in right up to my waist. Paul, who'd jumped at the same time, had just disappeared: he'd gone right through. He was groaning, and I'm pulling myself out and saying, 'Are you all right?' And he's saying, 'Get me out of here quick.' Because Cecil Chapman was out the back, had heard the crash and was coming in to see what had happened! I got the rope that I had tied to the spur and lowered that down. Chapman saw me and shouted, 'McGuigan! When I get my hands on you . . . !' But he hadn't got the key to get back into the store. By the time he had gone round, I'd got Paul up and out. We scarpered, disappeared for hours. I knew that if I sat it out long enough, Dad would have gone off with the band, Mum would be busy in the shop, and Papa Rooney would have gone home by the time we returned. So I sat it out, but I still got it anyway, and my Uncle Paddy had to go in and repair the roof. That was just typical of the kid that I was.

Then there was the time we went to Dublin Zoo. One of the highlights was a chimpanzee party, which featured these hand-trained young chimps. I was nine or ten at the time, and there was a stack of us, sitting round on little stools. What happened was that the zookeepers would lift the chimps up on to your lap, you'd stroke the chimp and they would feed you. I said to Dermot, 'Wait till you see what I am going to do.' They put the chimp up on my lap, and I was such a little scamp, I grabbed him in a headlock. The next thing I know, he is going mad: 'SCREECH . . . !' All the kids are shouting, 'AAARGH!' and flying everywhere, while I'm sat with this chimp in a headlock that he can't get out of. Dermot ran down to my dad and said, 'Dad, Dad! Barry's got the chimp in a headlock!' So he came charging up and the handler was furiously shouting, 'Let that chimp go, let him go!' It was completely stupid, of course. I got roasted by my dad the whole way back home. But that was the crazy sort of stuff I used to get up to.

I wasn't a big kid, but I had strength. That chimp could not get out of the headlock. He tried to but couldn't, because I was as strong as a horse. At school we had this game called Hardy Knuckles. On a cold winter's day, you would hold your knuckles out and say, 'OK, you hit me and I'll hit you.' Then they would smack yours and you would smack theirs. None of the boys could beat me, even in the classes that were two or three above me because I had big lumps of hands. Even then, I could really hit them hard.

I got into little squabbles and things, mainly the bigger kids having a go. There was one kid who came from a big farming family. He was a strong, physical guy and we had a row one time and he jumped on me. He was tough but we had a really good battle. There was another guy who was the same age as Dermot, and at that age a year and a half is a big difference. I had to defend myself against him, but I was pretty good at handling myself. I remember the last battle I really had in school: I was about twelve or thirteen and had just started boxing at the time. This kid was two classes above me and we were down in the handball alley (Gaelic handball is a different game from normal handball, a bit like squash or racquetball) when something happened and he said, 'Me and you in the back garden.' I thought, Christ, and was worrying about it all afternoon. But I could not back down because I would have lost face. We went out back after school, squared up, and I banged him three or four times, until he hit the deck. That was the last battle I ever had at school: once I started boxing, I never, ever used my fists outside the ring.

I loved school. I loved English, and that became my favourite subject. I loved history and was pretty good at geography and then I went to a vocational school and did woodwork and technical drawing and metalwork. But it's the teachers that really make an impact on you. In my junior school there was a guy called Paddy Kennedy. He was the sternest teacher in the school but he was absolutely brilliant. A woman called Mrs Goodwin was a tremendous help to me as well, as was a teacher called Dan McGuire. I struggled a bit early on, and went to St Patrick's High School, which was the vocational school. I did well there, though. I liked my English teacher, Peter Duffy, and a guy called Stephen Trant. Stephen Trant was a great help to me. I also got fantastic support and encouragement from my metalwork teacher, Eamon McGuinness. I got into history and loved reading about that, Irish history in particular. I enjoyed the course books and I remember Peter Duffy saying to me after I had done my Intermediate Certificate, 'You have done surprisingly well here, Barry. You are just below honours.' My self-esteem was massively boosted by that.

I did well in my Intermediate Certificate and then did the first year of my Leaving Certificate (the equivalent of A levels in the UK). By this point, the boxing was beginning to take off, and it was hard to find time for both. With all that sporting success, school seemed less important. I started doing less well and had to retake the year. I was with kids that were a year down from me, and after about four weeks I'd had enough. I remember saying to my mum, 'I can't do it. I can't work in the shop, train twice a day and do my homework, there's not enough time in the day for it.' Her response was, how dare you! My father was in bed, having got back from a gig at three in the morning, but I raised him and said the same thing. And he said, 'Promise me you will read lots and learn as much as you can and just be a glutton for knowledge.' I loved reading anyway so I said, OK, and went back out. And Mum said, 'Well? When are you going to school?' And then my dad took her off and that was it. It was a gamble, and of course it paid off with the boxing and everything, but it's something I regret, not finishing school. Looking back, I wish I'd stuck it out.

Back when I was a young kid, I used to hang out with a bunch of lads: Leo Strong, a guy named Liam Flanagan, his brother Eamon, and a whole load of others. Leo Strong was a massive Tottenham fan so we all supported Spurs. He lived on MacCurtain Street, and so we called ourselves the MacCurtain Street Hotspurs. I don't know whether the other guys still support Tottenham but I certainly do.

This one day, I must have been about eleven or twelve, we were down Analore Street, which was one of the roads that came up to the Diamond. We were messing about in this old derelict house when we found this pair of boxing gloves. Goodness knows what they were doing there. They were an old pair of red gloves, looked like 1950s gloves. They were competition gloves, would have been eight ounces. I suppose there must have been about ten of us there, in this derelict room with a bare wooden floor, and someone suggested we have a fight. So we had one glove each, and took turns to box. I remember that I had the right glove, and we were thumping away at each other. It soon became clear that I was better than everyone else. I was hitting the others hard, and remember thinking that these guys, even the older ones, were frightened of me.

Up to this point, I'd always been more interested in football than I was in boxing. I'd watch the big fights on the TV when the BBC showed them – Muhammad Ali, Henry Cooper, Jack Bodell, Brian London, people like that – but it was that afternoon on Analore Street that really sparked it off for me. Finding the gloves in that derelict house was the start of it all. I remember heading home and wanting to talk to my dad about it, but he was away with the band at the time. So it was a few days later before I caught up with him. He came back and as soon as I saw him, I asked, 'Dad, is there a boxing club round here?' And that is how it all began.

Chapter 2

The Opening Bell

My dad told me that there used to be a boxing club in Clones back in the 1950s. He said he'd been there and trained a bit when he was young. I don't think it ever went any further than that: he never had any actual contests. That club was long gone, so we had to look further afield. There was a club in Monaghan but that was thirteen miles away. There had been a club in Smithborough, but that had closed down. The nearest club was in a place called Wattlebridge, right on the border. The club was in the South, but the quickest way to get there was by travelling along the treacherous border roads.

We drove out to this club, and it was in this old Victorian-style school building. It was early summer, and we went to have a look around, but no one was there. The windows were high, presumably to stop kids looking out when it had been a school. But Dad lifted me up so I could have a look and I was fascinated. I saw the roped-off ring: it wasn't an elevated ring, it was just a roped-off section. The hall was a long rectangular shape, and down at the bottom was the ring roped off from the wall. It was very simple: just plain ropes and a wooden floor. There was a long beam at the top and a floor-to-ceiling ball – a speed bag as it is sometimes called – and a heavy bag. There was an old fireplace and a cupboard, which they obviously kept all the gear in.

We waited outside the club for about an hour, but nobody turned up. We drove down into Redhills, which was the nearest village, but there was still no sign of anyone. We must have gone back and forth three times, and it was only on the third time that we saw this guy walking up with a rucksack. He was a small, dark-haired guy called Michael Lyttle, appropriately enough. Lyttle looked like a boxer, so we followed him in the car: God knows what he must have been thinking. He walked up to the club . . . and just carried straight on. We were just about to drive away when my dad said, 'I am just going to ask him.' He asked Lyttle, 'You don't know anything about the boxing club, do you?' And Lyttle replied, 'I'm just going there now.'

It turned out that the boxing club was run by a couple of local farmers, Tom Conlon and Padraig McCafferty, and because it was harvest time, they were out working in the fields. Their most successful boxer was a fellow called Paul Connelly, who had won the Irish Senior title, which was quite an achievement for such a small rural club. He became a policeman down in Dublin, I think. With Conlon and McCafferty not around because of the harvest, the key to the club was with an old army guy called Mick Fitzpatrick, who lived about half a mile down the road. That was where Lyttle was going, to go and get the key. And we just went, 'Ah, brilliant.'

We could only stay for half an hour because we had done all this waiting and Dad was playing that night. But we got inside the club and I was immediately taken by the smell of it and the atmosphere. I watched Lyttle hitting the floor-to-ceiling ball, which he was pretty good at. I tried hitting it a few times myself and got a look at all the equipment. It all really whetted my appetite. I asked Lyttle when he was coming next, so we'd come when someone was around. It had only been thirty minutes or so, but I couldn't wait to go back. It was love at first sight, really.

I had only been going to the club for about two or three weeks when I had my first fight. I can't have been there more than about three or four times. How it worked at that level was that there'd be an amateur boxing show every week or couple of weeks, and you'd drive to different places in the country to take part. It just so happened that a couple of weeks after going to Wattlebridge, there was a show on in my home town. I hadn't really learned much at all in those first few sessions: I hadn't really had any coaching but had just done a bit of skipping, and hit the punchbag and the floor-to-ceiling ball a bit. The most I'd learned was from watching Lyttle to see what he did, and doing my best to copy him. Even so, it seemed a great opportunity, to fight in Clones in front of my friends.

I went along a little bit in hope: there was no guarantee you'd get a fight, it all depended who else was there. But as it turned out, there was a guy called Ronan McManus from the St Michael's club in Enniskillen. Tom Conlon said to his coach, Davy Campbell senior, that he had this kid who wanted his first fight. Campbell told him about McManus, who'd already had a couple of bouts but was still basically a novice. They measured us up, and McManus was a bit taller than me, and a bit heavier, but it was near enough and we agreed to fight. I was wearing a black string vest, shorts and a pair of 'gutties' we called them, like a well-worn pair of plimsolls. I was nervous as hell.

The show was in the Luxor cinema, and I remember there was loads of shouting as I was going towards the ring. It was meant to be supportive but didn't make my nerves any better. My Uncle Dennis was the timekeeper, and the referee was Albert Uprichard, who later became a good friend of mine. Albert was from the Lawrencetown ABC (Amateur Boxing Club) near Banbridge in

Northern Ireland, and he was a very upright old English-style amateur boxing coach. I didn't know any of that at this stage: he was just a tall, skinny man with a big moustache.

So there I was wearing a black string vest, and McManus came in with the proper St Michael's ABC colours on: satin shorts, the works. He looked the part, and he looked like someone who had done it before, but there was no backing out now. Albert called us into the centre of the ring, and gave us his instructions. 'I want a nice clean fight,' he said. 'No hitting with the inside of the gloves, and when I say break, you break. Good luck, boys,' Albert added, and then turned and walked away. I watched Albert go, looked across at McManus and thought, what do we do now?

This was my first contest, remember, and I didn't really know how things worked. I thought that must be it, the fight must have started. So I went for it, launched into McManus with punches flying everywhere. McManus was a bit surprised, but he wasn't just going to stand there and take it, and started returning punches. The crowd were laughing their heads off, hysterical at all this. Albert the referee turned back round to see what all the noise is about, and he yelled at us to stop. McManus and I were pulled apart, reprimanded and sent back to our corners.

The crowd were in hysterics. My Uncle Dennis was laughing, too. Albert let it calm down a bit and then said, 'OK, seconds out, round one.' The fight started properly and I just picked up where I left off really. I was just like a windmill, and completely overwhelmed the guy. McManus just could not keep me off him. There was no style or technique in what I was doing, I was just full of adrenalin and throwing as many punches as I could. I'm sure I'd cringe if I could see the fight now, but this windmill approach sort of worked, and McManus didn't get a chance to do anything. The crowd were going crazy, whooping and cheering, and I won.

I was so excited. I got a trophy for winning and ran all the way back to the shop to show my parents. My dad wasn't there as he was away doing a concert, but I showed my mum and said, 'Look! I've won! I've won!' Mum went, as only a mother could, 'Oh, that is brilliant, that is terrific. Now can I get back to serving the customers?' So I then went back down to watch the rest of the bouts, proud as anything, keeping tight hold of the trophy. I've still got it, you know, still have it at home. When my parents' house went up in flames on the night I won the world title (about which, more later), the trophy was just about the only bit of my boxing memorabilia that survived. As time has gone on, that first trophy has become even more special.

It was hard to get away from the Troubles, growing up in the seventies. It was impossible in fact in a place like Clones. There's something about being brought up in a border town that makes you acutely aware of what is going on. Clones is in the South, but in some ways was as much tied in to the North. There are seven roads out of Clones, and most of them went north before you went south. It was like going to the club at Wattlebridge: you had to crisscross the border several times to get anywhere.

Clones is in Monaghan, which is one of the three Ulster counties in the South, the others being Cavan and Donegal. This political splitting of Ulster occurred with the Anglo-Irish treaty of 1921, but in some instances, certain sports for example, the concept of Ulster as a whole still continues. This is true in rugby union for example, as it is for Gaelic games and for boxing. Which is how, as I made my way in amateur boxing, I had this situation where I would fight for Ulster, and then for both Northern Ireland and Ireland.

Clones' position on the border has always been important for the economy of the town, for better or for worse. For a while, it was an important railway town, a crucial junction that linked Dublin and Belfast, North and South, with trains coming in from Enniskillen, Armagh, Cavan and Dundalk. It was an important market town because of that: because of the good links, you had people coming from all over, and the place prospered. When the railway closed down at the end of the 1950s, however, that had a huge impact on the town.

The Troubles flared up in the late sixties, and the links got even worse. Clones started becoming badly affected in the mid-1970s. The border roads and bridges were suddenly the front line and were constantly being blown up by the British Army in an attempt to control the border and stop the terrorists slipping in and out of Northern Ireland. This had a huge effect on the economic lifeblood of Clones. There were towns in the North that were closer to Clones than the ones in the South, but people from those places would stop coming over. With their direct route into the town closed, people were reluctant to take the long way round, where they would have to go through an army checkpoint, which was always painstakingly slow. The local people and the business people knew that this was bad, and would go out to fix the roads, to fill the holes to keep them open. There'd be another explosion, they'd go out to fill the hole again, and that went on for years.

The Troubles had a big effect on Clones. Religion had never been an issue in the town and had always been fairly well balanced: in the sixties, it was probably about 60 per cent Catholic to 40 per cent Protestant. What your religious views were didn't really matter. My wife Sandra and her family are Protestant, and had the rival shop on the opposite side of the Diamond to us. But we both served customers from both communities, and didn't think twice about it. Despite my grandfather's past, politics was never mentioned in our house. We'd talk about things like the bridges being blown up, but we'd never discuss the politics of it all: we were more into survival. A customer was a customer, and that was the way it was at home, in the town, when I was young. Once the Troubles started, however, things began to change. Some of the Protestant community felt concerned, almost intimidated by what was going on. And because we were so close to the North, some of them moved back there. The Protestant community began to shrink, and has never really built back up. I'd say the split is about 95 per cent to 5 per cent now.

The Troubles impacted on the town, and it impacted on my boxing career right from the beginning. I'd only been going to Wattlebridge ABC for a few months when I had to change clubs. That was because I used to travel there by bicycle: I'd cycle over the border roads with a friend of mine called Noel McGovern. You could get to Wattlebridge without going over the border, but it was very much the long way round, about eight or nine miles. Or you could cycle out on the Cavan Road, and either go over the blown-up bridge, or carry your bike over, depending on the state of it, and carry on that way. You'd go over the border about four times, south–north, north–south, south–north–south, but it was by far the shorter way. It would be pitch dark on the roads, and all we'd have to see by was a flashlight, and sometimes not even that.

One particular night, Noel and I were heading back to Clones with no lights. We were coming down this steep hill at breakneck speed, came round the corner, and straight into this police and army roadblock. We were coming down the hill so fast, we were lucky they didn't shoot at us. There were so many terrorist incidents around this time that the police and army were always on high alert. The army would come in camouflaged, and the police would use infrared lights to monitor things. It was all as low profile as they could, so we didn't see them and they didn't see us.

Noel and I came round the corner to see two guys lying flat on the ground, being surrounded by both police and soldiers. You can just imagine their reaction when we appeared out of nowhere at high speed. They were waving God knows what and shouting at us, 'What are you doing on this road? You're not supposed to be here! You could have been killed! Get the hell out of here! Now!

Get out of here!' Looking back, we were incredibly fortunate that they didn't open fire on us.

We got out of there sharpish, and had to go the long way back. It took us another hour or so before we got home. Of course, my mother wanted to know what had happened and why it had taken me so long to get back. There were a number of incidents around this time – the infamous 'pitchfork murders', when two Catholic farmers were stabbed to death, took place only a couple of miles further down the road – and my parents decided it was just too dangerous for me to continue cycling over to Wattlebridge. I had to find myself another club.

I left Wattlebridge ABC and joined up at nearby Smithborough instead, which as luck would have it, had just reopened. There was a coach there called Danny McEntee, who was to have a big impact on my early career, and another called Frank Mulligan, who would play an important role later on.

Danny McEntee was both a great guy and a successful fighter himself: he boxed for the St Macartan's club in Monaghan, and had been Irish Junior champion, an Irish Senior finalist and had boxed the great Nino Benvenuti, the Italian world middleweight and world welterweight champion. He had a strong boxing pedigree from which he drew in his training. Danny was an excellent coach, self-assured and confident, and his training methods were all about instilling technique. One of the things I remember about those early sessions was his insistence on everything being repeated and repeated, until I got them right: he was quite 'old school' in his methods, which in terms of learning the basics was exactly what I needed. Danny recognised my potential straightaway, and that I was relying too much on my power. He knew I needed to improve my technique if I was going to impress as a fighter.

Danny was very thorough in his teaching methods, and very

descriptive, too, in what he wanted me to do. He taught me so many things: about blocking and parrying, about the idea of putting punches together in combinations, how to transfer my weight from one foot to the other. Technically he was brilliant and he was very patient with beginners like me. I never got to know him personally – it was more of a teacher–student relationship – but his influence at that stage of my career was immense. Danny changed my style so I was more cultured as a fighter and not as reckless. There was more cunning to my moves with his training: I would feint and try and draw leads, slip and counter. Danny was very good at instilling that and made me a much better, much more subtly aggressive fighter.

Frank Mulligan, by contrast, didn't have Danny's success in the ring: I think his career only stretched to two or three fights as an amateur. He couldn't match Danny in terms of technique, but he compensated with his energy and enthusiasm. Frank's greatest strength was on the mental side of boxing: he was very good at working on your mind: building up your confidence and encouraging you. He could make you go into the ring feeling ten feet tall, and that you had the ability to beat anybody. He put the hours in, too. Frank would thumb a lift from Smithborough to Clones, and come and train in the loft gym we'd put in at home. We'd do the pads and the bags and the skipping, put in two sessions a day.

Sometimes Frank's enthusiasm and lack of boxing experience would come together. He was always keen to get in the ring with me, put the gloves and the headguard on and do a bit of sparring. I remember on one occasion in Smithborough he was spraying punches at me, and telling me to come back at him. 'Come on, come on,' he encouraged. I threw a right, which missed, and then a left hook which caught him flush on the chin. Wallop – down Frank went, and didn't get up.

Oh my God, I thought. He's not moving. As hard as I tried, I couldn't get Frank to come round. This was an afternoon session, and there wasn't anyone else in the gym at the time. I thought, what do I do now? I came out the club and looked around to see if there was anyone who could help. Of course, there was no one about! The priest's house was about 150 metres down the road, so I ran down to that, and was hammering on the door and ringing the bell. But there was no answer. By now, I was panicking and ran back to the club: you can imagine how relieved I was to see that Frank was groaning and starting to come round!

At Smithborough I moved on from the shows and tournaments I'd fought in at Wattlebridge, and started fighting in competitions. The first one I won was the Mid Ulster title in 1975. I went forward for the Ulster title, and beat a guy called Hawkins from the Holy Trinity club in the semi-final. That was a bit of a surprise: he'd gone to the All-Ireland and won a title, so he was expected to beat me easily. But I won the semi and got through to the Ulster final. That took place at St George's Hall in Belfast, a beautiful old Georgian place round the back of the City Hall. My opponent was Garry Spears, a fighter from the White City club in East Belfast. Spears was a step up in class again: he had three or four All-Ireland titles under his belt, and he outboxed me. I tried really hard and pushed him back but I could not get to him. He had these quick, stinging little punches, and I could see that technically he was better than me. I came home disappointed that I hadn't won, especially as I felt I'd been working and training really hard. I realised how much more I would have to do if I was going to beat an All-Ireland champion. I went home then and licked my wounds and started getting ready for the next season.

The following year, I entered a tournament called the Golden Shamrocks, which was open to every club in the country. I fought my way through to the final, where I was up against a guy called Jimmy Coughlan from the Transport club in Dublin. He had won five national titles and was a beautiful boxer, very tall for the weight and very experienced. He did not know who I was, and didn't care quite honestly because he was capable, he thought, of beating everybody. It was at the National Stadium, in front of all the officials, and I don't think anyone gave me much of a chance. Coughlan outboxed me to begin with but as the round went on, I started nailing him and hitting him. I could see it in his eyes, I could see the shock on his face when I hit him because he didn't think I could hit properly. In the second round I caught him with a great punch. Bang! He went down. You could hear the sharp intake of breath that came from the crowd. I just dropped him like a stone, the national champion. Coughlan got up and the referee gave him a count. I went across the ring, banged him again, hit him three times and he was wobbling again but the bell rang to end the round. I went back to my corner and Danny said, 'Calm down, calm down. You will catch him again. But this time get closer. As soon as the bell rings get out and get on top of him.' So I went out in the third round and I knocked him out. Flat. I think everybody was shocked at how hard I could hit, I was only fifteen. We had about seventy people down from Clones and they went crazy. It was brilliant. I had won the Golden Shamrocks and had knocked out the five-times national champion.

It was time for the Ulsters again, but by this time, the Troubles in the North had escalated dramatically. There were a lot of random killings and we were worried about going to these fights and having to travel back late at night. Frank Mulligan, who was the club secretary, wrote to the Ulster Council, asking for permission to take part in the Leinster Championships in the South instead, which took place about the same time. They were fine about it, and Leinster were fine about it as long as nobody objected. But we got down there and a couple of the Leinster clubs did object on the grounds I was from Ulster: former opponents, who knows? So I'd missed the Ulsters and couldn't fight in the Leinster Championships either. I was gutted at the time. I was gutted that having beaten Coughlan so convincingly, I had to sit things out, while he went through to win the All-Ireland title again.

It wasn't until the next year, 1977, that I got the chance to fight in the Ulsters again. I'd gone up in weight to seven stone seven, and won the Mid Ulsters with two stoppages and a pull-out. I got through to the Ulsters final, where I beat a guy called Danny McAllister from the Oliver Plunkett club. Danny was a little chunky guy, winging punches and wanting to have a fight with me. I punished him and outboxed him and that felt good, to show that I had another element to my fighting.

That was the first time I really showed I could box as well as fight – using the technique that Danny was teaching me, instead of just relying on my raw power. Even at this early stage, I always loved my training: well, except for getting up early in the morning to go running. I enjoyed my roadwork and the gym sessions, and got into the groove of learning my technique: I'd shadow-box whatever Danny was teaching me first, then move on to trying it out on the pads, and then take it into a sparring session. That can sound a bit repetitive, but when you can feel the improvement in your performance, then you know all that hard effort you've been putting in has been worthwhile.

As well as getting the training from Danny, I was also beginning to really get into my boxing around this time. My dad would regularly go to America: he'd go and do his residency over in New York, and he would bring back tapes of fights for me to watch. That's when I first saw Roberto Duran and fighters like Carlos Zarate and Alexis Arguello. I loved Duran and remember watching him beat Ken Buchanan by a technical knockout in round fourteen at Madison Square Garden. There were plenty of boxers closer to home who had a big influence on me as well. I was interested in Mick Dowling, who was a very good Irish boxer at the time: Charlie Magri I followed right through from the ABAs, and couldn't believe it when he was flattened by Ian Clyde at the Montreal Olympics: John Conteh, Alan Minter and John H Stracey I watched.

Everyone remembers the heavyweight division in the seventies and of course I watched all those big fights, but in terms of my own fighting, I was always interested in the lighter guys, to see what I could pick up. The welterweight fighter Dave 'Boy' Green was someone I loved to watch. He was a bit rough-and-tumble, and I liked the fact that he was aggressive and wasn't afraid to walk in there and get stuck in. Jim Watt I also admired as a fighter; Maurice Hope I thought was a great technician. I remember watching Jimmy Flint, an explosive featherweight fighter from Wapping – he could knock guys out with a left hook or a right hand. So while I enjoyed the drama and spectacle of Ali and the heavyweight fights, in terms of my own boxing, it was the smaller guys who probably had the bigger impact.

Having won the Ulsters, I went down for the All-Irelands. I fought the West of Ireland champion in the quarter-finals and knocked him down in the first round. The semi-final was tougher, that went into the third round, and then in the final, which was down in Limerick, I was up against Martin Brereton. I'd beaten him on the way to winning the Golden Shamrocks and beat him again to win the All-Ireland. He was tough and strong, but I'd improved technically since the last time I'd fought him, and this time I really hurt him.

I was All-Ireland champion, which just felt fantastic. We had a big crowd of people down from Clones, and I remember this long and happy journey on the coach back home. It was a big thing for the town: Clones had no heritage in boxing, and now they had a guy who'd won the national title. The local paper was the *Northern Standard* and it gave me great write-ups: Paddy Turley was a huge boxing fan. The *Irish Independent* had been there to watch the fight too: the report said I was exceptional, and that I would go a long way.

By now things were starting to mushroom. People were beginning to get a sense of how good I was. It was getting to the stage where not many of the guys in the club would spar with me because I was too good for them and even some of the bigger and more senior guys wouldn't do it because they did not want to be hurt. I remember I used to spar with a guy called Barney McBride: he was a middleweight who got to the All-Ireland Junior finals. He only lost that to Sean Mannion from Mayo, who later went on to fight for the World Light Middleweight title against the incredible Mike McCallum. So McBride was good and he was a grown man and I was sparring with him. We had these really flat-out sparring sessions and despite his years, his weight and his experience, I gave as good as I got. But not many of the guys would spar me at the club and I had to start travelling for sparring. We would go down to all sorts of different clubs, travel two, two and a half hours for good-quality sparring.

I remember that summer going down to spar in the National Stadium. Gerry Storey from the Holy Family club in Belfast was also the national coach. He had spotted me and asked if I would spar with the Irish senior light flyweight champion, Phillip Sutcliffe. Sutcliffe was getting ready for the European Senior Championships in Halle in East Germany. He was older than me by a couple of years, which made a big difference at that age (though I'd actually beaten him on points in a tournament a few months earlier). He was fitter too: I realised that I would have to up my level of fitness again if I wanted to compete at the next level. I trained with the national team and that was the first time I came across interval training, practising these intermittent, explosive bursts of speed. The training was good and the sparring was as well: Sutcliffe went out and won a bronze at the championships, but I more than held my own against him in the gym.

At the end of the year, I went in for the Irish Juniors. I moved up in weight again, to bantamweight. I got through to the semi-final and fought a guy called Mick Holmes from the Phoenix club in Dublin. Holmes was a little chunky sort of fighter, so it should have been easy for me. But my technique was terrible. It was like I had gone backwards. I lost on a majority decision and couldn't have any complaints. I had been dreadful. I would get my revenge over Holmes before long, but at the time it felt a bit of a setback. And to make matters worse, Danny McEntee was involved in a bad accident soon after. I went to see him, and he was lying on his back in a bad way, couldn't move. He had to step down while he recovered and Frank Mulligan took over as club coach.

Mulligan had never done much as a fighter like Danny had, but he was still a good coach, with a good boxing brain. He would come and train with me and we would do two sessions a day. We would do pad work and did lots of rounds, working on combinations and keeping the jab really working, using my boxing skills more than my aggression. After losing to Holmes, it was all about bringing back the boxing.

It sounds a slightly crazy idea, but having lost in the Irish Juniors, I then went in for the Ulster Seniors at the start of 1978. It was a step up again, but I'd trained really hard, honed my boxing skills and felt that I was ready. The Holmes fight had just been an aberration. The semi-final, my first senior fight, was against Noel Reynolds from Lisburn ABC. He was a tough, tough cookie but I gave him a beating. I dropped him and badly hurt him. He came up to me afterwards, and said, 'How old are you?' I said, 'I'm sixteen, almost seventeen.' He couldn't believe it. 'You're *sixteen*? I've never been hit like that in my life.' My opponent in the final was a guy called Sean Russell, and Reynolds said, 'You are going to knock him out.' Russell had been at the fight (he'd got a bye into the final), and he came into my dressing room when Reynolds was there. Reynolds repeated what he'd just said: 'The kid is going to knock you out, Sean,' and Russell just laughed.

Sean Russell was a good fighter. He was in his early twenties and full of confidence. The crowd for the final the following week was full of his supporters as well. But I wobbled him in the first, had him down twice in the second, and he didn't fancy it in the third. I don't think he could believe it and neither could his supporters: I was only sixteen years old, the youngest ever Ulster Senior champion. That really made people sit up and take notice.

The fight was on BBC Northern Ireland, the first time I'd been on TV. We couldn't get back to Clones in time to watch it, so we piled into the Four Seasons hotel in Monaghan instead. There was a whole host of us, a guy called Trainer from the club, a couple of the Tiernay brothers, all kinds of people. We scrambled to the corner where the television was, and everyone in the hotel gathered round to see what was going on. 'Is that you?' they asked, when I came on, and we all watched and cheered. It was weird seeing myself on screen: it was the first time I'd ever seen myself box. I thought I looked a little reckless and lost my composure a bit, and I had this mop of raven hair flying about. But it was great to watch. I remember Harry Thompson, who was doing the commentating that night, saying, 'McGuigan is a bit rough, still a bit raw, but this fellow has got *serious* potential.'

Chapter 3

Amateur Dramatics

My whole life I wanted to win the Olympics. I used to have this thing I made at school. I made a little T-square in the woodwork class and I wrote on it, 'Please God let me win the gold medal in 1980'. That was my goal, my focus and everything my amateur career was geared towards achieving.

After winning the Ulster Seniors, I was picked for the Ulster team for a first international fight against East Germany in Belfast. I guess I should explain that historically Ireland was divided into thirty-two counties, and that you box for a 32-county team. Ulster consists of nine counties, though only six of these are in the North: County Monaghan, where Clones is, is in the South, along with Cavan and Donegal. My parents' families were from the North, so that was why the guys picked me, though if you want to be pedantic, I should not have been there. But that was why I represented Ulster, as well as Northern Ireland in the 1978 Commonwealth Games, and Ireland in the 1980 Moscow Olympics.

My opponent for the East Germany match was Torsten Koch. Koch was six foot, wiry and muscular with great technique: he would later go on to win the European senior silver medal as an amateur, which shows you how good he was. He was tall, had these great long levers and he could really whack you from distance. Koch had fought Gussie Farrell, the Irish senior champion, had unanimously outpointed him, wobbled him a few times and gave him a standing count. I thought it was going to be a bit of a job beating this guy.

I boxed him in the working men's club on the Shankill Road. This was right in the middle of the Troubles and everybody would have been acutely aware of where I was from. But I probably didn't realise because it was just like normal. Everybody treated it like normal. In fact, if anything we were given special treatment. We were escorted in and escorted out and well looked after, everybody was lovely to us.

It was a phenomenal night. Club Sound, who were a popular show band at the time, were playing that night and Dad got up and sang a couple of songs, which brought the house down. That put the icing on the cake. The crowd gave me unbelievable support, and I paid them back by beating this guy, beating him comprehensively. I stayed on top of Koch throughout and never gave him room. I had to, because I could feel the power of the punches when he did have distance, and the sharpness of his punches. I kept on top of him and he couldn't cope with the pace and pressure that I put him under. The fact that I'd got a unanimous decision against someone who'd beaten Gussie Farrell was a huge boost to my confidence.

The next big date in the boxing calendar for me was the 1978 European Junior Championships, which were due to be held at the National Stadium in Dublin. As you can imagine, I really wanted to get in the team for that one. I entered the Irish Under-19s and found myself up against my old nemesis, Mick Holmes, in the final. I was up for that one, and really wanted revenge. I was on form and feeling lively, my punches were hitting the mark, and I had developed my boxing skill. I am going to really give it to you, I thought.

Holmes walked in and I boxed the hell out of him. The first round I hit him with a good left hook – Bom! – and down he went. Second round it was the same: down he went again. This time when he got up, there was no bell to save him. I walked in, properly flattened him and the referee stopped it.

I entered the Irish Seniors, and guess who I found myself up against in the final? This time I didn't knock Holmes out, but I still beat him comprehensively. I had him wobbling and he got a standing count, but he got through the fight. Actually, he hit me with a good left hook at one stage and I remember the ringing in my ear. Overall, though, I gave him another hammering.

I presumed I was in the team and went into camp to get ready for the European Juniors. The camp was in Drogheda, which is halfway between Belfast and Dublin along the east coast. We trained there and went back and forth between Drogheda and the National Stadium. I remember we were out playing football, when one of the guys who was watching called out to me, 'McGuigan! Have you seen the paper?' I said no. And he passed me his paper and I read that I wasn't old enough to fight in the competition. You had to be seventeen and a half, and I had only just turned seventeen. So I went in and asked, 'Is this true?' And they said, 'Yes. Sorry, you can't box.'

I think it was just some official mistake, but it was very hurtful for me, to have found out like that. It was really upsetting. I felt badly treated, badly let down by them all. What made it even more difficult to accept was that Mick Holmes, who got my place, went on to win the silver medal, losing in the final to a Russian guy called Samson Chachatrian. Holmes lost by a smidgeon, and having just beaten him myself so convincingly, I know I would have won the gold medal. The gold medal in Dublin in the European Junior Championships. That would have been really something.

*

There might have been a rivalry with Mick Holmes but it was always a professional rather than a personal thing. Out of the ring, it was all friendly. We'd play football together and again, it would be competitive, but that was because we all liked to win. It was never nasty or malicious and the banter, of which there was lots, was always good-humoured. That was true with all boxers in and around the national team: there was a great spirit between us, and lots of joking and messing about. Sammy McDermott, who fought at light flyweight, I remember we used to take the mickey out of all the time.

There were some real jokers in the pack, and none more so than the featherweight Kenny Webb. I remember we were flying out to East Germany for a competition one time and he brought with him this lung tester. This device had a tube that you blew in to, to try and turn the turbines round inside it, and a couple more tubes at eye-level. You had to give a really good blow to get the turbines to turn round: you had to scrunch your eyes up and go for it. What Kenny did was to fill the turbine with soot, so when you shut your eyes and blew it – boom! You got two black panda eyes. Kenny pulled this trick on everyone: even the East German officials.

When I didn't make the team for the European Juniors, I received some comforting words from Gerry Storey, the coach of the national squad. 'Don't worry about it,' he told me, 'something else will come round for you.' Sure enough, a week or two on, not even a fortnight later, I found out that I had been picked for the 1978 Commonwealth Games in Edmonton, Canada, a selection that more than made up for my earlier disappointment.

Storey was the coach for the Northern Ireland team, too, and I learned a lot from him. For the first time I found myself throwing sequences of punches, rather than individual punches. A one-two, a one-two, step away, jab. He showed me how to put five or six punches together, throw combinations in a way that I had never done before. I was at the point in my career where I was getting a bit older and more mature as a boxer, my timing was improving and I felt confident in the ring. I had a razor-sharp jab, my right hand was very hard, and I had a good left hook. What Gerry did when I went to camp with him was to help put them all together. Ta ta ta ta ta ta – bang! They were fast combinations and it felt phenomenal.

Going to Canada was an exciting experience. I would have loved to have seen more of the country when we were there, but the training schedule meant that there was little time for any sightseeing. The thing that sticks out in the memory was just how hot it was. It was the height of summer and, coming from Ireland, I really felt the heat. I remember being worried when we got over there that I had lost all the fitness I'd gained back at the training camp in County Down: there I was doing ten 120-metre sprints, with a ten-second rest between, but in Canada I could only do seven before I was wrecked. I was concerned it was the altitude, but it was just the weather and I worked hard to get myself as sharp as I'd been in County Down.

The athletes' village was arranged alphabetically by sport, so the boxers were in with the bowlers, you know, crown green and all that. They were the greatest guys, just fantastic. We stayed in these high-rise apartments at the university campus: Hugh Russell was my room-mate. I remember we'd travel around in these big yellow buses to get to our training. We'd go over to the ice-hockey rink, where there were rings set up, and do our sparring there: with the Australian team, if I remember rightly.

Being so young, it was a real buzz to be away from home. This feeling was reinforced by being able to meet the other competitors in the athletes' village. This would usually be at meal times, when everyone ate together: they did a particularly mean American breakfast, complete with hash browns. I remember chatting with Steve Ovett and Daley Thompson, who were both incredibly friendly and down-to-earth. I also met Don Quarrie, the Jamaican sprinter who'd won 200 metres gold at the 1976 Olympics.

The one time we did see a bit of Canada was when we headed out into the countryside courtesy of Dennis Belair, who was a big name in Canadian boxing and had a good relationship with the Ulster boxing team. Belair took us out of town, about forty miles into the countryside, where we spent the afternoon shooting. We shot rabbits and did some clay-pigeon shooting: the targets would be fired up in the air, and we'd take aim from the other side of the lake.

When the training was over and the boxing tournament began, my first opponent was a Scottish guy called George Lowe. I beat him, and then defeated Michael Anthony from Guyana to reach the semi-finals. This time my opponent was a Canadian, Bill Ranelli, so you can imagine the amount of support he had. He was a local guy and boxed a bit like Mick Holmes, only more aggressively. This was where all the hard work with Gerry really paid off, and I knocked him out with the best combination of punches I'd thrown. I hit him – boom! – and he wobbled and went down. The referee gave him a standing count, and then said, 'Box on.' I ran across into his corner and unleashed this combination: I must have hit him with at least ten punches. I hit him several times on the head, his legs went and that was it. The crowd, which had been really boisterous before the fight, was completely silent.

The final was against Tumat Sogolik from Papua New Guinea. They said he was a 24-year-old Papua New Guinean customs officer, but he looked more like he was 34, and was the biggest bantamweight I have ever seen in my life. I got to the ring for the final, stepped up and just went, 'Holy . . .' when I saw him. He wasn't tall, if anything he was slightly shorter than me, but he was massive, huge arms on him. I don't know how on earth he made the weight. But he made it anyway and I knew I had a real fight on my hands.

In the first round, I outboxed him. I was outboxing him again in the second and about halfway through I remember thinking, I'm just going to throw the right. I went to throw it, but he beat me to the punch. Jesus Christ, I'd never been hit like that in my life. I thought the house had fallen in on top of me. I didn't go down, but the ref gave me a count. Sogolik came running after me, but I had the presence of mind to grab and hold him and clear my head. I started getting back into it and the bell went for the end of the round. In the third I used my jab, and moved around. I kept missing him by a fraction with the right hand, and I was just thinking I'll really go for it this time when he caught me again. I didn't go down, but my leg went and the ref said, 'Stop!' and gave me another count. Sogolik came roaring after me but once more I was smart enough not to get caught again.

It was a close decision: very, very close. Des Lynam, who was commentating on the radio, thought I'd won it: Harry Carpenter, the legendary BBC commentator who was the reporter for the TV, thought I'd lost. But amateur boxing is about the quantity of punches as opposed to one-off quality punches. It's about how many times you hit the target area. Though I'd had the standing counts, over the course of the whole fight I felt I'd outboxed Sogolik. I thought I'd done just about enough to win and I was right. Sogolik may have landed the bigger blows but I hit him far more than he hit me. I got the points and the gold medal.

It felt incredible. I was only seventeen and here I was, with the gold medal in my first international tournament. I was one of the youngest champions they'd ever had, certainly in boxing. It was an amazing tournament for Northern Ireland, too. The team won a whole string of medals: another gold, a silver and a couple of bronzes: an achievement only bettered in 1998 and 2010 (in 2010, Northern Ireland set a new record, getting five boxers into the final and winning three gold medals: the most successful boxing nation in the entire tournament). We came home to a great reception: a crowd turned up to meet us at the airport at Aldergrove and I won the BBC Northern Ireland Sports Star of the Year. British Airways sponsored the award and the trophy was a triangle with a Concorde inside it. I went on to win the award so many times that they eventually gave it to me to keep. I still have it somewhere.

By now, I was finding it increasingly hard to make bantamweight. In October 1978, I went to Rotterdam to represent Ireland in a multi-nations tournament and struggled to hit the limit of eight stone seven. We stayed on a boat in the harbour, and I remember running along the harbour, really sweating to try and make the weight.

They introduced these new gloves with stuff in them called closed cell foam, which reduces knockouts by 60 per cent. I remember hitting these guys with everything and they could take it but I was bouncing punches off their heads. It definitely seemed like I had lost a bit of power. I beat a Czech guy in the first round, David Rose of England in the semis and Russell Jones of Wales in the final. Jones took some stick but I beat him unmercifully and won the award for best boxer of the competition.

After that, I decided to move up to featherweight. My first fight after stepping up was in a Scotland–Ireland match at the National Stadium in Dublin. That was a crazy night. The capacity is a couple of thousand or thereabouts, but there were loads more watching than that. It was a sellout and they broke the doors down to cram in and watch. They were standing in the wings and the galleys, everywhere to try and cheer on a cracking Irish team: Phil Sutcliffe, Gerry Hamill, Mick Holmes, P J Davitt, Kenny Beatty and the Christle brothers, Mel, Terry and Joe, also fought that night.

I boxed this guy called Neil Anderson, a southpaw. It was my first fight at featherweight and I noticed immediately that he was stronger than the bantams were. I hit him with some really good shots but I could not get rid of him. I beat him, but knew I was up against fighters who were physically stronger and could take a better shot. I began to fill into the weight and went into the Ulster Seniors as a featherweight for the first time. It was the first fight my mother ever came to watch, and boy did she choose the wrong one.

I remember that I'd had my hair permed. It's a bit embarrassing now, but it was the in thing at the time, and Sandra, who I was going out with by then, was working at the hair salon, so I decided to have it done. I was boxing in the final against a guy called Kenny Bruce and I remember my mother was late arriving for the fight. She was just coming in, concentrating on reaching her seat, and she wasn't really watching, and then she looked up and saw me. I had this curly hair and had got cut right down the face. My mother just said, 'Oh my God,' turned around and walked out. She never came to watch me box again.

What had happened was that I had backed Bruce up to the ropes and gone to throw a right hand to the body. He had put his head down and I ended up hitting him on the top of his head. I got his teeth in my nose as I'd gone in and got cut again as he'd hit me in the process. The blood was pouring and I must have looked a right mess. Under the Irish rules of the time, what happened was that if the fight lasted more than one round and got stopped for a blood injury, then whoever had won the opening round was declared the winner. I'd won that comfortably so I was still Ulster champion, albeit at a different weight.

I got the cuts stitched and had to take time out for them to heal. After that, my next fight was against Torsten Koch again, in another international match against East Germany. This time the fight was on his home turf. We flew to East Berlin and drove 300 kilometres down to a place called Erfurt, and somewhere along the way I caught this terrible bug. A really bad, sick stomach. To make matters worse, the roads were dreadful: it was so bumpy, it was like driving on cobblestones. By the time we got to Erfurt, all the weight I had put on in becoming a featherweight had gone. I was back down to eight stone seven, back to being the weight for a bantam. I wasn't myself. I wasn't strong. The fight was closer because of that, but I still beat him.

East Germany at the height of the Cold War was a strange and threatening place. Our hosts were keen to impress upon us throughout our stay what a prosperous and egalitarian country East Germany was. They were also eager to discuss the country's past, and took us to the Buchenwald Memorial and the remains of one of the Second World War's most notorious concentration camps. The East Germans wanted to show us their abhorrence at what their countrymen had done, and how different things were now under communist rule.

The potholes and bumpy journey down from Berlin, however, suggested a somewhat different perspective on East Germany to the official version we were being given. The East Germany I witnessed felt run-down and bleak, and somewhat behind the times. The one exception to this was the boxing facilities we were allowed to use. We were put up in university accommodation, and at the bottom of the high-rise apartment block we were staying in was this amazingly kitted-out gym. It was real state-of-the-art stuff: the gym had what looked like tennis balls attached to the walls on some sort of wire. These would be hit against the wall and bounced back for the boxer to hit, to help improve their accuracy. This might sound like something out of a James Bond film, but they also had this mechanical punching mannequin, which could throw a left jab at you: the idea being that it taught you how to parry and slip the punch. The East Germans were deadly serious about their sport and would go to great lengths to win; it was later revealed that the use of anabolic steroids and performance-enhancing drugs was systematic and widespread. I don't know if that was the case with boxing then, but I do remember one opponent coming into the ring and giving off a strange chemical smell. God knows what that was about.

The other thing you couldn't escape in East Germany was the 'big brother' feel that permeated the country, and the sense that the Stasi, the state secret police, were never far away. It felt like everyone was watching you to start with, but pretty soon you realised that they were all watching each other as well. One of the other boxers out there was the light heavyweight Tony Deloughrey, who had brought some jeans across with him to sell: the students were all desperate to buy denim. In doing so, he tried to strike up a romantic relationship with one of the female students – something that got stopped extremely quickly. Our team coaches were told in no uncertain terms to make sure nothing of the sort happened again.

Because my weight was down, the Germans then wanted me to fight their bantamweight, Mario Behrendt. Behrendt was unbeaten: a good, hard-punching southpaw. His father Wolfgang had won the Olympic gold medal at the 1956 Olympics, and had beaten Freddie Gilroy, a Belfast boxer, in the semi-finals. Mario had been groomed as a boxer from a young age and was a big, big bantamweight. He was much bigger than me, and I was a featherweight.

I was ill and I was light and everything else, but I agreed to fight him. Behrendt hit me a lot, hurt me with some shots, made me think, oh, this guy can hit. The only way to beat him was to take it to him. If I'd have stood off, he would have clipped the head off me. So I took it to him and in the second round I caught him: what a shot I hit him with! That completely unnerved him. I hit him again near the end of the round, completely nailed him. He didn't get a count but you could see it put the fear of God into him. After that he was on the defensive. I backed him up and put him under pressure. He still hit me, but I was catching him a lot by the last round. It was a close decision, but I deserved to get it.

From East Germany, my next competition was another multi-nations tournament, this time in Romania. The tournament took place in Constanta, on the Black Sea. It was a holiday resort but, like in East Germany, you could never quite escape the feeling you were being watched, and that everyone was curtailing their behaviour accordingly. The mood wasn't quite as oppressive as in East Germany, and the people were slightly friendlier in their demeanour towards us. But it was made perfectly clear to us that on no account were we to misbehave. The other thing that I really remember about the visit was the thunderstorm on the first night we were there: I've never experienced a storm like it. We had these metal shutters right down over our windows, but even so, the noise of the thunder was incredible. It was quite a welcome!

I beat three Romanians on the way to the gold medal: the junior, senior and military champions. The military champion in the final, that was the first time I had ever got dropped with a body shot. I'd gone back to the ropes, and thought I had heard the referee say, 'Break, step back.' So I relaxed and loosened my guard. But then the soldier buried his southpaw left hand right in the pit of my stomach. I went oh! . . . gasp, and it didn't feel too bad. Then I went . . . GASP, knelt down and couldn't breathe. The referee gave me a count and I looked at the corner and I thought I was never going to be able to breathe again. I had the presence of mind to run away, for about thirty seconds I ran and ran and ran, started catching my breath again until the bell went.

Benny Carabini was in my corner, a little fat guy from Dublin, who was on the central council of the Irish Amateur Boxing Council and our coach.

'What happened to you?' he asked.

'I could hear the ref,' I wheezed, '. . . jab to the body . . .'

'Come on, kid,' Benny replied, 'lift it up.'

He made me stand up and breathe, and bend over. It took the full sixty seconds to get my breath back. Of course, the Romanian came out and was rushing after me. But I steadied myself, steadied myself, and hit him . . . bang! His legs sagged, and the referee gave him a count. I hit him again but by that stage I had clearly won: he'd only hit me with the one body shot. I won the final and once again won the award for best boxer of the tournament: a great way to finish the year, and the decade, and to set myself up for the Olympics.

I'd been working towards the Olympic Games for four years, but 1980 couldn't have started much worse in terms of my preparation. I had been chosen for an Ulster versus Leinster match, fighting against Ritchie Foster at the National Stadium. I had come to the ring with bandages on my hands, but had just a little bit of sticky tape at the back of my hand to hold the bandage on. I got to the ring and the glove officials said, 'You are not allowed that, you can't put that on your hand.' It's only a bit of tape, I argued, but the guy wasn't having any of it.

'You are not allowed to do that, you'll have to go and get that changed,' he insisted, pointing back to the dressing room.

This is ridiculous, I thought. I'm about to step into the ring. So I just took the whole lot off. I ripped the bandages off in a rage and went into the fight with bare hands beneath my gloves. I beat the living daylights out of Foster, needless to say, dropped him three times. But I knackered my hands up something awful in the process. I chipped a bone on my left hand, on the knuckle. You can still see it now. It wasn't much but it was enough. I had to go and see an orthopaedic surgeon, who injected around my knuckle with cortisone. It accelerated the healing, but I still missed the Ulster Seniors.

I got myself back into shape again for the Irish Seniors: got sharp, even if I didn't have any sparring beforehand. In the semis I fought Damian Fryers, a really strong, stocky guy from the Holy Trinity club in Belfast. I outboxed him but in the process chipped my bones again and couldn't box in the final against Mick Holmes. I was back in the routine of rest and cortisone injections to try and get myself ready for the European Juniors.

The Juniors that year were held in Rimini in Italy. The team was made up of a fantastic group of lads, and we got up to all sorts of mischief while we were out there. Ritchie Foster and Gerry Hawkins in particular were always up to something. Hawkins was so small he was known as 'Diddler', but when we went to Rimini, he more than held his own. While we were staying out there, we decided to hire a load of scooters for the day. You had to hand your passport over to the rental place both to prove your age and in case there was any damage. Martin Brereton was the only one of us who had a licence, so he got given a bike with gears, while the rest of us had to make do with these tiny scooters.

It wasn't long before we started mucking about, Ritchie and Diddler in particular. We rode the bikes down to the seafront, and decided it would be fun to buzz along the beach. So there we were, spraying sand everywhere and people shouting at us and complaining: it was all good fun, but as we got to the end of the beach, word had obviously got out about what we were doing, because there were the Italian police, parked up and waiting for us. We did a quick U-turn, as you can imagine, and went as fast as these little scooters would allow back along the beach, with this police car trailing us on the road at the top.

We made it off the beach and headed back into town, switching this way and that, trying to leave the police behind. I can't remember who decided, but we cut into this park, thinking, they can't follow us in here. We were bombing along, pleased with ourselves that we'd lost them. Ritchie and Diddler, meanwhile, were continuing to wind each other up as they'd been doing all day. As we were riding along, Diddler stuck his foot out and knocked Ritchie off his bike: Ritchie went sprawling and his bike went smack into a tree! Ritchie was furious, and went running after Diddler, but Diddler was too fast for him, and off he went.

Ritchie's bike was absolutely ruined: the front of it was completely crumpled. Brereton and I helped him carry it back to the rental people who, as you can imagine, were far from happy, and refused to give us back our passports until we'd paid for the damage. Ritchie, Brereton and I had to empty our pockets – we had to hand over every last lira we had before they gave us our passports back. Diddler and the others, who'd already returned their bikes without having to pay anything, thought the whole thing was hilarious.

In the tournament itself, I won my way through to the semi-final, which was against Yuri Gladychev of Russia. Gladychev was the world junior champion, which rankled slightly: I had wanted to go to the 1979 World Junior Championships that took place in Tokyo, but for some reason or other, the Irish hadn't sent a team, and Gladychev had ended up winning my division. So he was a good fighter, no doubt about that. He was clever, too, but even so, I beat him clearly. Yet somehow the judges gave it to him, three votes to two. The funny thing was that they were trying out a seven-panel jury in that tournament, and all of the seven judges on the panel got it right and gave the fight to me, but they weren't allowed to overrule the original decision.

I was angry, angry and gutted. I was furious because you know you are in the lap of the gods, the judges make the decision who wins, not you. It was a foul decision and the crowd knew it. The Italians howled at the result and when I got on the podium to get my bronze medal they cheered, 'Ireland! Ireland! Ireland!' That felt good, but it didn't overcome my disappointment of not winning.

Once again, I had no time to brood because within a couple of weeks I was back down to Drogheda, getting ready for the Moscow Olympics. I was picked as captain of the team, which meant a lot to me. We trained in Drogheda in the Holy Family club along the Boyne. We stayed in the Rossnaree Hotel and in the morning we would run down to Bettystown beach, do our sprints along the beach and run back. Then we would do weights in the afternoon and sparring in the evening. We trained really hard.

At the very end of the sparring, the last sparring day, we all had to do six rounds. I sparred two rounds with Phil Sutcliffe, who was the bantamweight, and I was outboxing him. Then they put in Damian Fryers and again I sparred very well. And then they put in this guy, Tommy Davitt. Davitt was a pro welterweight, pro light welterweight, and probably weighed near eleven stone, ten stone ten. In the fifth of my six rounds, he slipped my jab and threw a left hook . . . bang! – he hit me underneath the ribs and he cracked my ribs. I finished the round, but immediately felt the impact. Afterwards, boy it was painful.

I remember arriving at Moscow Airport and being taken to our accommodation, which again was on a university campus. Everything looked clean as we drove in, almost too clean. The streets seemed strangely empty too, in a way that reminded me of my visit to East Germany. Throughout my time in the Russian capital, I don't think I saw any dogs or birds anywhere. The whole place felt strangely sterile. That atmosphere made its way into the athletes' village as well. There was still the camaraderie I experienced at the Commonwealth Games, but it seemed more restrained. Movement was a lot more restricted as well: you had to keep your pass and credentials with you at all times, and needed identification to be allowed to go anywhere.

I had to train but because of my rib injury I could not spar. Between the end of the sparring, travelling to Moscow and getting back into the gym, I had probably lost about two and a half weeks of training. Not only was my rib painful, but my hand was beginning to play up again. It was sore and started to ache again.

My first fight was against Isaac Mabushi of Tanzania. I knocked him down in the second, gave him two standing counts. The bout was stopped in the third round. I remember watching the fight afterwards and Harry Carpenter saying on the BBC commentary, as I walked back to the corner, 'It looks like McGuigan's hand troubles are over and he now progresses to the next round.' But exactly as he was saying this, I was saying to Jerry, 'My hand has gone again.'

It was throbbing as I was going back to the corner. But because my next fight was two days later, there was no time for recovery, no time to think about it. I fought a guy called Wilfred Kabunda from Zambia. He was a big, tall, stringy featherweight. I had a local anaesthetic, which you were allowed to do, so I could not feel anything in my hand, could not feel my hand at all. The hand didn't bother me during the fight: I boxed well and felt I clearly won the fight. Yet somehow they gave the victory to him. My second bad decision in a matter of months, and I was out of the competition.

My next fight would have been against the guy who won the gold medal, the East German Rudi Fink. This time it was Kabunda who got the raw deal. He beat Fink from pillar to post and they gave the victory to his opponent. I don't know what it was all about, whether these were just rotten decisions or something more sinister. There were stories about corruption and Iron Curtain countries doing each other favours: one particularly colourful suggestion was that they were putting rat shit in the foreign athletes' food. I know our team manager, Eddie Thompson from Belfast, was very sick for months after the games.

What I do know is that for the judges, I was just a number. I might have been nothing to them, but for me, the Olympics had been everything. Everything not just for me, but for the hopes and aspirations of all the people around me, those who'd supported me and helped me. People like the Monaghan Men's Association who had saved up and given me money every week to support me (that had come about through Frank Mulligan, who had a contact there:

the organisation would have dinners to raise money for local causes). It was all just so gut-wrenchingly sickening. Everything I had done, everything everyone had done, had meant nothing.

I saved up the money I was given for being out there, and bought Sandra an engagement ring with it: that was about the only good thing to have come out of the whole experience. I didn't go home straightaway: the whole team stayed to the end. It was boiling hot and every day Martin Brereton and I would go down to the track in the athletes village where we were staying and we would lie out on the pole-vaulting mat and get a bit of colour. I watched loads: I was in the stadium to see Sebastian Coe beat Steve Ovett for the 1500-metres gold medal. I remember seeing the 400-metre relays, and the closing ceremony. And, of course, we had one boxer still in the competition: Hugh Russell, our flyweight, boxed brilliantly to win a bronze medal. We were all so proud and screamed ourselves hoarse supporting him.

The thing about boxing is that when you're in the ring, you know whether you have won or not. And although he would never admit it, your opponent knows too. But that is part of amateur boxing; you have to say that's it, get up and get on with it. After the European Juniors and the Olympic Games, I'd had enough of my career being blown apart by bad decisions. I went home and said, right, that's enough for me. It's time to consider turning professional.

Chapter 4

Turning Pro

I was interested in the thought of turning professional from quite early on in my amateur career. I had gone over to have a look at Terry Lawless's gym in east London when I was sixteen, to get a sense of how they trained. The gym was above the Royal Oak in Canning Town, and I would stay with my Uncle Leo in Highgate, and get the tube out from there. I remember telling Lawless how old I was and he didn't really believe me. 'You are sixteen?' he said. 'You are the most muscular sixteen-year-old I have ever seen in my life.'

I went back to Lawless's gym again after I had won the Commonwealth gold. Again I wanted to watch the training, to see the likes of Charlie Magri and Ray Cattouse close up. I wanted to spar with them too, to test myself against them. One of the main reasons I wanted to go was to ask Lawless when he wasn't busy – he was always looking after his guys – whether I was big enough to move up to featherweight. His advice to me was, 'If you are good enough, son, you are big enough.'

It was an exciting time for me, to go over and stay in London: I was still only a kid. I learned all the routes on the tube to go across town from north to southeast London. I would travel down, go in and bandage up, tape up and spar. I sparred with Charlie Magri, who was getting ready for a title fight. He was heavy, a sort of slightly bandy-legged big, big flyweight. He probably had an extra bit of weight on and was heavier than me as a bantamweight. I remember the first day I came in he was training, and he finished and put a big blanket round him to get the heat up, just to sweat out, because you could sweat out probably another two pounds if you do it right. Put a towel over you or a blanket over you and your woolly hat and it just pours out of you.

Magri was getting ready for a European flyweight title fight against an Italian called Franco Udella. I had been watching him spar and I thought it was all fairly tame. Even so, I did my gloves up and was a bit nervous and apprehensive as I stepped into the ring. The bell went and I walked across to Magri and hit him with a jab. His head went back, and blood started pouring out of his nose. We started to go at it: wham, wham! I was told to take it easy after that: 'You don't go hell for leather, son,' Lawless told me. 'Just box, go through the movements. You don't have to throw everything in your punches.' We went through to the end of the round. It transpired that I had broken Magri's nose and they had to postpone the European title fight.

The next time I visited, I sparred with Jim Watt, who had just become world champion. I sparred six rounds with him and did very well. I frustrated him so much because of my head movement: I was moving and jabbing and throwing loads of punches. He found me a handful to cope with. Couldn't catch me, he even says that today. But I did six rounds with him and I thought, wow, I've done well here. I got out, and then Jim did another six rounds with somebody else. By the time he finished, he had done fifteen rounds of sparring. That was the difference with their training – they didn't spar to knock someone's head off. So I picked that up and took it back to my training.

Spending time in Terry Lawless's gym was a good learning

curve for me. I went back to my amateur career confident that I could be a featherweight, pleased that I had done well against decent fighters and impressed with the professional setup. All of which stayed in my mind as the end of my amateur career played out.

By the time I got back from the Olympics, the contrast between the professional and amateur worlds could not have felt starker. I was so disillusioned with what had happened in Moscow that I actually thought about giving up boxing altogether. That's enough now, I thought: I have wasted enough time and have had too many raw decisions. After I came home, Sandra and I went to work for a guy called Sweeney in Dublin who was a friend of a friend. We went down to Dundrum in south Dublin to run a hamburger joint. It was sort of a trial run, to see how it worked. Anyway, I lasted about a week of flipping burgers and it nearly drove me flipping mad. I started training again before the week was out. There wasn't a local club, so what I ended up doing was asking Sandra to help me. In order for me to do my pad-punching, what we did was tie a mattress around her, and I'd punch that. It didn't hurt her or anything, but goodness only knows what anyone looking in through the window would have thought!

It wasn't just the bad decisions that were affecting my amateur career. By now, I was reaching the end of the road with my coach Frank Mulligan. There's no doubt I had learned a lot from him over the years, but we had been together for so long that I needed someone else to continue improving my game. I'd enjoyed working with the national coach and could see that his different way of doing things was bringing fresh ideas to the way I was fighting.

Secondly, Frank's personal situation was beginning to get in the way of our relationship. I should mention that in 2009, Frank was sentenced to six and half years for sexually abusing teenage boys. It goes without saying how utterly revolted I am with what he did:

his actions were evil and unforgivable. The incidents he was found guilty of all happened several years after we'd parted company, but even so, it's difficult for those terrible events not to cast a shadow over our earlier relationship. I should stress that nothing like that happened with me: instead the issue that ended things between us was Frank's drinking, which was damaging our working relationship.

I remember saying to Frank, I've agreed to take part in this match against West Germany, and I need to get ready for it. I went down to the club and he was on the drink. I told him that I'd had enough of this, and said that if he wasn't dry in two days then that would be it. I'd had enough letdowns in my amateur career by now: I was deadly serious about what I was doing, and couldn't tolerate this, couldn't deal with things being done in a half-hearted way.

'Look,' I said to him, 'I am boxing this guy in ten days' time and you are not in a fit state to work my corner. How am I going to get ready? I need to go to somebody who can help me. And you can't help me like this.'

Frank said he'd be all right, that he'd be ready. I knew in my soul he wouldn't be but after all the time we'd been together in the club, I wanted to give him a chance. This was the Monday and the fight was on the Friday week, so I gave him two days. I said, 'I'll come back on Wednesday, and you had better be ready.'

On the Wednesday, Dad and I went out to see him, but he wasn't around. We spoke to his mother, who was a lovely woman, and Dad asked, 'Where's Frank, where's Mulligan?'

'Oh, Paddy,' she says, 'he's in the tavern.'

'How long has he been in?'

'All day, last night as well.'

So my father and I went into the village to see Ben Toal, who was a cousin of Frank Mulligan. Dad goes in and says, 'Have you seen Frank?'

'He was in here last night,' said Ben, 'he was in here this morning.' He said, 'Go up to the postman's house.'

Dad and I went up to the postman's house and I remember sitting in the car down at the bottom of the steps, and saying, 'Don't bother, Dad, we will just . . .'

But Dad went up to the postman's house and as he was walking up the steps, he could see Frank in the front room. They were so blind drunk, him and the postman, that they didn't even see my father. Dad walks up and knocks on the door, and all he could hear was this scrambling: 'You go . . . no, you go . . .' Eventually the postman opened the door and he was as drunk as a skunk. My father said to him, 'How are you doing?'

'Hello,' said the postman.

'Have you seen Frank Mulligan?' Dad asked.

'Frank Mulligan?' The postman acted all innocent. 'Frank Mulligan . . .'

My Dad, who could see him, said, 'He's standing behind you, you clown.'

'Oh, *that* Frank Mulligan!'

My father just brushed past him and went up to Frank. 'I thought you weren't going to drink,' he said.

'I haven't . . . I haven't.'

'What's that in your hand?' Dad pointed to the bottle of whiskey he was holding.

'It's . . . Cidona.' (Cidona is a non-alcoholic apple drink.)

My father just said, 'Good enough. On you go, mate, that's good enough.' And he jumped into the car and we drove straight to Gerry Storey in Belfast, and carried on training without Frank. I sparred that night and the Friday night, sparred the following Monday and a light session on Wednesday and then we drove to Dublin on Thursday. I got up Friday morning and, for the first time ever, I had to go to the scales twice to make weight as a featherweight. I fought against the West German and Gerry Storey did my corner. I boxed well, and it was nice to get a win under my belt again.

It's said that bad luck comes in threes. I don't know about that, but certainly bad decisions seemed to turn up in that number. I agreed to fight in a multi-nations tournament at Wembley Arena, this ABA centenary event. I boxed a fellow called Pete Hanlon from Gloucester who was in the Moscow Olympics representing Great Britain at featherweight, and I beat him and battered him to get to the final. Then I boxed a guy called Ian McCloud from Scotland. He was a southpaw, a tricky, awkward southpaw. I won the fight easily, but they gave it to him, which seemed to me another lousy decision.

That was it for me with the amateurs. Here I was, just getting started, and these guys were winning fights over me when they shouldn't have been. There is something wrong here, I thought. I need to get out of this game. 'I've made my mind up. I'm turning pro,' I told Gerry. Gerry asked me to hold on until the Ulster Seniors and, because he had helped me a lot, I agreed. I did the Ulster Seniors and won them again for the third time. I boxed Damian Fryers from the Holy Trinity and broke his ribs in the second round. I won the title but it didn't change my mind. I was turning pro.

I had been approached by a number of promoters to turn professional. Terry Lawless had shown an interest before the Olympics. Mickey Duff had written to me. Eddie Thomas, who looked after Colin Jones, wanted to look after me, and a number of others were interested. I also had an offer from some Irish guys in America and that was the other option open to me. Then Barney Eastwood came in and showed an interest. He approached me, funnily enough, through Gerry Storey.

The immediate advantage that Barney had over the others was that I could fight at home. I would not have to travel away. I was very much a home bird and my family was central to my success, the support structure that I had from my extended family. Fighting at home was going to be an extension of that and therefore it was much more appealing to me than moving. There was no guarantee, I was told, that I would get any better money by moving anyway and so I never got to the stage of negotiating with the others. Because I was interested in Barney Eastwood, the other discussions never really materialised.

I felt I had boxed my whole life in the North. I had represented Northern Ireland at the Commonwealth Games and won the gold medal. This seemed to me to be the obvious way to go. So my father and I met up with Barney at Ballymascanlon Hotel in Dundalk, just out on the Carlingford Road. Barney was there along with another chap called Davy 'the Hat' Donnelly. We had a second meeting in his house in Holywood but I more or less knew after the first meeting that I would probably sign with him.

Barney and I clicked straightaway. I liked him: he was quite assertive, but warm. I remember asking him whether he would prefer for me to call him Barney, BJ or Mr Eastwood and he said, 'I'd prefer you to call me Mr Eastwood.' So that is what I called him from there on in. At the second meeting, I think I met his wife Frances and her sister Martha, and I met their father, he was called Mr Monaghan. I can't remember if it was that night, but I met the boys, too: they were all my age, some of them older, some of them younger. I liked them all, I thought they were a nice family. I thought, yes, we are going to do a deal.

Barney was interested in bringing professional boxing back to Northern Ireland in a big way. We are going to kick it off again, he said, we are going to really start it again, do a brilliant job and we will have it like it never was before. That appealed to me as well. At that time, professional boxing was a bit hit-and-miss, if you'll pardon the pun. Charlie Nash fought occasionally in Northern Ireland, and I had actually gone to watch him box in Derry in this freezing-cold leisure centre one night. But those sort of big fights in the North were sporadic. There was a guy called Damien McDermott but he fought only very occasionally and hadn't fought in a long time. To be part of reigniting the interest in pro boxing again, that was exciting.

We did a deal for my first ten fights and had a signing session at the Royal Avenue Hotel in Belfast for the media. A guy called Harry Doherty was the legal witness. The press were there, some TV and radio and we did a load of interviews. It was a huge day for me, you know. I was just twenty when I turned professional. It felt a big deal.

When I started training, I thought I was going to meet up with Gerry Storey initially. But Storey didn't agree or couldn't agree or whatever it was. I don't know what actually happened with him. Storey was out and a guy called Eddie Shaw was in. I went to meet Eddie and we trained in the Immaculata club in Belfast and it was a formidable place I'll tell you. We had to go through the Divis flats and the Divis flats was a square-shaped high-rise set of apartments, flats, and the army was ensconced on the top of them; it was a Republican part of town. You would walk into the gym at your peril because kids would throw things down on top of you. I used to meet Eddie Shaw at the National Forresters club that was about 300 metres away from the Divis and then we would walk in. I say 'walk': we would do commando runs, zigzag so no one could throw anything on top of us, before getting to the gym.

The gym was in the basement of all of this. It was actually a very good gym, the Immaculata. It had a very good reputation. We'd train there and do a bit of sparring, but most of the time we had to travel to get sparring. I did a lot of pad work with Eddie, we would do the bag and work with another guy called Ned McCormick. Ned was a very funny character. We worked in that gym and then we would go to the Holy Trinity, for example, for sparring and we would go up to St Agnes's to get sparring up there. We would travel around, go wherever the sparring was.

My debut fight as a professional was against Selvin Bell on 10 May 1981. It was a Phil McLaughlin bill in Dublin, at the Dalymount Park football ground. I was on the undercard of Charlie Nash defending his European title against an Australian-based Italian called Joey Gibilisco.

I remember the weigh-in, thinking I was a big featherweight but turned out to be nine stone on the button: Selvin Bell was nine-two. We got to the show and even though it was May, it was freezing cold: at this time I had never fought without a vest, which didn't help. It was a miserable evening weather-wise, and damp: they'd put a mat down over the grass but that was sodden too. I was told not to go out in my boots, that I would soak them. I made sure I put something over the top, and put these plastic bags over and Sellotaped them round so I wouldn't get my feet wet.

I was supposed to go on before the main event so I put on my boxing boots, put the plastic bags over them and started making my way towards the ring. I got about ten or fifteen feet from the ring and the floor manager came running towards me saying, no, we can't, we can't do it. They wanted to put the Charlie Nash fight on first for the television. I was nervous about the fight but had to turn around and go back to the dressing room.

Some fighters will go out and watch the fights before they box but I never like to do that, I just like to concentrate on what I am doing. I went back to the dressing room and listened to the commentary. Gibilisco hurt Nash, and dropped him. Nash got up and fought back and got back into the fight but Gibilisco hurt Nash again. Nash again fought back but with less vigour this time and then Gibilisco finally knocked Nash out: stopped and dropped him. I thought, oh shit! I am going to have to come out now and follow that. Some of the crowd will have dispersed. And those that are left will all be down in the mouth.

It was about ten o'clock by the time I came out, and quite a strange atmosphere. But I was pumped up with it being my first pro fight and I just took Selvin Bell apart. I measured him up in the first round and then hurt him in the second. I never let him off the hook and dropped him with a body shot. I dropped him with a head shot and then the referee bawled at me and jumped in to stop it. I remember all my family and my fans were there to support me. They were all shouting and screaming and jumping up and down and Harry Mullan, who was the editor of *Boxing News*, said, 'You would think McGuigan had just won the world title, instead of being the 43rd man to have beaten Selvin Bell.' When I won the world title he said, 'I take it back.'

Selvin Bell was my first win as a professional: my first defeat, however, came far sooner than I'd have liked. Having defeated the Liverpool boxer Gary Lucas in four rounds on the undercard of the Jim Watt – Alexis Arguello fight at Wembley, I took on Peter Eubank at the Brighton Corn Exchange on 3 August. One of the reasons I'd wanted to turn professional was to get away from those ropey decisions that I got in the amateurs. I wanted to fight longer fights where I could really show my class, and where there could be no arguments about who was the better fighter. And yet here I was, in just my third pro fight, back in the same situation as before.

Peter Eubank comes from a family of boxers: there is his brother Chris, of course, and also his twin Simon, another fighter. He is a Brighton kid, so the fight was a home fight for him, and it might have been the reason that referee Roland Dakin gave it to him. Eubank was a tough kid, for sure, but there's no doubt that I won it by a mile. Yes, he was brave and got up and threw punches, but they all hit my arms and missed. I put him down, beat him from pillar to post and yet somehow Eubank won 78½–78. Even his own fans howled at the decision.

I was confused and angry. I'd lost my unbeaten record as a professional even though I thought I'd won and everyone who was there was telling me the same. In the end, I dealt with the defeat by telling myself that I beat Eubank, but that I just didn't get the decision. I put the referee's opinions aside and considered it a win. That was it. I made the decision to fight again very quickly, and put the defeat behind me. The last thing I could afford was to dwell on what happened, as my next opponent was someone who was a serious step up in class.

Out of all my early fights, the contest with Jean Marc Renard was probably the most important. Renard was a really good young boxer: he was unbeaten in his six fights and could really fight: '*fantastique*' they described him as, back in Belgium. Renard would go on to win European titles at two different weights and challenge Antonio Esparragoza for his world title, so he was a class act. His calling card was his tremendously laid-back left hook: he'd invite you to throw your right hand at him and then, once you were committed, he'd lean back and beat you to the punch.

This was a decent fighter I was taking on, and it was important that I won. If I had lost that fight on the back of the Eubank one, it would have really shaken my confidence. It could also have had a detrimental effect on my career. But beating Renard was more than just about getting back to winning ways. It was also important as a measure of myself as a boxer: I wanted to prove to myself and the paying public that I could do the business against anyone, the good fighters as well as the journeymen.

There was another reason that the Renard fight was significant, and that's because it was my first professional fight at the Ulster Hall in Belfast. I had boxed in the Ulster Hall several times before as an amateur, and I loved it. But this time was different: as a professional, I needed to show that I was someone who was capable of pulling in an audience. I had to prove not just that I could box, but that I was box-office as well.

The Ulster Hall is a brilliant venue for boxing, with an atmosphere that is all its own. Opened in 1862, it was built as a multipurpose hall, but always with music in mind – at one end there is a stage with this fabulous, enormous pipe organ – and perhaps that's why the noise is so electrifying. The hall has played host to some big names over the years: the Rolling Stones performed in 1964, and Led Zeppelin played 'Stairway to Heaven' live here for the first time in 1971. Before all that, back in the 1950s, the Ulster Hall was a hugely popular boxing venue, with regular fight nights both on Saturdays and during the week.

Because of the acoustics and the shape of the hall, when you put the ring in the middle of it, it felt like the guys were beside you. It was as if they were sitting in your corner, cheering you on. As a fighter, it's a huge boost to come in to that level of support, to hear this amazing atmosphere echoing all around. The Ulster Hall fans really know their boxing, too. There is no fooling them: their knowledge and understanding of the sport is second to none. If this most discerning of audiences decided to get behind you, you knew that as a fighter, you must have been doing something right.

I don't think the place was quite full for my first professional fight in the Ulster Hall, but those who did come that night got more than their money's worth. It was a great contest, with two good boxers going flat out. After the allotted eight rounds were over, the referee Harry Gibbs gave it to me by a single point, 79–78. In those days, a point was worth two rounds, so that meant I'd won the fight by five rounds to three. I thought I was a clearer winner.

My plan was to keep the tempo high because Renard didn't like to fight at pace. So I kept changing direction, going in and out of punching range, and tried to keep on top of him. Renard wanted to unleash his left hook but I was being clever, pretending to throw the right hand so he would fire off his left hook and then I'd pull back. I was jabbing and hitting him with a long right hand and double-jabbing and throwing the right. The double-jab always left me vulnerable so I made sure I was hitting him: jabbing to the head and then pile driving the right hand into his body. As clever as I was being, he still managed to hit me with his hook a few times. And then, in the seventh round, he caught me perfectly. Wallop. Before I knew what was happening, I was on my arse.

Looking back, this was a real test-of-character moment. There's a question mark over any boxer about whether they can take a whack, but the truth is that until it happens to you in the ring, you don't really know. As I sat on my backside I remember thinking, I was caught there. And then, a split second later, what the hell am I doing down here? I bounced back up right away, and knew immediately my legs weren't gone or anything: it was just a terrific shot, and a flash knockdown. In fact, I was up so quickly that the referee assumed I'd just tripped over, and didn't even give me a count.

The referee wasn't the only one to think that. Back in the corner at the end of the round, Eddie Shaw asked me, 'Did you trip?' Ned McCormick, his second, was in the corner too, and he knew right away what had happened. 'You must be joking,' he said. 'He was knocked down; those long arms got him with a great left hook.' They had a bucket of ice and water, and an old sponge, and they soaked the sponge in the icy water and went 'whoosh' with it in my face. It was freezing cold and the shock of it made me go 'Aaargh!' but I needed my head clearing and it did the trick. I came out then and I really gave it to Renard in the eighth and final round.

The crowd knew that I was the real McCoy after that. They knew I had fought a very good kid, and I had beaten him clearly. I had taken a shot, got up, fought back and had my opponent in trouble in the next round. So there was no doubt that I could take a whack either. After a performance like that, the crowd would have been left thinking, well, this guy has got something. They had been treated to an entertaining fight as well, which was no bad thing for future business.

At the end of the fight, the crowd showered the ring with 'nobbins'. Nobbins was an old way of appreciating a good fight: the crowd would throw coins into the ring as a mark of respect for a good contest. This was before the launch of the pound coin, so the fans would throw ten- or fifty-pence pieces. The fact that the audience considered the Renard contest to be a 'nobbins fight' was an indication of how good it had been.

Jean Marc Renard had been an opponent who could walk the walk. By way of light relief, my next fight, again at the Ulster Hall in October, was against someone who was better at talking the talk. Terry Pizzaro from Florida was a late replacement for my original opponent, Sylvester Price, but made up for lost time by telling anyone who would listen what he was going to do to me.

'I'm gonna kick his ass!' he bragged. 'I'm gonna beat him so bad!'

All of which was great in selling out the hall, a show of support that Pizzaro was unsurprisingly dismissive of: 'They'll need to get in the ring to hold McGuigan up,' was his response. A couple of days before the fight, Pizzaro met my father, shook his hand and apologised for what he was going to do to me: 'I'm sorry, but I'm going to beat your son badly.'

I remember saying 'he's whistling in the dark' to all that. Pizzaro was a decent fighter, but his jabbering was certainly better than his jab. It bucked me up so much that by the night of the fight, I was really ready to go to town on him. Even then, he didn't let up: Pizzaro kept his act going right up to the opening bell: he clambered into the ring and danced around it, playing up to the crowd, waving and all that sort of stuff. He did this shuffle, beating his chest, and told me again he was going to give me a hammering.

Pizzaro was flash, you know, fast. I looked at him for the first round because he was quite tricky, but after that I'd seen enough and just set about him. I was missing him with punches that would have taken his head off and then finally in the fourth round, pom pom pom . . . BANG! I caught him with a body punch and he hit the floor. He was lying on the floor roaring and screaming – 'Aaargh! Aaargh!' – making so much noise that the crowd were laughing at him, you know. Even after the fight, he still didn't shut up: 'Gawd, you hurt ma ribs!' he winced. 'Man,' he continued, 'you a busy bee, man!'

With the Renard and Pizzaro fights, it was clear that we had an audience in Belfast, so it wasn't too difficult to entice Peter Eubank over for a rematch in December. We knew that we would pull in the crowds, and there'd be a lot of press because he had beaten me the first time. I also knew that without Eubank's home-town advantage, there'd be no ropey decisions to fall foul of, and no arguments about who was the better fighter.

Eubank wasn't cocky coming in to the fight, but he was certainly very confident. One of the strangest episodes I remember was when his manager Tony Brazil, who I think must have been into his fifties, ended up being one of his sparring partners. We had offered him some fighters to spar with and Eubank took our offer up, but then he also sparred with his own manager. This was presumably to maintain his sharpness and to shed those last few pounds, but I saw the two of them a few days before the fight and Tony Brazil's eyes were black and blue. Eubank had hit him on the nose and bashed him up. Brazil just looked as though he had been in a car accident. It was terrible. I thought, God, you do that to your manager?

The Ulster Hall was packed this time. The fight was a really good one but I was always in complete control. The longer the fight went on, the more I ground him down. In the sixth round, I had him in desperate trouble. I was all over him and thought the fight was going to be over there and then. When the referee jumped in, I thought it was to end it but in fact he was separating us as he thought he'd heard the bell. As it turned out, the noise was so intense that he'd misheard: there were still twenty seconds of the round to go. By the time everyone had worked out what was going on and the round was restarted, Eubank had recovered. The moment had gone.

I had put so much exertion into trying to finish him off in the sixth that I took the seventh round off, just picking him apart again, and softening him up near the end of the round. Eubank's powers of recovery were incredible, he had this amazingly tough chin like his brother Chris, but in the eighth round I really set about him. I wanted to stop him so badly so it wouldn't go to a points decision so I pounded him all over the ring and this time, when the referee pulled us apart with twenty seconds to go, it wasn't because he thought he'd heard the bell. I had got my revenge fair and square.

Six days after beating Peter Eubank, Sandra and I got married. It hadn't gone down well with the in-laws, arranging the fight so close to our wedding day, but we wanted to get married and that was that. There was no point in holding back any longer: I had my career to be getting on with and Sandra was working in the hair salon, so we were just trying to be as industrious as we could. Of course, it didn't help that in the process of beating Eubank I got a little cut on my eye. On the morning of the wedding, I had to have my stitches out, and thankfully they'd done a good job – you wouldn't think I was damaged at all.

It was a winter wedding and it was snowing, or a little bit of light sleet as we called it. We got married in Sandra's church, the Church of Ireland, and had a blessing in the Catholic church afterwards: my brother Dermot was my best man. It was a lovely day and a wonderful reception at the Lennard Arms, my father-in-law's hotel – it was a real coming together of family and friends. And even though it was less than a week after the Eubank fight, I felt fantastic, no after effects at all.

Sandra is a remarkable woman. I was attracted to her from the first day I set eyes on her back in the early 1960s. She was and still is a beautiful-looking woman. She's always had great bone structure, fabulous brown eyes and she had a great shape: even as a teenager she looked like a woman. I finally plucked up the courage to ask her out on her eighteenth birthday. Sandra has a very good business brain and she is a hard worker, she has a gregarious personality and finds it easy to network and get along with people. She would have been a great success as a businesswoman had we never met. Apart from anything else, she has been the most fantastic mother to our four children and a fabulous wife to me: just incredible in every way, she's kind, selfless, generous and exceptionally loyal. I am still madly in love with her after nearly thirty years of marriage. She has been an incredible support to me over the years.

It definitely made a difference to my career, being in a stable relationship, being with her. I know so many great guys – great, great guys – who were sensible, level-headed, solid as a rock and then they met up with the wrong girl, and it destroyed them. Destroyed them. Couldn't keep it together, went off the rails, bang. So I know I have been exceptionally lucky. I really mean that. None of this would have happened without Sandra.

Chapter 5

Young Ali

Getting married didn't stop the fights coming thick and fast: I remember going on honeymoon to Tenerife, and skipping away on these beautiful marble floors to keep myself in shape. In early 1982, I continued my winning streak and people started talking about me as a possible British title contender: I beat a tough Spanish fighter called Luis de la Sagra on a points decision, then despatched both Ian Murray and Angel Oliver in three rounds; Angelo Licata only lasted two rounds, while my second contest with Gary Lucas only lasted the one. Then on 14 June 1982, I fought against a Nigerian fighter called Asymin Mustapha, who boxed under the name Young Ali, at the World Sporting Club in the Grovesnor House Hotel, Mayfair. The fight should have been all about impressing the watching officials from the British Boxing Board of Control. As it turned out, the night was memorable for all the wrong reasons.

The thing I remember most about the build-up to the fight was the battle with my weight. I hadn't actually hit championship weight – nine stone – for any of my fights since my pro debut. For the Gary Lucas fight, I'd weighed in at nine stone three, and for the two fights before that I'd been nine stone two. So I had to prove to the BBBofC that I could make nine stone or thereabouts before they'd consider me for a shot at the title.

I remember it was quite a struggle to get down to the weight and had been more difficult to achieve than I'd expected. What you do to get your weight down, certainly the way we did it all those years ago, was that you went through what we now know as a catabolic state: basically, you shrank your stomach and your body. You ate a couple of meals a day, your body would shrink and you would lose both fat stores and, unfortunately, muscle mass. Nowadays they have a much more scientific approach and you are able to predominantly eliminate the fat and retain the muscle mass. But no matter how much and how strict and how good the diet is, you will still lose lean muscle mass if you are dropping a considerable amount of weight.

On the morning of the fight, we weighed in at the Board of Control office, which was close to Piccadilly Circus. Ray Clark was the secretary of the Board of Control and I remember getting on these big scales and making the weight. I was there with Barney and Paddy Byrne: Paddy was both a fighting agent and cuts man, and played a significant part in my career the whole way through. A very funny guy, sharp as a tack, he was like the camp jester and great to have around. He knew his boxing, too – he'd looked after Paddy McGuire, who'd won the British bantamweight title, and in the 1970s had been involved with the McCormick brothers from Dublin. Both had won British titles, one at light welterweight, the other at light heavyweight, having made the decision to take British citizenship to be able to do so. Paddy was already familiar with the way my career path was playing out, and was a great source of advice.

After the weigh-in, Paddy, Barney and I walked down to Fortnum and Mason and we had breakfast. I had a normal breakfast, scrambled egg or something like that, but then decided I would have an ice cream. It was a complete mistake: as soon as

I ate it I felt bloated, this big dollop of ice cream on top of a substantial breakfast. All that hard work getting my weight down, and now I just felt dreadful.

I had never been a big fan of the boxing setup at the World Sporting Club anyway. The fights took place at the Grosvenor House Hotel in Mayfair, and the feel couldn't have been more different to the Ulster Hall. Back in Belfast, I fought against a backdrop of noise and support, in front of a crowd who really knew their boxing. At the World Sporting Club, everyone was dressed in black tie, and they sat round eating dinner while you boxed. Some of them ignored the fight completely, and didn't even appear to be boxing fans at all. It was a strange, sterile atmosphere for a boxer to fight in.

The venue for the dinner-boxing show was the Great Room, a large and commanding space that, believe it or not, started out life as an ice rink. It was the home of the Park Lane Ice Club, a high-society meeting place that boasted royalty among its members: it is where the Queen learned to ice-skate. In the 1930s, the rink was boarded over to create the largest ballroom in Europe: the Great Room is now a popular venue for awards ceremonies and other prestigious gatherings. The dressing rooms were up at the top, and I remember walking down this elaborate-looking staircase and around the tables to the ring. Everyone was dressed in black tie and eating. There was the occasional bit of applause, but nothing more than that. I remember coming to the ring in this strange atmosphere and looking up at Young Ali. He looked tall and slender, as opposed to a short, stocky muscular guy.

Ali had been a bantamweight originally, but had outgrown that division, stepping up to superbantam and now featherweight. The fight started off, and immediately I could tell he was tough. I was hitting him with some good shots but he was quick and competitive. He took it to me some of the time but I never backed up so I took it to him as well, and he was happy to have a fight with me. When he engaged me he was tough: he would fire shots back but I was soon getting the better of the exchanges. He would back away, but I was having success here too. I'd push him back and we'd do the old attrition stuff of trying to catch each other with clean shots as we broke away from close exchanges. It wasn't easy because he was difficult to hit, but I bounced a lot of punches off his head and hit him hard to the body. I didn't hit him enough to the body, really, but his defence was not as good when I threw punches at his head, so that's where I was concentrating.

I rattled him several times, but he'd keep coming back: he had good powers of recovery. Young Ali hit me with plenty of punches too, so it was competitive, definitely, for the first couple of rounds. But I kept banging away with my combinations and started taking control of him. He was losing the rounds, though only by a little bit: I wasn't beating him all over the place or anything like that.

I was aware that the Board of Control were looking at me as someone they could potentially put into an eliminator fight. I really wanted to impress them, and remember trying hard, really hard. In the fourth round I made a big effort to get rid of Young Ali. He'd been in trouble in the third so I really went for it. His recovery was good, however, and near the end of the round he made another spirited effort and came back. When I got back to my corner, I remember saying, 'Oh, this is a tough kid, he is tough!' In the fifth, I decided to take a round off. I'd have another look at him, box him more, but not put the same energy in as my effort in the previous round. So I used my movement, outboxed him and took the round that way. I was told later that when Ali got back to his corner he was complaining about his jaw: 'I can't feel it,' he was saying, 'my jaw feels like it is floating around.' The corner men told him to keep going and get through it, encouraged him that he would be all right and sent him out for the sixth.

I came out for that round thinking, right, I am going to go and get him now. I stepped it up and began to set about him. This time,

Ali started to wilt and I hit him with the long right hand, right on the nose. I had hit him with a couple beforehand and he was starting to go so I went bom, bom . . . Bam! I hit him and the reaction was incredible. His head swung round and he just fell down. He fell down and I went to the neutral corner. There wasn't lots of screaming and shouting or anything like that: my uncle was there and my cousin, and there was a bit of cheering from them, but otherwise the audience response was all fairly muted.

I went to the neutral corner and Ali did not get up. The referee counted ten and he still didn't move. The doctors were in immediately: they didn't have paramedics or stretchers in those days. They crowded over and after three or four minutes, I was beginning to wonder what was going on. I remember someone coming over to me and saying, 'This kid, this kid is badly hurt.' I couldn't believe it. 'You must be joking,' I replied. 'No,' he said, 'he's very badly hurt.'

I just thought, oh my God. We took the gloves off and waited, and it was all a bit confused: there was no announcement or anything like that. I was still in the ring and was just getting out of the ropes when apparently he came round and they helped him to his feet. I thought, that's a relief. I remember looking and clapping but they were around him when they were lifting him, so I couldn't really see him properly. It's said he put his hand up to the crowd, but I don't think he did, I think they just lifted him to his feet. They tried to let him stand, but then Ali just fell and they cushioned him and let him go back down to the ground. I remember looking back as I climbed up the stairs to my dressing room, and the Board of Control officials and his corner men were all down on their hunkers again.

To be honest, I didn't think anything of it at the time. I didn't think anything of it at all. I thought that once I had seen him get to his feet that he was all right, he'd recovered. I went up to the dressing room and started getting changed when someone came in and said again, this kid is really hurt. But he got to his feet, I said. No, this guy said, they thought he was collapsing again. I went and had a quick shower and it was all very subdued. I came out of the shower and dried and put my clothes on, and Ray Clark came in. 'That young man is seriously injured,' he told me.

So we knew at that stage that it was very bad news. They took Ali to the nearest hospital, rather than a neurosurgical one as they do now. These days, we know all about the 'golden hour', that critical time period for sorting things out. But whatever hospital they took Ali to, by the time they registered him and put him in and everything else, the golden hour had long gone. He was in there, and then they took him to another hospital and registered him again: it was only then that they operated.

They tried to stem the blood clot. What they do is an X-ray first of all to find out where the bleeding is. Then they shave the head and cut into the skull, take the skull cap off where the bleed is and then try to fuse the bleed. They leave the skull open so the brain is allowed to swell and then come back down again and then they put the skull cap back on. So they tried to operate on Ali but couldn't stem the blood flow. I'm not sure exactly why they couldn't. All I know is that Ali didn't recover from it and he remained in a coma. After about a month or so, they flew him back to Nigeria, where they kept him alive with a respirator.

It was a very strange time for me, and incredibly difficult to deal with. There were so many conflicting emotions: sadness at what had happened; anger that I'd been put in this position; uncertainty as to how to proceed. I hadn't taken the game up to do something like that to somebody. I wanted to get the better of my opponent but I never wanted to hurt them, and certainly not permanently. It shocked me, profoundly shocked me. I found out that Young Ali's wife was pregnant and that he'd come over from West Africa on his own, to earn some money and go back to her, and then this had happened. I was very down about it, very upset. I was questioning why I was boxing, whether or not I felt I could continue.

It was a strangely lonely and isolating experience to go through. The only fighter I was aware of who'd been in a similar situation was Alan Minter. In 1978, Minter had knocked out the Italian Angelo Jacopucci to win the European middleweight title: Jacopucci died a few days later as a result of the blows he'd received during the fight. At this stage in my career, I was just a young fighter starting out: I didn't know Alan at the time, and wasn't in a position to discuss my situation with him. For all the fantastic support I got from Sandra, Dermot and everyone else, I felt on my own in coming to terms with what had happened.

I was desperate for information, and to find out how Ali was doing. Why had they taken him home? I wasn't sure whether that meant there was a chance that he would recover, the way some people with brain damage can get physiotherapy and treatment and they can help them and give a reasonable quality of life. Or had they taken him back to die? It was difficult to get any answers: the Board of Control didn't inform boxers, you know, didn't want to alarm them. So I picked up bits and pieces here and there, and tried to make sense of the situation.

It was a terribly strange thing. Everyone thought I was a nice kid. People liked me, yet here I was, having almost killed somebody, and it was all legal and above board. Because of what I did, when I was in the ring, I was legally allowed to almost kill someone. What must people have thought of me? I found myself asking why it happened to Ali and not to me. I went to church and prayed a lot. The people that I always had faith in were those at the Poor Clare Monastery in Belfast because of their amazing dedication – they had given their whole lives to God. Some of them have been in there sixty years. I visited them a lot during this difficult time, and their words were a great support. 'There is nothing you can do, Barry,' they told me. 'Just leave it in the hands of God and just hope that by some miracle, he will recover.'

I was like that for ages, just thinking, wandering around. But I couldn't carry on like that. As Ali stayed in a coma for weeks and then months, the harsh reality was that I had to make a decision. OK, I thought, what are you going to do? Was I genuinely willing to give it all up and do something else? Sandra was pregnant and working six days a week in her hair salon to make ends meet: it wasn't just did I want to stop, but could we afford for me to go back and do something else? And how would that have affected my life? Would I have been able to give up my boxing dreams and get a regular job? What I did is that I tried to say, look, what would happen if the positions were reversed? What would happen if he had been the one who almost killed me? Young Ali would have carried on, fighting and earning for his family. And I made the decision that I would have to continue.

I think, in fairness to Barney, he didn't interfere. He said, just let yourself come back to it naturally. And eventually, that's what I did: I made the decision to continue. I started to pick up the training again, and although it was difficult at first, my brother Dermot was brilliant. He said, 'Come on, Barry, try and get on with it. You know, that's it, this is the reality.' I am sure he was deeply affected by it but he still tried to get me out of the reverie I was in. He's right, I realised. I've just got to get on with it.

It was four months between the Young Ali fight and my next contest, against Jimmy Duncan. It was the longest I'd been out: I'd been fighting so regularly before the Young Ali fight, that it was going to take a while to return to full speed. It wasn't just the physical shape I had to get myself back into. With everything that had happened and Young Ali still in a coma, there was a question over my mental state that I had to deal with as well.

The Jimmy Duncan fight was by no means a gentle

reintroduction to the ring. Duncan had had seven fights – six wins and one loss – and we were looking at this as a possible eliminator for a British title fight. Which meant that I had to work on my weight once more, and get it down to under nine stone. The fight itself went OK, and I stopped him in the fourth round. But the key moment for me had happened the round before.

I'd had Duncan in trouble near the end of the third. He was looking vulnerable, you could see it in his eyes that he was going. I was right in front of him, and I was going to whack him one, when I paused. I had him in trouble and I just stopped. I thought, what am I doing here? I didn't want to hurt him. I totally stopped in the middle of the punch. In that split-second timing where you hit him or he hits you, I paused and he hit me with a left hook. It brushed off and hit me on the cheekbone. I realised what was happening and thought, Christ, this is serious. So I pulled back out again and got away. I cleared my head and I started again, looking at him, getting set to open the jab, when the bell went for the end of the round.

I came back to the corner and Eddie Shaw was on to me instantly. What was all that about? What was that about? And I said, it was nothing, Eddie, I just paused. But Eddie knew. He spat some verbal at me: 'Don't fucking do it again,' he said. That sorted me out. After Eddie had sworn at me, I was all right. I came out in the next round and I knocked Duncan out.

The referee went back and told the Board that they should be considering me for a title fight. So we then got a final eliminator, back in the Ulster Hall against Paul Huggins from Brighton. Funnily enough, I met him again about a year ago. He had been down and out but became a Christian and turned his life around. He is working in Hastings, his life is back on track and he is doing well, which is a great story. Huggins always was a tough opponent, a wear-them-down attacking fighter. He was a gung-ho, come-forward sort of guy, and had the power to knock you out. I had to show my boxing ability to deal with that. I boxed very well, very clever that night: I was constantly on the move, circling one way around the ring and then the other, making myself as difficult to hit as possible. In the fifth, I wobbled Huggins with a right hook and a left hook. His legs went and the crowd was screaming. The referee jumped in and stopped it.

The Huggins fight was the final eliminator for the British title and, unlike the Jimmy Duncan fight, I'd come through with no qualms. I'd had no hesitation, no worries, and felt I was getting back to my old self. My career was moving forwards again and I was in line for a title fight. But a few weeks after the fight came the news I'd always dreaded hearing. Young Ali wasn't showing any signs of recovery, and his family had made the agonising decision to switch the machines off. He died on 13 December 1982.

I now know that Young Ali was never going to recover because I have learned much about the intricacies of what a subdural haematoma actually means. Having pressure on the brain for a long period of time means more than likely that your long-term brain function is going to be severely compromised and your chances of recovery are poor. A typical subdural haematoma injury is when a blood vessel on the surface of the brain tears, then a clot forms between the brain tissue and the skull wall. This puts pressure on the brain and if that pressure is not removed very quickly the patient ends up with varying degrees of brain damage and sometimes can die from their injuries. Boxers who dehydrate to make certain weight categories are supposed to be more susceptible to this, yet there are many boxers who have had no trouble making weight but have still suffered from a subdural haematoma. Nobody knows why it happens to certain boxers and not others. It was suggested that Young Ali had an unusually thin skull but I'm not sure whether that's true or was just a rumour: from what I've been told it seems to me that it was just one of those rare but fatal boxing injuries.

In 1982, they didn't have the procedures in place that they have now. These days, the nearest neurosurgical hospital is made aware that a professional boxing match is taking place nearby and that in the event of a boxer suffering a head injury they will take him to that hospital. We now have paramedics ringside who are experienced in treating head injuries, and every professional boxing show that takes place in Britain also has to have an anaesthetist ringside. Finally, every boxer that has a BBBofC licence has to have an annual MRI scan of their brain. It's a far better system we have these days, and just a tragic shame that we didn't have such a setup when I was fighting.

Two and a half years later, when I was getting ready to fight Eusebio Pedroza for the world title, I thought of Young Ali. When a fighter is left alone with his thoughts, loads of things go through your mind. Before a big fight, these sort of things can enter your head. Sometimes they do, sometimes they don't, it depends on the individual. But that night I thought about Ali.

After I won the title and was being interviewed by Harry Carpenter on TV, I took the opportunity to talk about him. I wanted to win the title and dedicate it to Young Ali because of what had happened. I wanted people to remember him, to remember the guy who was involved in that tragic fight with me. I wanted to be able to say that it wasn't just an ordinary fighter who had beaten him, but a world champion.

I was in tears when I was talking to Harry Carpenter about Ali. I sort of stuttered through what I wanted to say, but even with all the noise and the excitement and all the buzz, Carpenter was able to pick up what I was saying. And he interpreted and explained it to the millions watching on TV. It was an important moment, simple as that, and I was hugely emotional. It meant a lot to me that at the moment of my biggest victory, I was able to remember Young Ali in that way.

Chapter 6

Leave the Fighting to McGuigan

I decided to box professionally in Northern Ireland with a British Boxing Board of Control licence because, as I mentioned, I could live at home. Professional boxing had been very successful down through the years in Northern Ireland with the likes of Rinty Monaghan winning British, European and world titles, John Caldwell doing the same and Freddie Gilroy winning British, Commonwealth and European titles. These fighters had enjoyed fanatical support when they were boxing and, while those years had long passed, I always knew that potential was there for it to return if the right boxer came along.

Boxing out of the South of Ireland was always going to be much more difficult. First of all, there didn't seem to be an appetite for the game in a professional sense in the Republic. Secondly, there were very few licensed fighters and the organisation that administrated the professional game at that time, the Irish Boxing Board of Control, was effectively a one-man band. There was controversy surrounding Charlie Nash's European title-winning contest against Francisco Leon that took place at the Burlington

Hotel in December 1980. The organisation was re-formed in 1981 as the Boxing Union of Ireland and its first show, ironically enough, happened to be my professional debut: the main event was Charlie Nash versus Joey Gibilisco in a European lightweight title fight, where Charlie was knocked down a number of times and lost his title.

The BUI was a fledgling organisation with very few actual boxers on their cards and, in fairness, very little recognition at that time. By contrast, the BBBofC was a world-renowned body recognised by the WBA and the WBC, the only world bodies at this point. The BBBofC had serious gravitas. Many fighters on the strength of being British champion were able to get a shot at the world title, so the decision to go down that route was a no-brainer.

To indicate how apathetic the general public were to professional boxing back in 1981, you only have to look at my pro debut on the above-mentioned Charlie Nash European title undercard. It was held at Dalymount Park soccer stadium in Dublin, where the Irish national team played their matches. It had a capacity of 30,000 but on that evening there couldn't have been more than a few thousand people there. Even when the great Muhammad Ali fought Al Blue Lewis at Croke Park in 1972 there were no more than 10,000 people in an arena that can hold 80,000. It was embarrassing and must have cost the promoters a small fortune, despite the fact that they would have received substantial television money. Amateur boxing, by contrast, was very successful and maybe that was the problem: all the shows at the National Boxing Stadium on Dublin's South Circular Road were very well attended.

These days professional boxing is very successful in the South of Ireland due in no small part to the success of boxers like Steve Collins and particularly Bernard Dunne. While Collins based himself in England for the latter and most successful part of his career, Dunne was a Dubliner fighting out of Dublin, after starting

Left: My first Holy Communion, aged 8, 1969.

Above: Summer 1973 in the back yard. Back row from left to right: 'Papa' Rooney, my grandmother 'Doty', and Uncle Paddy. Front row: My cousin Pat, my sisters Rachel and Rebecca and myself.

Left: Summer 1977, after winning my first national juvenile title.

Relaxing with my Commonwealth Games teammates, 1978. Left to right: Myself, Gerry Hamill, masseuse Ray Smith, Kenny Beatty and Kenny Webb.

Winning Commonwealth gold as a seventeen year old, 1978.

My final eliminator fight for the British title against Paul 'Fireball' Huggins, 1982.

Morning run on the beach at Ballyholme, Bangor: my training camp, 1983.
Pacemaker Press International

Celebrating after beating Valerio Nati to become European champion, November 1983.
Action Images / Mirrorpix.com

Mum and Dad
in the gym that
Dad made for me
at the back of our
house, 1984.
Express Newspapers

With my father
Pat in 1984.
Tony Fisher / Daily Star

Barney Eastwood
and me after
another hard day
at the office, 1984.
Michael Fresco

Press call with
Frank Bruno
before facing
Farid Gallouzc,
March 1985.
Mirrorpix.com

Above: My dad sings 'Danny Boy' before the Pedroza fight, June 1985. Pedroza is trying to stare me down (I'm just out of shot on the left). Mirrorpix.com

My first real breakthrough against Pedroza came when I knocked him down in the seventh round. Pacemaker Press International

Pedroza and I
battle it out in
round eight.
SSPL / Getty Images

'You'll be a good
champion': Pedroza
congratulates me
after the fight.
Express Newspapers

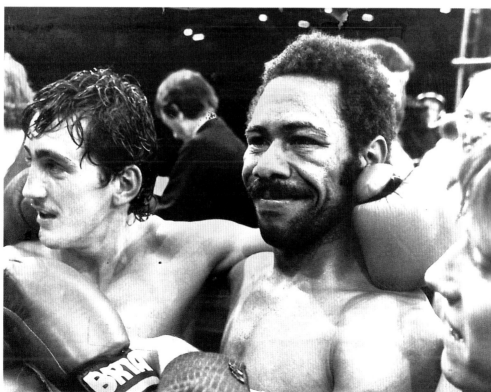

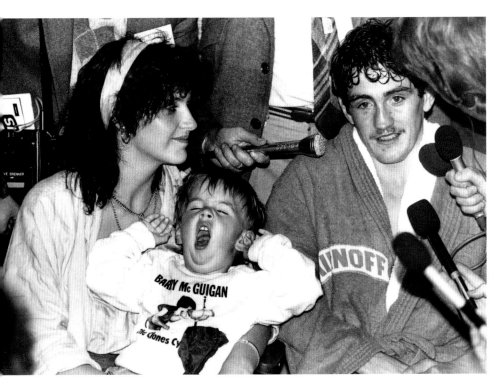

Meeting the press after the Pedroza fight with Sandra and an exhausted Blain.

Monty Fresco / Daily Mail / Solo Syndication

My mother and me after coming home to Clones, following the Pedroza fight.

Express Newspapers

his career being based in the USA and being managed by none other than the all-time great Sugar Ray Leonard. When he returned home Bernard built up a huge following and RTE, the state-run television station, got huge ratings when Dunne boxed.

Mel Christle has been involved in the BUI since its inception and he is now the main guy running what is now a very active and successful boxing organisation. Mel is one of three boxing brothers who are a unique family: they were very successful amateur boxers representing the national team many times. Mel was a heavyweight, as was his brother Joe, while Terry was a big-punching middleweight. The Christle brothers belied the notion that boxers are not the most intelligent people in the world: as well as running the BUI, Mel is a very successful barrister; Joe has enjoyed careers in both journalism and the law; and Terry, who had a professional record of fifteen fights and thirteen wins with nine knockouts, is now a surgeon in the US.

Recently I was present at the first-year celebration of Muhammad Ali's visit to Ennis, County Clare, to receive the freedom of the city: Ali's paternal great-grandfather Abe Grady was from Ennis. The day I was there I met a nice guy called Michael McTigue, a descendent of a great old Irish fighter of the same name, Mick McTigue. Mick McTigue fought and won the world light-heavyweight title way back in 1923 from an African champion called Battling Siki. It took place in the La Scala Theatre, Dublin, right in the middle of the Civil War. Right up to when the bout actually started there were gun battles going on out in the nearby streets. They must have stopped to allow the boxing contest to take place and for people to get in and out of the venue – totally bizarre. McTigue won an unexpected lopsided decision over twenty rounds. The younger Michael told me that my victory over Danilo Cabrera in February 1986 was the next world title-winning performance from an Irish professional boxer since his great-grandfather lifted the title almost sixty-three years before.

That was how sporadic professional boxing was in the South of Ireland.

The only other way of being successful in the pro game was to uproot and head to America and try to cash in on the Irish-American audience the way John Duddy has done so successfully over the last five years. For me that was just a nonstarter because I was too much of a home bird and simply could not have been away from my family. I was determined that I could kick-start the interest in pro boxing in Northern Ireland and that if things worked out the way Barney and I had planned we could capture the imagination of the whole country, North and South.

I always believed – and still believe – that a boxer has to become part of the community. For a fighter to build up a solid base of support, he has to be authentic, he has to be home-grown. To give you just one example, there are a couple of amazing Cuban boxers based in Ireland at the moment but the crowds just don't turn up to watch them. The Irish don't care about them: it's only a small amount of boxing fans, the real enthusiasts, who appreciate them. Being home-grown is an important part of a boxer's image: the more a fighter can make local people and journalists feel as though they are part of something, that everyone is embarking on the 'journey' together, the stronger their fan base will be.

The North was right beside me: if you went half a mile out of town, you were there! I had boxed for the provincial title; all my titles were fought in the North. I was in many senses a northern kid. As an amateur, it had never really been an issue: as with other sports like rugby union, the Irish Amateur Boxing Association was an all-Ireland body, and selected fighters from both North and South. It was only now I was a professional and a title contender that I had to make a decision one way or the other.

I knew that by going north of the border, going to Belfast, I was going to bring all the southern guys with me. So we would have people like Martin Breheny from the *Irish Press*, we would have Tom Cryan from the *Irish Independent*, we had Shaun Kilfeather for the *Irish Times*. We had Gerry Callan, who wrote for the *Sunday Tribune*. We had Eoghan Corry, who wrote for the *Sunday Tribune* – we had all of the southern Irish press who came with us too. Then in the North we'd have Alex Toner and Paddy Toner from the *Daily Mirror*, Michael McGeary and Denis O'Hara, who wrote for the *Irish News*, we had George Ace, who wrote for the *News Letter* and Jack Magowan, who wrote for the *Belfast Telegraph*. It also helped enormously that the editor of *Boxing News*, the trade paper, was a Derry man, Harry Mullan, and he was a huge help as well. We had all of these guys and they were all part of my success story.

The journalists from both North and South understood the sensitivities and the practicalities of where I was coming from, and where I was going from a political sense: everything I did took place against the backdrop of the Troubles. When you look back on it, it was an incredible social-history story: the political hurdles we had to jump, just to be able to fight. We had to find out how best to do it, to navigate our way around upsetting people.

I knew that I'd have to get British citizenship to fight for the British title. We always thought it would not be a problem, that we would just go and apply for it. But I was worried about the fact there had to be forms signed and all that, and especially because the political situation was so delicate at the time. I ended up getting help from the SDLP's Paddy Devlin. He was a big politician, a Catholic guy: his politics were all about peace and reconciliation. So he helped us with the passport, and got all the issues sorted out pretty quickly.

I remember that my dad had reservations about it, just because it was a big thing to do in those days. Terrible things were happening in Ireland. It was not like we were going to be able to get a passport without there being some publicity, or some news story about it. So I think that was his major concern. But as it turned out, it all moved along fairly quickly. There weren't any threats. Not at that point anyway.

The Republican side of politics would have known that British citizenship was the direction my career would have to take, and on the deeply Republican side of things there would have been a lot of resentment. There would have been a small section of the community for whom what I was doing would have been anathema. But I did not know those people: I never came across them and they never got in my way. There would have been undertones in certain places, Republican territory, where my actions would not have been appreciated, but these were the sort of neighbourhoods I'd generally steer clear of.

Sometimes you couldn't avoid it completely. Take the Immaculata club, where I trained: I had to go through the Divis flats to get there. That was staunchly Republican. Part of that would have been because the army was stationed on the roof, and because of the intimidation the local residents were under. It would have made them rebellious. But I would cut through and go to the gym. And I knew there were boxing fans in these areas too, deeply knowledgeable boxing fans, ordinary people who knew who the bad people were too, and they would have stayed a distance away from them. The guys that didn't like me didn't like anybody. They were misanthrope 'hate the world' types.

It wasn't until 1985, after I became world champion, that I did get a genuine threat. Someone contacted the *News of the World*, and whichever Republican organisation it was told the newspaper that they were going to kidnap me. I think it was genuine enough because they were keeping an eye on me, the security forces on both sides. Remember that I lived right on the border. By this point, I lived along an unapproved road outside Clones: I lived in the North but it was effectively the suburbs of Clones. Because of that, there was always the potential I could be nabbed. So the security forces on both sides of the border looked out for me. When I had to travel to certain places I would get an escort, following in the distance.

I was issued with a gun as well at that time and was taught how to shoot. I couldn't hit a barn door, but I was taught how to handle the gun properly. I kept it for a couple of years, I think, and then I had to give it back when I moved to England. I had to have a licence for it, had to keep it in a metal box locked and all that sort of stuff. To be honest, I didn't want to keep it.

One can only speculate as to the motivation behind those making the phone call to the *News of the World*, but my feeling was that the kidnapping threat wasn't political. I don't think it was anything to do with my taking up British citizenship, but it was everything to do with my high profile as a sports star. The threat occurred not long after the kidnapping of Shergar, the racehorse. That incident was all about the ransom, and attempting to raise funds for terrorist activities. My suspicion is that the same thinking was behind the threat to me: that if they got hold of me, they could demand a massive sum for my release. What I suspect the terrorists then realised was that because of both my popularity and my non-political stance, kidnapping me had the potential to backfire. Perhaps that is why, thank God, the threat never materialised.

There was one incident that happened during this period that seems funny now, though I can assure you it wasn't at the time. I was world champion, and had been over in Cavan doing an exhibition sparring session. It was a good gym in Cavan and the event had gone well: I sparred with a guy who'd been flown over from England and also with Dermot. Once the session was finished, Dermot and I headed back to Clones. I was driving an Alfa Romeo, which was a sponsor's car and so had my name written on the side.

The road from Cavan to Clones, like so many in the area, crisscrossed the border between North and South. I didn't have an escort that day and was doing my usual thing of flying along, really pushing the car to its limits. Except this time, I pushed it too far. The car was a rear-wheel drive and I went into this corner too fast and the back end stepped out. I tried to control the car, but overcorrected in the process. Before I knew what was happening, we went flying over this hedge into a field, rolling it over three times. One of the wheels came off, and the stereo speakers, which were still blasting out music, had ended up in the front (it was Eric Clapton singing, ironically enough, 'Coming for to carry me home'!).

Dermot and I were lucky not to have been seriously hurt, but the car was a wreck and so we walked back up to the main road to flag down a lift. But in between us getting picked up and getting back home, an RUC patrol drove past and saw the car. They saw this wreck in the middle of the field with my name on it, and put two and two together to make five. The next thing that happened was that back in Clones, Sandra was answering the door to the Garda. The officer explained about the car and asked her whether there might be some obvious explanation, like I'd gone fishing or something. At this point Sandra, who knew exactly where I'd been, was starting to get worried. Fortunately, at that precise moment, Dermot and I arrived, and she knew that everything was OK. We can laugh about it now, but at the time, the incident gave her a real scare.

The only time that anyone made a sectarian comment to me was in 1986, after I had lost the title. I had been to see a friend of mine near Dungannon. I was preparing to take part in a car rally, and we were meeting with the co-driver. We'd gone to have a look at the car, which was a Ford Orion but with an Opel Manta engine in it: a Ford Orion is normally a front-wheel drive but they had put in a rear-wheel-drive engine. So it was a reconfigured car and we met and checked the vehicle and then had dinner.

I came out of the meal and I was driving a big ice-blue Mercedes-Benz 560. I turned left and drove up to a T-junction and there were three guys standing by the side of the road. They were in their early twenties and just as I was about to pull off – looked right, looked left, everything clear – one of them shouted, 'McGuigan, you fucking Fenian bastard.'

I stopped the car. I was shocked – nobody had ever said that to me before. I reversed back to the T-junction, put the hand-brake on and jumped out. I ran round the front and said, 'Which one of you brave men said that?' They didn't say a word, didn't say anything. So I jumped back into the car and drove off. They were just taking the piss, you know. If I had driven on they would probably have shouted something else. But I'd confronted them and they'd chickened out. That was the only time it happened, ever. I never experienced any other sectarian abuse, before or after that incident.

It was always amazing, the amount of support I had. People would go out of their way to accommodate me. They would go out of their way to support what I believed: my belief in peace, tranquillity and harmony. Even though they may not have had the same political views, people went out of their way to try and feel the same way as me. Certainly at the time they were around me, all that period of time, they tried to get a sense of what I believed in. I always felt that was a really good thing: if nothing else it was good for them to know that there was an alternative, a peaceful view to the political situation, and they could experience that.

People still come up to me and say it was a frightening, terrifying time back then, and yet when I fought it was just like a complete panacea, it was just amazing. 'Leave the fighting to McGuigan' was the slogan at the time, and for those few hours I was in the ring, it allowed people to do just that. I am so proud of that, more than anything else. I am proud that I was able to offer something other than the violence at the time, to be able to spread that hope.

*

My British title fight was supposed to be against a guy called Sammy Sims from Newport, but he vacated the title, as he'd decided he was going to go for a European crown instead. There were two Stecca brothers from Italy: there was Loris Stecca, who was the older fellow, and Maurizio Stecca, who won a gold medal at the 1984 Olympics. Loris Stecca was the European champion, and Sims decided he would vacate the British title and fight him instead. It was a neat way of getting out of having to have the fight with me, though it didn't quite work out for him. Sims gave up his British title and was then beaten by Stecca in seven rounds. The British title became vacant and the two top contenders were myself and a guy called Vernon Penprase. So that was the fight, and I started my preparation.

There was a gap of five months between the title fight and my previous one, and that was because I had started to get ready for Penprase and caught one of the worst flus I ever had in my life. I was getting ready down in Bangor on the seafront in a place called Beresford House, which is where we used to stay. It was two big Victorian houses side by side and they joined them together through the main hall and made it into a huge big guesthouse. It was owned by a girl called Jean Anderson, a nice lassie, and it was run by her and her husband Robert: he was a travelling salesman.

Ken Buchanan the former lightweight champion of the world and an outstanding box/fighter, came over and helped me get ready for the fight. Buchanan was a smart mover and boxed like this guy Penprase, so sparring with him was good practice. We were sharing the same room: it was a big old room with two double beds in it and we had a bay window at the front, and I was in the bed nearest the window. Buchanan was writing his memoirs at the time and he had a typewriter, an old tic-tic-tic typewriter. And I caught the most dreadful flu I have ever had. I was absolutely sick as a dog. I would fall asleep and wake up, go to sleep with this tic-tic-tic and wake up with this tic-tic-tic, and couldn't work out was going on. I felt completely out of it.

My training totally stopped. I couldn't run, couldn't eat, couldn't do anything. Eventually I started to pick up a little bit but it was far too close to the fight date. This was about three weeks before the fight was due to take place, so the fight had to be put back. I was taken to hospital and Barney was advised that it would be wise to postpone it, as I would never have been ready in time. The fight was rescheduled for April, about a month afterwards.

The fight against Penprase finally happened on 12 April 1983. It took place in a vibrant Ulster Hall, packed to the rafters with noisy support. It was the first time I'd fought since Young Ali had died, and there was this question mark over me, too, as to how the flu bug had affected my training. It was an important evening in more ways than one. But I felt good by the night of the fight. I had only had a short space of time to recover from the flu, but I came back, worked hard and got into great shape. My recovery time was good – I had only just turned twenty-two years old – and I felt I was really hitting my natural strength and power.

Penprase was a good fighter, a good boxer. A blond kid who still looked like a teenager, he was born in Plymouth and lived in Devonport. He was a good talented kid, a good talented boxer. Considering all the fuss about the build-up, the applying for the British passport and problems in my training, the fight was some-what brief. In fact, it was one of the shortest featherweight title fights in history, the shortest that century at the time. Penprase just had no idea that I was as good or as powerful as I was, and I took him completely by surprise. I knocked him down twice in the second. The second time Penprase tried to get up, the referee saw the state of his face and stopped it there and then.

It felt brilliant getting the belt, so brilliant. My dad was there and all my family was there and the place was packed to the rafters and it was just really amazing, an amazing time. I knew that the British title was just the start, that this was not going to be as much as I could achieve. I knew that it was the start of something that was going to be very significant: my first professional title, but certainly not my last.

Chapter 7

America and Europe

I can never emphasise enough how important good-quality sparring is in getting ready for a fight. This is where you try things out, where your trial and error starts and finishes. If you don't do it in the gym, you'll never do it in the ring. You try things out in sparring, and once you've got it, you do it again and again and again until it is second nature. You need someone watching you, telling you that's not good enough and to do it again: you need that person telling you when you've got it right, and saying, now do it right again. That is how it goes: over and over again. You would be crazy to try something in the ring that you have not practised thousands of times before in sparring.

The first part of the process is actually watching a fighter, seeing them in action and thinking, oh yes, I want that move. In the early days, I used to get these grainy old videotapes from a friend of my father, who worked for ABC in America. We would get these old grainy tapes of people like Roberto Duran, Carlos Zarate, Alfonso Zamora, Alexis Arguello, Carlos Monzon and early Marvin Hagler, this old stuff which would be shown over in the States. Dad would bring them back when he was over there singing, or we would get them sent over. They'd be Betamax tapes, so we'd convert them and I would watch them over and over until I wore them out.

It was great to see these fighters because you could see the movement they had, their technique, and I studied them closely. We did not have slow-mo or anything like that on our video recorder, so I would break the moves down by literally stopping them and moving the tracking, going through them literally frame by frame to work out what they were doing. Then Dermot and I would go up and practise them in the gym. You'd practise on a punchbag, punch ball, wall pad, pads, focus pads: once you've got it worked out, the next stage is implementing it in the sparring sessions in the gym. Then, and only then, would you carry it over into a competitive contest. That is the way it works.

It is always an advantage to have seen your opponent in action before a fight. I would say that if you got hold of a couple of videos of a guy fighting a couple of distance fights, then you can near enough work out for sure what he is going to do. You can work out what his style is and work out the way he fights. At the same time, it is important not to be over-reliant on videos, because once you're into the ring, it might all be different. You might have sparred with fighters who are similar in style, but they will never be exactly the same. You need to be able to cope with that – that's why you need to give yourself options, and put the hours in practising your moves.

It's difficult to imagine now, with DVDs and the Internet and YouTube and everything, but for my early fights, we didn't really have anything to watch. We only had word of mouth to go on: he is a tough little guy, or he likes to come forward, he likes to circle to the left and so forth. So you just had to get on with it. Later on, when we did start getting videotapes through, they could sometimes be a mixed blessing. I remember that getting hold of a video of Danilo Cabrera, the opponent for my second world title defence, was as much of a hindrance as it was a help. The video was over a year old, and he looked quite an ordinary fighter. But he had improved dramatically since then, and so we were caught unawares by that. That is a terrible realisation when you are half-way through a fight and realise, fuck, this guy is going to be in here for a long time.

The videos I got of Bernard Taylor, he was so good in them I had to stop watching. I turned the videos off at first because I found myself thinking, how am I going to beat this guy? But I went back to the tapes and worked it out. I thought, I know the way he fights, he likes to fight at a distance and box. So I'll stick on him like shit to a blanket, I am going to put him under so much pressure he won't be able to breathe, and that is what I did. But if I hadn't seen him, I wouldn't have had the level of intensity in training I put in to be able to close the ring down. If I hadn't watched those videos, it would have been a big shock when I stepped into the ring, and the fight would have been half lost by the time I'd figured out what I had to do.

In July 1983, I went to America for a couple of weeks. The primary reason for the visit was to take part in a couple of fights, but it was the sparring I did when I was over there that was to have the bigger impact.

The first fight took place in Chicago. We stayed in a hotel in the west of the city, and were looked after by a big guy called Monaghan. He drove us around Chicago and showed us the sights. Apart from the boxing, it was the weather I remember more than anything about Chicago. It's not called the windy city for nothing, and the gusts coming in off the lakes were something else. We also had tremendous thunderstorms, which petrified Eddie Shaw something rotten: it was probably a good job he didn't come to Romania with me back in my amateur days!

We sparred at a gym in the Spanish area of town. I think we went to the gym because of John Collins: he was from Chicago and one of the top middleweights at the time. It was a typical old-school gym, a huge old hall with a long wooden floor with a ring down at the bottom. There was one punchbag attached to the ceiling: you could hit the bag and have to wait ten seconds for it to come back again.

The gym itself might have been poor, but the quality of the sparring was exceptional. The one I remember in particular was this Mexican guy called Pajarito Marquez. Marquez campaigned at super featherweight, but he was heavy. He had just taken on Jackie Beard, who was one of the top featherweights in the US; though Beard had beaten him, Marquez had given him a really hard fight at short notice. We got Marquez in to spar and every day was like a war. He'd bring with him this whole posse of Mexicans, ten or twenty people, and because the ring was about five foot off the ground, they'd all stand there looking up and shouting abuse at me. Marquez couldn't speak English, so there was no communication, just intimidation from his support and punches winging their way from start to finish.

Every day I was there, he would come in and we would do four rounds. He was blown after two and he would get out after three, but I'd keep insisting that he do another round or two. I wanted as much sparring as I could because it was a great experience for me. Marquez could hit hard, really hard, and was bordering on world class at a weight above: I wanted to see how much I could stick it out with such a tough, tough Mexican. It was a good exercise and every day I would get the better of him, just. I got the better of him and then the last couple of days we made him do four rounds. Marquez was not happy about it because he was tired and I would beat up on him in the fourth round, really try and hurt him. So we sent all these Mexicans home unhappy, every day, but boy, they were tough sessions, tough as hell.

After Chicago, we moved to New York. That was great: I got to train at Gleason's Gym and went running in Central Park. One of the standout moments for me was when I got to meet one of my boxing heroes, Roberto Duran, who was in town to promote his upcoming fight with Marvin Hagler. Paddy Byrne, Barney and myself were invited to come and see him at a restaurant by Luis Spada, his manager. I wasn't quite sure how he was going to react to me, because back in Ireland I had named my dog after him, a fierce German shepherd. But he was fine about that, and gave me a hug. I sat there and watched amazed as he put away three chickens: you'd never have known he was in preparation for a fight.

We also went to the press conference Duran and Hagler were having to promote the fight. This took place in a huge hall underneath Madison Square Garden, which could hold 2,000 people itself. As well as all the media, a lot of boxing people had turned up: Ray Mancini was sat there with what I thought was a stunning young woman. It turned out to be Vikki LaMotta, the former wife of Jake LaMotta, whose story Martin Scorsese told in the film *Raging Bull*. Vicki LaMotta by this point was in her fifties, but you'd never have known!

Duran turned up to the press conference in this ice-blue suit, and he was noticeably over the weight. I remember him raising his hands like he'd won the fight, and there were these big sweat patches underneath his arms. Compared to how friendly Duran had been to us, Hagler was somewhat more guarded (though that might have been because we'd been hanging around with Duran and Spada). He was always very serious when he was a fighter, and would stop himself from becoming too friendly (something that completely changed, I should add, once he retired). That was what he was about and I both understood that and was fine with it: just to be there, to say hello and soak it all in was more than enough for me.

At Gleason's Gym I sparred with a couple of Victor Valle's fighters: Vinnie Costello, one of the top American super featherweights, whose brother Billy was soon to be the WBC light-welterweight champion; and Tony Santana, who was also a world-class super featherweight. It was exactly the same as with Marquez: they wanted to get the better of me and decapitate me.

Costello and Santana were continuously trying to get one up on me. Every day I would come down and they would put one in, one out, one in, one out and I said no, no, no, you have got to do at least two rounds at a time. They would try it on, but I would still wear them out. They would give me quite a bit of stick but I would always get the better of them. Valle had this little flyweight kid as well, a really polished beautiful box-fighter, and would throw him in at the end. So I would do four rounds with the two guys, and then they would put the flyweight in with me. It was exciting stuff: everything in the gym would stop, the guys tapping the bag would come and congregate round the ring to watch this white Irish guy. I remember after one session that Santana said to me, 'Hey, man, you fight like a brother,' and that was a huge compliment.

What stood out for me compared to the sparring I'd had back home were two things; firstly, the intensity of the sparring, and secondly, how technically good the fighters were. They were always in the position not to get hit with punches, taught to keep their chins down so they would not get caught with a counter-punch. And even if they did get caught with a counterpunch it would hit them on the head as opposed to the chin. They had a term for it, when your chin was protected, they'd say that every-thing is in the groove. The fighters would be taught with the glove under the chin, punch the bag with a glove under the chin, and even when they were fatigued, they'd still keep their chin tucked. From a technical perspective everything was very, very solid.

Victor Valle trained his fighters well. But I also learned that they didn't work as hard or with the same intensity as I did after the sparring. When I finished sparring I would hit the bag or hit the pads or I would skip or do something more. My sparring was very good and intensive, but afterwards I would work at the same intensity on the punchbag and the floor-to-ceiling ball, and I would always do a good ground-work routine. I would go to a number of the bags, punch like hell, and throw loads of shots. I think that impressed them, too: Valle's fighters had a much more leisurely approach after the sparring had finished. So I think they were impressed with my work ethic.

I met Bobby McQuiller out there too. Bobby was very, very impressive. He had boxed Sandy Saddler back in the day. He was so slick, was a great conditioner and he had a very sharp mind for an old guy. He had a great boxing brain. He was a great help to us and he said he would come to Belfast and bring a few of the guys with him for me to spar. Bobby did that and Barney started bringing in South American sparring partners and suddenly it gave me that extra element to my training. We started getting American sparring partners and Barney had connections in South America and he started getting in Panamanians, Dominicans and Puerto Ricans to come and spar.

This was very, very important in moving my career on. English and European fighters just weren't in the same league: if I could spar with top American and South American fighters, then I knew that I was really able to hold my own with the top guys. The fighters we got in were better technically and they were tougher. Even bantamweights and featherweights were as tough as lightweights, light welterweights. That was the difference. I could never keep British fighters for more than a few days – I don't think I ever sparred with a British featherweight. The lightest guys over here were lightweights and even then they would only last a day or two.

The fight in America was actually the second one I'd had since winning the British title. Six weeks before, I fought a guy called Samuel Meck at the Navan Exhibition Centre. This was another of those attempts to fight in the South and see what the response was like. To garner some publicity, we did the weigh-in on the *Late Late Show*, on the Friday night, and the fight was on the Saturday. It did the trick because the place was packed, every bit as atmospheric as the Ulster Hall. What it showed was that I could travel and take that sort of support and atmosphere with me.

Samuel Meck was from the Congo but based in France. As strong as a bloody horse, he was so tough it was like he was carved out of marble. Because I just attacked guys non-stop, I knew that he was going to be a hard nut to crack. He turned out to be just that. I stopped him in the sixth round but he certainly took some stick. I hit him with twenty-two unanswered punches and the crowd went bonkers. He was one tough guy but I was punching him all over the ring, before referee Fred Teidt stopped it.

Then we did the fight in America. It was meant to be two fights, one in Chicago, the other in Atlantic City, but the second one never happened. It was a BBC show: Frank Bruno and Lloyd Honeyghan were on the bill as well and it all took place at DaVinci Manor. DaVinci Manor was a crumbling old Victorian hall that was half empty, and it was so quiet that I could hear the American commentator calling the fight as I was boxing. My opponent was a fighter called Lavon McGowan, and the fight didn't last beyond the first round. I hit him with a right hand to the head first and he went down. I whacked him again with a right hand to the head and the next thing I hit him with was with a brilliant left hook to the body. He let out a roar because he wasn't expecting me to switch to the body and it really hurt him. He was never going to get up after that: if you had counted a hundred over him, he still would not have got up.

The other thing I remember about America was that Dad had been to see Mike Tyson sparring the previous year, and came back absolutely raving about him. Dad used to go out to a place called Dirty Nellie's, which was an Irish club in the Bronx, and he would do a six-week or a three-month stint there. There was this lawyer, Rudy Greco, who used to represent some of the boxers who didn't have much money, and he asked Dad to go with him to the Catskill gym to see this sixteen-year-old kid. Dad came back raving and said, 'The kid is incredible. You have got to put all your money on this kid. You've got to remortgage your house, this kid is going to win a world title.' He was joking, of course, about the betting, but he was deadly serious about Tyson!

My next fight after that was back in Ulster Hall in October. Hugh Russell, who had won the British flyweight title, was supposed to be defending his title at the Ulster Hall. But he picked up an injury, and I got a message asking if I would replace him boxing a guy called Ruben Herasme. Herasme was a Dominican based in Florida and he was flown in to fight me. I took the fight at, I think, two weeks' notice, but I was in good shape. I got a couple of spars in and you can see from my weigh-in that I weighed nine stone one and a half, so I was on the money with the weight.

The fight lasted two rounds. He was strong to begin with, but I pulverised him with a left hook to the body and he just crumbled. I hit him with one and it sort of glanced off him but half winded him, and he went down. He took a standing count and got up again. I threw another three shots to the head and he lifted his hands up. I went for the head again and he put his hands up and I buried a left hook into his body and he was screaming. He hit the floor and that was that.

Between the fight in America and the defeat of Herasme, the biggest thing to happen to me that year was the birth of my first son, Blain, on 25 August. He was born in St John of God's Nursing Home in Newry and the nuns looked after Sandra – the place was just pristine, spotless, and they were so good to her and to me. Blain's name is a bit unusual, but I remember a fighter from the

States called Blaine Dickson, and always loved the name: in actual fact it has the same meaning as Finbar, which is my name (my full name is Finbar Patrick McGuigan). I took the 'e' off it: I liked Blain, so that was it. It is a great name, as I say, a unique name. My son's name is Blain Finbar so effectively it could be Finbar Finbar.

Blain was a good baby and Sandra breast-fed, which I was delighted about because I didn't have to get up at night! He was a summer baby and everybody doted on him. Everybody loved him. My mum and dad loved him too, he was their first grandchild. Everybody was just doting over him and he was a nice pleasant baby and he didn't cry too much and he slept pretty well. It was just the nicest time. At that stage we were living outside Clones and had bought this house: it was out on the lake and needed renovating. There was a grant in the North that you could get, you could get a certain amount to help you build or repair an old building, provided it was kept in the same configuration and so on. We rebuilt the house with effectively the same sort of shape but made a few different alterations to it. We lived beside the lake and it was a wonderful time.

Having a child didn't really affect my attitude to work, to boxing. If anything, it reinforced the family thing, it helped put my roots down. Sometimes, of course, you'd be woken in the night and you would not get a good night's sleep, but when I was between fights I always trained at casual times so I could accommodate that. I would train at all sorts of hours: I remember after the world title fight I would be coming back at eleven o'clock at night and I would say, 'Dermot, do you want to come?' and we would go and do fifteen rounds at the pads.

For me, it didn't matter about the time as long as I had done the work. That was my attitude. Not every fighter is like that. I remember reading about Henry Cooper, and he used to get up at four-thirty or five in the morning to beat the traffic in London. He would go out running then to avoid the fumes. He'd go back to bed after that, then get up, have his breakfast and then train again. All his training was done by two in the afternoon and he had the rest of the day to relax or whatever. Whereas my normal routine would be to get up at about eight o'clock and go for a run. I would come back in, have a light breakfast and then go back to bed again. I'd go to the gym about half-one or two. I'd finish and have something to eat immediately and then would have a proper tea in the evening. In reality, that was the wrong time to eat because you go to bed on a full stomach: it was counterproductive, but we did not know then what we know now as far as nutrition is concerned.

It wasn't long after I had won the British title and people would come into the town and go to the shop just to see me. They'd drive from twenty miles away and my mother would go, come on in and I'll make you tea. It was like open house. They would say, 'Oh, Barry, I've brought my cousin up to say hello to you', 'So, how are you doing?', 'Can you do some of your boxing?' and so on. My mother would never say no to people: 'Go on in there, you might see him,' she'd say. And we would be in the gym up the back and people would come in and watch us training. They would meet my dad, the famous singer, and so it was lovely. When Blain was born that just added to it all. He and Sandra got a lot of attention.

My last fight of 1983 was a big one: a European title fight against the Italian Valerio Nati. Like the British crown, the title was a vacant one: just as Steve Sims had vacated the British title, so Loris Stecca gave up his crown rather than fight me. Valerio Nati had been European champion at bantamweight before moving up to featherweight: he'd actually lost to Stecca earlier in the year, so this was his second shot at the title.

The fight took place at the King's Hall in Belfast. It was a gamble because it was the first time I had ever fought there. I'd always packed out the Ulster Hall, but the King's Hall was a far bigger venue: the Ulster Hall in those days had a capacity of about 2,000 (that was before it became an all-seater venue). The King's Hall had an official capacity of about 8,000, but you could squeeze 10,000 in at a push.

It was a bit of a gamble putting the fight on there, but it paid off all round. Nati was a tough little guy for about five rounds and then I started to break him down. He saw that and he capitulated. He got sick to death of being hit in the body and went down in the sixth. I hit him with three decent shots. He went along and I chased him, he went down and he took the count and the referee stopped it.

Nati was a tough guy, but he was a bit of a moaner: he kept on complaining that I was hitting him low. The truth was that my shots were borderline shots. There is a very fine line between hitting the guy with a perfect body shot and hitting him on top of the cup. I never, ever hit people down low on the cup. But I hit him right on the waist, right in there, and there is a fine line as I say. And often what would happen is you would sweat and perspire and all the guys had oil on them, so when you actually threw that punch, you would hit him and it would slip off, it would slip and hit the top of the cup. Nati complained, but it was just some moaning to try to get me disqualified or to get a point deducted.

Nati's problem was that my body shots were really hurting him. I lifted them up into the ribs and round the side of the elbow, and there was nothing he could do. I would work hard to make him move his elbow, sucker him into lifting his protection and hitting him where I wanted. I would open him up with a light shot on the forearm, then the money was in the last one. It is the most horrible thing, because what happens when you get them there, you paralyse the lungs and there is nothing they can do about it.

That's why a body shot is different from a head shot. The thing about a head shot is that if you get hit with one you go 'whoa' and feel woozy, but if you can grab your opponent and hold him, your head can clear and you are OK again. Hit your opponent with a body shot and it does not go away. I'm not talking about the stomach – you can work hard and have a wall of steel there. In my prime, I could let a heavyweight hit me flat out with their bare fist there. Not a thing would it do, not a single thing. But the one area you can't build up is round the side, because there you have the concertina of the floating ribs to protect the bell shape of the lung. It sits on the side there, it is soft and it goes in and you cannot do anything about that.

I realised that the way to hit people there is that you have got to trick them. You have got to hit them to the body to get a head shot in. You have got to throw head shots to bring up the hands and then you can bang the body. I worked that out and I was noted as an exceptional body puncher. I was a good body puncher because I worked meticulously at it. I remember seeing a photo of Alexis Arguello throwing a body shot and his elbow looked like it was at the strangest angle. But what he was doing was not trying to lift with his body shots. Arguello was cutting across because he was driving into the side with his body shot, and that's what I worked out. It was such a devastating punch that when I would turn my hip, you could hear the whiplash. A devastating punch but very difficult to catch your opponent with because he would always block. So you'd find a way of tricking him, getting him to make a little space and then . . . bang!

I didn't care how good the guys were, I didn't care how strong they were. If I hit somebody with a proper body shot it would take them out, every single time. Nati didn't like that, but he wasn't alone in that. There would be plenty of other fighters, world-class fighters, who were about to discover the same thing.

Winning the European title was great, though it felt more of an important step along the road than an achievement in itself. Perhaps it would have meant more if I'd fought the reigning champion, rather than Stecca relinquishing his crown. What felt a bigger deal was fighting in the King's Hall: packing that out was not only something special for me as a fighter, it also raised the interest of the American TV networks, and the big-name fighters they could bring to the table.

Chapter 8

Gearing Up

To step up from European champion to thinking about the world title, there was one remaining question that needed to be answered about my boxing. Just as the Jean Marc Renard fight had been important earlier in my career, in showing that I could take a whack and that I could pull in an audience, so I now needed to prove that I could go on and defeat a real top-level fighter. Even having beaten Valerio Nati, I knew I was still about a year or so off challenging for a world title. To get that shot, I was going to have to take on some tough opponents over the next twelve months.

In January 1984, I fought the Zambian boxer Charm Chiteule at the King's Hall in Belfast. Chiteule had already fought at world-class level, he was definitely a world-class guy: he'd gone ten rounds with Azumah Nelson back in 1982 for the Commonwealth title; in 1983, he'd lost to Refugio Rojas on points for the USBA super-featherweight title. Chiteule had a top-level team behind him as well: he was managed by Mickey Duff and trained by George Francis. Francis had trained people like John Conteh and Cornelius Boza Edwards, a whole host of world-class fighters, and would go on to work my corner on the night that I won the world title. So I knew I was going to be in a tough contest.

Chiteule was a counterpuncher, a lazy counterpuncher: he'd step back and throw these long, rangy, arcing shots. He could take a punch, he could fight at pace and bang a bit as well. He wasn't a devastating puncher but he could hit hard. I pursued him from start to finish and backed him up, but he was a classy fighter and clever with it: he hit me with some really good punches. On top of which, he stuck his thumb in my eye. That was because of the horrible gloves that we wore. They hadn't got attached thumbs, so if you put your fist out a certain way, the thumb would sit out. Chiteule caught me with his thumb and my eye just went. I could hardly see out of it. I had to grit it out after that to beat him.

Part of the problem that night was expectation: because I'd won my previous fights so convincingly, the press assumed that I would beat Chiteule easily. That was never going to happen, because he wasn't that sort of a fighter. As a boxer, you can only do what your opponent lets you do, and as much as I'd have liked, I didn't impose myself on him quickly enough and get a grip on the fight as I'd got used to. I was hitting Chiteule to the body really hard, but he was a big tough guy and it had very little effect on him. At which point I knew this one wasn't going to be over quickly, that I was going to have to grind him down.

It was a hard fight. I was getting the better of him, but it was only from the seventh, eighth, ninth that I started to beat up on him. Finally, in the tenth, I set about him. There were about forty seconds to go, and I battered him. I bounced several left hooks off his head, and he was gone. Before it could go any further, the referee stepped in and stopped the fight.

For me, what I showed that night was that I could take out a guy who was both a decent fighter and also a difficult and awkward opponent. But because the press had been expecting an easy victory, for some of the journalists the jury was still out as to whether I could cut it against the top fighters. Because my eye had puffed up quite badly, I did not get a chance to prove them wrong for another three months. But prove them wrong I did, against the talented Dominican Jose Caba. Caba was a tough little fighter, again with world-class pedigree. He had fought Eusebio Pedroza in Italy the previous October and, although he didn't win, had gone the distance with the WBA featherweight champion. He'd lost on points and had caused Pedroza problems in the process.

Caba was a dangerous puncher: he swung punches from a low centre of gravity. He was short and thick-set, and I knew he was going to come at me. I decided the best way to counteract that was to box him. Instead of my usual style of attacking all the time, I changed my game to meet him head-on in the middle of the ring. I fought tooth and nail to hold on to that position, making sure he couldn't back me on to the ropes. I allowed myself room to take a step back, but that was it: I kept myself in the centre of the ring. I decided I'd box him for as long as I needed and then, when he started to wilt, I would automatically fall into what I did best: pursue him, and attack.

I boxed beautifully that night, really did a number on him. I showed my boxing skills against a world-class opponent, which wasn't my usual thing. Caba walked on to punches for the first five rounds. In the sixth he started giving, and I backed him up. From that point on I was relentless and never left him alone; I kept hitting him with combinations and banging his head up and down, sickening shots to the body and to the head. I had taken all the sting out of him and he was beginning to fade. I was really hitting him by this point, sitting down on my punches, biting the canvas with my feet and really letting my shots go with power. About a minute into the seventh, Caba started to go. It was a flat-out pace, and I was hitting him to the body and the head, picking him apart when the referee jumped in. If he hadn't, I'd have knocked him out, no question.

You can never say in boxing that just because one fighter beats someone more easily than another, that it follows they are the better fighter. It doesn't work like that. You couldn't say that because I stopped Caba in seven but Pedroza could only beat him on points that it followed that I would beat Pedroza. Beating Caba was a gauge, no more than that, on the level that I was fighting. But as gauges went, it was a good one: the fight showed that I could compete on equal terms with the best, and that was a great boost, a shot of confidence for me. I definitely felt I was on course for a crack at the big one.

Moving towards a world title wasn't the only consideration in choosing my opponents, however. Being British and European champion, I had to make mandatory defences of my titles. These contests were frustrating 'treading water' fights compared to the calibre of the other opponents I was taking on. I had three such fights over the next nine months, and none of them lasted more than four rounds.

The first defence of my European title was against the Spaniard Esteban Eguia. Statistically he was a good fighter, with a track record of forty wins, four losses and three draws. But I just bashed him, blew him away. I knocked him down three times, and the fight was stopped in the third. The fight took place in June, and more interesting than the contest was the fact it was held at the Royal Albert Hall. It was the first time I'd fought in London since the Young Ali fight two years earlier: the thinking was to see what the support was like fighting in London and to build the growing interest in the media. I remember training down at the Thomas a Becket gym and putting in some really good sparring sessions. The media would come down and watch us, and I was beginning to make a big impression on them.

The other reason the venue was interesting was because the Royal Albert Hall was where my dad had sung in the 1968

Eurovision contest, sixteen years before. I was certainly aware of that. I remember him saying, 'I was here'. Years later, I got the chance to sing at the Albert Hall myself, when the singer Paul Carrack, who I'd become good friends with, invited me up to join him on one of his songs. I got on stage and told the audience, the last time I was here, I'd knocked a Spaniard out in three rounds. So the Albert Hall is a special place for me, with many happy memories.

The next mandatory defence was a European one, and by default a British one too, against Clyde Ruan in December. Again I was heavy favourite to win, and knocked him out in the fourth. Afterwards, Ruan said fighting me was like fighting a ghost. By which he meant that he couldn't deal with my head movement. I kept putting myself in position and snapping his head back with a jab, then I would slip, slip and do nothing until he would step up again. As soon as he was set to punch, I would slip, slip and wait, then I would let go with my own shots. I was trying to set him up for the knockout punch.

There is a great picture of Sean Kilfeather, the *Irish Times* journalist, when I knocked out Ruan. I hit him with a left hook and he went flying across the ring, falling down right where the reporters were. They all went 'Eughh!' and all pulled back because blood was coming out of Ruan's nose. And there's this photo of Sean Kilfeather showing this partisan support and going 'Yes!' and punching the air as Ruan goes down. And the referee Larry O'Connell counted Ruan out, and that was it.

Again, I remember the fight more for non-boxing reasons. Two days beforehand Papa Rooney, my grandfather, died. He was in Longford at the dog track and had a brain haemorrhage and collapsed. My Uncle Leo was with him going to the hospital in the back of the ambulance when he died. I was upset because he was very close to me: I had grown up with him. He would often go coursing and I would go coursing with him, myself and my brother Dermot. He was close to eighty years old and a great old character. He lived a good life and had died the way he would have wanted, at the trackside. My grandfather had worked in my mum's shop since she had taken it over in 1963 and we were close. I remember crying that night after the fight, and dedicating the victory to him.

After beating Ruan, I was encouraged by Ray Clarke of the BBBofC to give up my British title. They had given me Ruan as a defence and I had knocked him out. The board said to me, look, you are basically too good for anybody else. Give your title up, and we will give you a Lonsdale Belt (which British champions earn after two successful defences). So I gave my title up after the Ruan fight, though they never did give me a belt!

The third mandatory title defence, the second European one, was the biggest mismatch of the lot. Farid Gallouze was the French champion and number-one contender for the European title, but by the time we fought in March 1985, I was in a different league. The fight took place at Wembley Arena, on the same night as the Republic of Ireland were playing England in a friendly international at Wembley Stadium. The idea was that the fans would do both – watch the football and come straight over to the Arena to watch the fight. It was quite a walk and by the time the fans had shown their tags and rolled into their seats, the fight was over.

That was with me genuinely trying to hold Gallouze up. I sparred with him for the first round and I thought, this guy is hopeless. I went into the second round thinking, I want to knock him out now. I can't put on an act, I can't pretend any more, so I got rid of him. Half of the crowd were still coming up the stairs when I put him down. A lot of the fans were furious. They had come the whole way over from Ireland to try and watch both the match and my bout. They flung their tickets to the ground and walked out. I couldn't blame them.

*

The Eguia, Ruan and Gallouze defences were distractions from the bigger picture of pushing on towards the world title. In between these contests took place the fights that really mattered.

The first of these, against Paul DeVorce, took place back at the King's Hall just three weeks after the Albert Hall fight with Esteban Eguia. The fight was significant because it was the first time that American TV had taken a serious interest in my career. CBS had come over to show the fight live, and it was important for me to make a good impression. Television, for better or worse, plays a vital role in any fighter's career. I was lucky to fight at a time when the main channels took a big interest in boxing and that made a huge difference in terms of the sport's popularity and profile. BBC Northern Ireland had shown my fights from early on, and by the time I fought Vernon Penprase for the British title, my fights were being shown across the network.

Getting American interest was the next step up again. The package we could offer was a good one. Firstly, I was an exciting fighter, and with my aggressive style the audience was always guaranteed a good, action-packed fight. Secondly, there was the setting: the King's Hall had an amazing atmosphere, which again gave the fights a must-watch feel. Thirdly, this was all taking place in the middle of the Troubles, so they could come and do a big story about that. And finally, the time difference was perfect for an American audience. We'd fight at ten on a Saturday evening, which meant they could show the contest live at five in the afternoon, Eastern Time, which was perfect for their Saturday sports shows.

DeVorce was a very tough little guy, a little powerhouse. He was two inches shorter than me and built like a brick shithouse. I was a little apprehensive before the fight because he had a good reputation: he had twenty-two wins and only one defeat in his career, and that had been a points decision against Jackie Beard. DeVorce came forward in the first two rounds but I walked him on to some crackers, snapping his head back and hitting him with some really sharp hard hooks. I snapped the jab in his face and he stopped coming forward after that. I could see his face and his eyes lighten up and I thought, right, now you will get a bit of a taste of something. So I backed him up, and started pounding him, chopping away at him.

In the fifth round I hit him with a series of combinations followed by a left hook to the body. I hit him and he went 'Ooooh!' I hit him again and the referee jumped in to end the fight. His corner complained that the referee, Sid Nathan, had jumped in too soon, but there was no such response from DeVorce. There might be a slight cultural difference there: the Americans don't like fights stopped too soon because they like to see closer finishes; equally, you could argue that this view is too harsh, that in the US a guy has to be absolutely flattened before anyone would think about stepping in.

My next American TV date, between the DeVorce fight and the Ruan defence, was pencilled in for October against the Venezuelan fighter Angel Levi Mayor. Like Jose Caba, Mayor had gone fifteen rounds with Eusebio Pedroza, so he would have been another tough opponent to test myself against. I say would, because Mayor pulled out and his place was taken at short notice by Felipe Orozco. Orozco was no mug: he'd only been beaten once in his professional career and that was in a world super-bantamweight title fight against Jaime Garza a few months before. He was a tall fighter, five foot eleven, but more importantly, he was a southpaw. All my preparation had been geared to facing an orthodox fighter, and now I had to start again.

All my sparring had been with orthodox fighters similar to Mayor. So I didn't have long to get used to somebody in the opposite position in front of you. Above all, it is hard to land a jab on a southpaw. It is very difficult. You nearly always have to lead with a hook and that is a risk itself. But as luck would have it, on the undercard of the fight was Cornelius Boza Edwards. Boza

Edwards was the one-time world super-featherwight champion and, more importantly for me, a southpaw. So I sparred with him, and he was tough as nails. It was flat out, giving everything in those sessions. It was a great experience and it got me sharp for the fight. After those sessions, Orozco wasn't any bother: I came out of the blocks like a bullet and finished him off in two.

After impressing the American networks with beating DeVorce and Orozco, the TV people were keen to see me up against someone truly world class. The networks were saying, 'Now hold on a second here, how much longer are we going to wait? Give this guy a proper test. Give him a world champion who can punch.' And having despatched DeVorce and Orozco, they got their wish in February 1985, when I was lined up to fight against Juan La Porte.

La Porte was a top-drawer fighter, a real class act. He'd gone the distance against the great Salvador Sanchez as a young fighter and knocked out Rocky Lockridge, who would later win a world title at super featherweight. In 1982, he'd won the vacant WBC featherweight crown by beating Mario Miranda, a title he lost to Wilfredo Gomez on points after battling for most of the fight with a broken thumb. Two years after our fight, he took on Julio Cesar Chavez for the WBC super-featherweight title at Madison Square Garden and narrowly lost on points.

As well as being a fantastic fighter, La Porte was a classy guy as well. I was used to my opponents coming over and saying nasty things about me, how they were going to knock me out and all that stuff. Remember Terry Pizzaro apologising to my father for what he was going to do to me? La Porte couldn't have been more different. I met him about a week before the fight, as he was training at the same gym as me. This one time we overlapped, and he was over in the corner as I arrived for my session. 'Oh, hi, Barry,' he said. He walked straight across and said, 'I wish you good luck, man.' I had always done that to my opponents, always just walked over and said calm as you like, 'good luck', 'best of luck', 'may the best man win'. He'd done that to me and I thought, wow, that was a classy thing to do. I knew I was going to have a handful that day.

There was something quite special about La Porte. There's an old saying that empty vessels make the most noise, and there's something in that. Guys who are not confident in their ability are normally shouters and loudmouths. Guys that are confident in their ability don't need to talk themselves up. I always had the highest of respect for people who were just confident, self-confident without being overly bumptious. And that was exactly what Juan La Porte was like: he was incredibly composed. The King's Hall was rammed that night, absolutely packed, but none of that fazed him. There was a delay between La Porte getting into the ring and my arrival, I think because the American TV were wanting to build up the atmosphere. So La Porte was in the ring, waiting, surrounded by this huge wall of noise, a massive outpouring of support for me. A lesser fighter might have let that unsettle him, but it didn't make any difference to La Porte. He was supremely confident, never believing for one minute that he wasn't going to win.

La Porte was an amazing fighter, very very handy. He could punch with either hand: he knocked out Rocky Lockridge with a left hook and nearly took me out with his right. His punches were heavy: like a lot of Puerto Ricans he was naturally heavy-handed. So it was very tough, a tough fight the whole way through from start to finish. Ten intense rounds, flat out. I was dominating it and keeping myself ahead and constantly backing him up. I always felt like I was winning the rounds, I always felt I was in charge but knew that I could never switch off with him, never even switch off for a second, as I almost found to my cost.

I dominated most of the rounds but he definitely won a few of them. He hurt me in the fifth and then he hurt me really badly in the ninth. What happened was that he beat me to the punch. You can jab in two ways: you can either feel your way in with the jab, or you can jab really hard and sharp and snap their heads back. Either way, it is a committed shot. You are pushing all your weight from the back foot. You step into it, push your weight in, which means you are throwing your weight forward. So I snapped this jab in the ninth, put his head back and I thought I would do another one. I went forward again and before I could jab him … Bom! He hit me with this huge right. There was all my weight going forward for the jab and all the power from his heavy punch, and they met head-on with the most almighty wallop on my jaw.

This is the honest truth: when he hit me with that right, I was transported back to when I was a child and used to go to Mrs Keenan's toy shop down the road. For a split second, I thought I was in the toy shop again. I had the sense to grab La Porte, to try and allow my head to clear. It was a bit like when you've been walking along in the rain and get into your car: the windscreen steams up and you put on the fan to clear and it takes a bit of time before you can properly see out again. That was the impression I got when I looked at La Porte. I could hardly see him to start with, it was so fuzzy. Eventually Harry Gibbs the referee said, 'Break! Step back!' So I stepped back and La Porte winged another couple of shots at me that I just got out of the way of. I was so fit that my head cleared fairly quickly after that, and I got right back into it. I was back in it before the end of the round, but I went back to the corner at the bell and they gave me the old 'sponge in the ice-cold water bucket' treatment. And that *really* woke me up. I came back and the tenth was my best round of the whole fight. I had him out on his feet and his legs went, his legs sort of did a little jig. It was a great fight and a great performance.

For me, it was the best performance of my entire career. The Pedroza fight was the better night, but technically, this was the superior fight. That was partly to do with La Porte's style, too: if he hadn't been a guy that came at me and fought me, it would have been a different sort of fight. From a purely entertainment point of view, La Porte was a better fight than either Pedroza or Taylor. As a fight, it was non-stop. It was at that intensity right through. La Porte did not throw as many punches as me, but the ones he did throw, they hit and hurt. I had to fight relentlessly, and that made the contest good to watch.

There might be those who say, 'Actually, the best performance was the first five rounds by Bernard Taylor.' That was certainly a beautiful boxing display, but although I was getting outboxed, he never really hurt me. And for everyone who admired the way Taylor fought, there are plenty of others who loved the way I cut him down, stopped him in every position, and really ground him down. There's the Pedroza fight, of course, which is special because I won the title. I displayed a bit of everything in that: punching power, relentless aggression, non-stop fighting. And then there was the whole atmosphere and everything else. But in terms of performance, I still think that the La Porte fight had the edge.

La Porte was very complimentary after the fight, which again shows the mark of the man. The sports writers, people like Harry Mullan and Hugh MacIlvanney, all knew how well I'd boxed. But the one that sticks out for me was from Sugar Ray Leonard, who was there to commentate on the fight for CBS TV. He came to my dressing room after the fight and he was charming and generous. 'It was a pleasure to watch you,' he said. 'That was one of the best fights I have seen, and you are on your way to a world title fight.'

Chapter 9

Preparing for Pedroza

There were three world title fights I could have gone for, but Eusebio Pedroza was always the one I wanted. The IBF title wasn't a big deal at the time, and was held by a South Korean, Min-Keun Oh, who would never have come over to fight. The WBC title belonged to Azumah Nelson. Nelson had taken on the defending WBC champion, Salvador Sanchez, in 1982 and had lost. Shortly afterwards, Sanchez died, leaving the title vacant. It wasn't until the end of 1984, just a couple of months before the La Porte fight, that Nelson finally claimed the WBC crown, beating Wilfredo Gomez in Puerto Rico. He'd only just won the title, and so the credibility lay with Pedroza.

Eusebio Pedroza was a big deal. The Panamanian fighter had been the WBA featherweight champion since 1978, when he'd won it by beating Cecilio Lastra. Since then, he'd had nineteen successful defences of his title over a seven-year period: he was one of the longest-serving world champions in a long time, and his achievements were up there with the likes of Willie Pep and Sandy Saddler. Taking his crown would therefore be a hugely significant victory: if you beat Pedroza, there was no way anyone could argue that you weren't a worthy champion. And given Pedroza's pedigree and history, this was clearly the fight with the biggest box-office appeal.

The negotiations for the fight took place on the night I was fighting Farid Gallouze. Pedroza had been flown over and was put up in a top hotel to come and watch the fight and have the discussions, but he never showed up at the venue. I knew he was meant to be coming, but didn't know until afterwards that he hadn't shown. I never took much notice of who was in the audience in any case, because I was so switched on thinking about the fight. So much so that if I saw someone I recognised, I would deliberately block them out, so that I could focus on what I needed to do in the ring. It was only after the fight that I asked the question, was Pedroza there? And they told me that he didn't show. Everyone was really disappointed: they thought that the fight wasn't going to happen.

I was a bit surprised he hadn't come to check me out. I thought that was a sign of his arrogance. I guess he felt he'd been world champion for so long that he didn't care about what anybody else did: he wasn't going to learn anything by coming to watch me. He had boxed guys all over the world and thought I probably wasn't even as good as some of the guys he had beat, so why bother? That was fine. I didn't really care about that, to be honest. But what I did care about was that the deal was not done by the time the fight had taken place. I got a bit frustrated and thought, well, I'm just going to go home and enjoy myself and let's see what happens.

The next day, we heard that in fact they had been up all night discussing the deal. Barney Eastwood and Mickey Duff had gone back to them and entered into negotiations and it was sorted in the small hours of the morning. Word got back to us first before it reached the press but then it hit the media fairly quickly. The fight was on for 8 June 1985, and would take place at Loftus Road, the Queens Park Rangers football stadium in Shepherd's Bush.

In terms of the venue, the fight was a London one because there was no way Pedroza would have come to Belfast and fought me on my home turf. Loftus Road was chosen partly because of the television deal. The BBC had agreed to show the fight live, and I think I'm right in saying that it was the first time the BBC had ever done a live outside broadcast on boxing. They had done things like Cooper and Ali, but these had always been recorded and edited and put out some days later. The fact that Loftus Road was in Shepherd's Bush, and therefore close to BBC TV Centre in White City, made them feel a bit more confident in what they were trying to pull off.

It was a risk, certainly, what they were trying to do, but it was arguably the biggest fight to take place in Britain since Cooper–Ali and they decided to give it a go. It was a gamble that paid off tenfold: nineteen and a half million would tune in to watch the fight, and that's not counting the Irish guys who hadn't paid their licence fee. That's a huge audience for a boxing match: Bruno–Bugner and Benn–Eubank came close, but although they got amazing ratings too, about fifteen or sixteen million I think, the figures weren't as big as I got for the Pedroza fight.

To pull in an audience of almost twenty million, that indicates the sort of appeal that I had way back then. I'm sure a lot of that was to do with the Irish thing: I don't think I fully understood the sort of support and acclamation I got from both sides of the border. I certainly didn't realise it at the time, largely because I went out of my way not to read the papers in the build-up to the fight. The expectation was big enough as it was, and the last thing I wanted was to make myself more nervous by reading about it and heaping more pressure on myself. But because of the situation in Northern Ireland, because of the Troubles, the fight meant a heck of a lot to a large number of people. You have to remember how desolate things were at the time: a lot of organisations and big businesses did not want to go near the North because they thought it too risky. There was sadness and tragedy and people trying to get on with their lives in the midst of all that. The Pedroza fight just cut through all that: for a while at least, it gave everyone something else to think about, something to believe in.

With the Farid Gallouze fight little more than an easy workout, I was back in the gym on the Monday with my brother Dermot. We worked right the way through until I took a break out to Spain with Sandra and Blain. It was a break but I trained out there as well: I trained, ran, did press-ups, callisthenics and shadow-boxing. I didn't do so much as to make the holiday miserable but just enough to keep things ticking over, to keep myself in shape. We were out there for eight to ten days, and then I came back and started getting ready for the Pedroza fight in earnest.

My training routine was as follows: I'd get up at eight-thirty and do my road work, that would be a five- to six-mile run at a fast pace (I'd run sub six-minute-mile pace or half a minute slower, depending on how I felt on the day). I'd run along the coast towards Belfast Lough or away from Bangor towards a place called Ballyholme. I'd stretch when I came back, shower and have my breakfast, which consisted of a bowl of All-Bran, a couple of glasses of orange juice, a couple of glasses of water and a cup of tea. Then I'd head back to bed and try to get a couple of hours' sleep. Often I'd not sleep but I would lie there and rest and read a book.

I'd be up and about by lunch time, have a piece of fruit or a cup of tea then head to the gym for my boxing session around two o'clock. This session consisted of two or three rounds of shadow-boxing, then I'd glove up and get straight into sparring. At the start of my training camp I'd begin with four or five rounds with a couple of sparring partners and build to eight to ten rounds with up to three sparring partners. Then on one of the days I'd do fifteen rounds with up to five different sparring partners. (There were always several sparring partners at the gym because there were a number of guys getting ready to fight. There were always at least two or three South Americans.) When I finished sparring I'd take off the gloves and shadow-box for a couple of rounds or hit the heavy bag for a couple of rounds, then I'd do fifteen to twenty minutes of tempo skipping, then ten to fifteen minutes of ground work: this would include abdominal work for your stomach, and press-ups and neck-strengthening. I'd do some stretching (not enough) and finish, shower and head back out to our guest house in Bangor. I'd drink a load of water and have my main meal of the day at around seven o'clock at night. That would be typically chicken, steak or fish of some kind and vegetables: carrots, parsnips, broccoli, cabbage, cauliflower or whatever was going. Obviously we wouldn't have all those vegetables, only two or three, and sometimes we would have cream potatoes or roast potatoes. Then I would go for a walk with Sean McGivern around the marina or around the town and I'd go to bed around 11 p.m.

If you compare that type of diet to the modern diet you can see how nutrition has come so much more into focus in boxing. What I was effectively doing back then was putting my body into starvation mode and going through what's called catabolism, where your body eats itself. I was only really having one and a half meals a day, which as we now know is completely wrong. If you'd seen me six weeks out from the fight I looked really healthy and strong but a week before the fight I looked like I'd just come out of a prisoner-of-war camp – I'd shrunk, losing crucial lean muscle as my weight came down to nine stone.

My son Shane has become exceptionally good at diet and nutrition: he puts together diet sheets and strength and conditioning programmes for pro boxers all the time, so I asked him to show me the type of diet that he would put me on to make the weight and be as strong as I could be. Here's how it would differ: in the morning I'd do my run as before. I'd then have a whey protein shake and one hour later I'd have my breakfast, which would be a steak with one handful of nuts. Then I'd have my rest and four hours later I'd have my lunch, which would consist of chicken, fish or red meat with green vegetables (as much as I liked). Then I'd have an hour to digest my food and then do my boxing session. Straight after the gym session I'd have a protein shake and my evening meal would be salmon or fish of any kind with steamed vegetables. Comparing the two diets, it's remarkable to think that I could have had three solid meals per day (provided I stuck rigidly to what I was prescribed) and still have made the weight. The modern diet would have allowed me to retain as much muscle mass as possible, I'd have been a bigger athlete and undoubtedly a stronger fighter as a result, but we didn't have this knowledge back in the mid-1980s.

With the Pedroza fight, as with all my fights, I wanted to be able to get down to the weight early and hold it. It is tougher that way because you have got to watch what you eat and watch what you drink, but I always liked to have the satisfaction of finishing inside the weight. By the end of the sparring, five or six days out, I'd be going through the motions, just to break sweat really. At that point, I'd just shadow-box and skip: I wouldn't punch for five days before a fight. At this late stage, it's just about weight management and retaining your strength.

The preparation for the Pedroza fight went extremely well. We had the camp up in Bangor, and I remember going home for the weekend: Sandra would either come up to Bangor with Blain or I would head home to Clones to see them. I remember watching Dennis Taylor beating Steve Davis in the world snooker final at home and then heading back up to Bangor the next day. We stayed at Beresford House, which was right along the front on the promenade. It has all been modernised now and looks great but even back then it was very, very pretty: a wonderful place to stay. I ran every morning with my great pal Sean McGivern. He used to play soccer and was very fit. He was the only guy that could run at my pace and we used to hang out together in the evening. Sean became a trusted friend and remains my close friend to this day.

The sparring for the Pedroza fight was the toughest I'd had. So much so, in fact, that for a while in the middle it started to dent my confidence. We had a plethora of fighters who came in and sparred. I sparred with Americans and Latin Americans and with the guys that were in the gym. I did my initial prep with the local guys, people like Damian Fryers, Danny McAllister, Dave McAuley, Peppy Muir and Davy Irving.

Gerald Hayes came in for some sessions. He'd lost to Pedroza the year before in Panama City and knew exactly what I was up against. He was good, but getting on a bit: he was in the vet stage of his career, so I was hurting him and beating up on him and he didn't feel he could be of any benefit to me. But his experience against Pedroza certainly helped: when I was sparring the other guys, he would talk and shout at me: 'Move your head!' 'Show the body and switch it to the head!' 'Double the left hooks up!' He would talk tactics to me and coach me through the rounds.

Then Barney brought in a couple of guys from Panama: Ezequiel Mosquera, who was the national lightweight champion, and Jose Marmolejo, who was a top-five world-ranked feather-weight. In fact, he was so good that he was ranked third in the world, higher than me! Mosquera and Marmolejo were there to simulate Pedroza's style: Marmolejo in particular was extremely similar in the way he boxed. He was really tough and although he was a featherweight, was weighing a stone heavier than me. Mosquera was a lightweight but weighing over again – he was finishing the sessions at ten stone seven, which is welterweight level, so he was big too. The sparring sessions with these two were tough. I got hit plenty, and hit low. I had real wars in the gym with those guys.

For a week in the middle of training I found myself thinking, oh shit, this is going horribly wrong. Because I was getting hit too much and wasn't handling these guys the way I should have been. I remember my dad being concerned about how the sparring was going. I'd sparred extensively by this stage, and he was worried I was getting tired. I remember saying to the old man that yes, it's really tough this time, but I was a glutton for punishment anyway and loved to train hard, I loved to really push myself. But he was definitely right to raise it, because if you give a fighter too many hard spars, it can dent their confidence, no question. With Marmolejo and Mosquera, I wasn't on top like I was used to. There were definitely days when they got the better of me. You can't win every round in sparring and from a mentality point of view, it is important to realise that you can't expect to win every round in sparring. The key thing is not to get annoyed, but deal with it and improve.

Although I wasn't always on top, I knew these sessions were exactly what I needed: they were the dose of reality for what I would face in the ring. Pedroza was a different kind of fighter from what I had fought before and I needed to be ready for that. His was a different style: he fought at a different pace and threw punches from different angles; he hit you from distance and you couldn't hit him back again; he was tricky on the inside, he would tie you up and foul you – in his fifteen-round contest against La Porte, it was estimated he had fouled La Porte 110 times. Pedroza was absolutely brilliant at working his opponent out, diffusing their best weapons and stopping their attacks.

I knew I had to find a way to prevent Pedroza from doing all that, and the only way I was going to work out how to do that was by sparring with the quality of Mosquera and Marmalejo. It was hard work, not least because Marmalejo was arrogant as hell. You should have seen the way he would throw uppercuts and lift you round, lift you up and put you down, hit you as he pulled you down. It was obvious he'd been told to do that: get inside, put his head down, hit me low, do whatever he wanted. It was all to imitate Pedroza's style, and I knew that, but that didn't make it any easier.

Sometimes I would get so annoyed by the sparring that I wouldn't sleep that night. I couldn't sleep the whole night and I would have to do less of a run in the morning to get more sleep so I could be ready for the gym. That is how much it got to me. But it was all part of the preparation and it was important. Barney knew what he was doing and he was right to bring these guys in. He thought it might be a good workout, and sparring against the Panamanian pair turned out to be very good indeed.

The sparring was the most crucial element of the training, but it wasn't the only part of the preparation that was important. I also worked with the great Teddy Atlas on tactics. Teddy Atlas was a very good coach, and worked with the young Mike Tyson. Atlas had been over a few times and we worked out a plan to deal with Pedroza. He sent me a video of how he thought it should work, shot a little bit of video showing what I had to do tactically. Don't give ground in the middle of the ring, Atlas advised. Keep the pressure on him: move your head and jab with him. He said to make sure that when I attacked with the body shot that I came in close to the ropes. He thought I should double-jab as opposed to one, and that I should throw my right hand when Pedroza had his back to the ropes and a single jab when he was in the middle of the ring – because if I missed and Pedroza countered with the left hook, he could leave me looking foolish.

I watched tapes of Pedroza fighting as well. I watched his fights against Jose Caba, his ten-rounder against Gerald Hayes and his fifteen rounds with Bernard Taylor. I didn't watch any more than that because you can swamp yourself with it, and it can all become a bit much: you can make yourself bleary with theory. I watched those three contests and I was able to get enough from that. That was enough to figure things out, to discern what type of a guy he was, and what I needed to do to beat him.

Another element to the training was getting used to fighting outside. I hadn't fought in the open since my first professional fight against Selvin Bell. I was used to the support and atmosphere of the King's Hall in Belfast, but Loftus Road was going to be a different experience. There was no roof, so the noise was going to disappear up into the night sky, rather than bouncing off the King's Hall roof and coming back down to envelop you, like I'd been used to.

We did a training session out the back of one of Barney's houses in Holywood: I think it was his son Brian's house. It was a nice sunny day, and we set a ring up outside in the garden, and I did fifteen rounds. I sparred with Marmalejo and Mosquera, with an American super featherweight called Dwight Pratchett and a couple of the English guys. That was at my peak sparring: I did fifteen rounds with five different sparring partners. After that I knew I was ready to go the distance with one guy, however good he was.

Fighting outside was great. It didn't feel as hot or claustrophobic as I was used to, and it was a useful experience to have had. That's what good preparation is all about: simulating the experience you're going to face in the ring. That's true with the sparring partners you use, to get a feel of what your opponent will be like, and it's true of the conditions. If your fight is at two in the morning, then you need to practise fighting at two in the morning to adjust your body clock. And if your fight is outside, then you need to have a training session outside, so there are no surprises when the big night comes.

The hard work was paying off and the training was coming good. I got through my difficult week, got used to the Panamanians and began to start hitting and hurting them a lot. Right at the end of the training in Ireland, we had a press day in

Belfast, and all the media came to watch. It was meant to just be a sparring session with the cameras in there, but, of course, with the Panamanians it was all-out stuff. I was sparring with Mosquera and wobbled him with a left hook in front of all the press: I hit him and his legs turned to jelly. That was great for my confidence.

We began to wind down my heavy sparring in preparation for moving across to London. I was close to the weight and we were doing a final few rounds of sparring a couple of days before my flight. I did six rounds with three different guys, the last of whom was Davy Irving, a Belfast welterweight. It was literally the last round, with the last guy, in the last sparring session, and I threw this long left hook at him that pulled all the tendons down my arm. He moved into it and I didn't think he was going to, that was why it happened. I could feel it immediately and thought, oh Jesus, what have I done here? Everyone went, 'What's up? What's up?' and I said, 'It's all right, it's OK,' even though it wasn't. I finished the round, there were thirty seconds to go, and thought, what do we do now?

I knew it wasn't bone or anything but it was sore, really sore, and I knew I had done something to it. I was worried, of course I was. I never thought the fight would be off: there is never a fight where you are completely 100 per cent. It never, ever, goes like that. By the very nature of boxing, the pounding and the getting pounded, you're never going to be in perfect condition. So I never thought it was terminal, no way. But I knew it was sore and painful and was worried it might hinder my performance.

We flew over to London the next day. I was staying at the Holiday Inn on the Edgware Road, which was a lovely hotel and nice and central. I had a big suite to stay in, and in one of the rooms we pushed all the chairs back so I could shadow-box in there.

A physio called Deborah Good came in to work on my arm. We didn't want it getting out, so we contacted a British Board of

Control doctor, Dr Adrian Whiteson, on the q.t., and asked him to recommend someone. The press had expected me to go down to the Thomas a Becket gym on the Old Kent Road, so we told them that my weight was so good all I was doing was ticking over, and that I would just be doing some shadow-boxing in the hotel. Which was true, if not quite the whole picture. Deborah Good came in, a lovely girl, and worked on my arm every day up to the fight: she used this gel and a little electric pulse, and it got a lot better.

As well as the shadow-boxing, I'd go running in Hyde Park with Sean McGivern. We'd run down the Edgware Road, once around the park and back up to the hotel again. I'd go fairly early in the morning, around eight-thirty or so. There was no point getting up much earlier, because by this point I was gearing myself up to be in peak condition at ten in the evening. It was fairly quiet on the run: I'd have my hood up, so most of the commuters who were hustling and bustling wouldn't know who I was. I'd get beeped by the taxi drivers, though: 'McGuigan! We're rooting for you!' they'd shout. Back at the hotel I'd do some shadow-boxing, maybe a bit of skipping: light sessions, nothing too heavy. I'd move my feet, do some foot drills and work on my tactics, but nothing more by this point. I'd keep a careful eye on my weight: we'd go downstairs and use these huge scales that they had in the kitchen. They were really accurate, so I'd go down when no one was around, strip off and jump on.

These last few days I always found the hardest. The main training was done, the fight was still a few days off and you'd have these long lingering hours in between, saving your energy, not doing too much. I'd avoid the papers, wouldn't watch programmes like *Sportsnight*, but you'd still end up thinking about the fight, over and over and over again. Even though I was keeping away from the media, it was difficult to keep away from the magnitude of what I was trying to do. You'd try to dampen that down, tell yourself it was just another fight you were preparing yourself for, but it was hard to kid yourself. It didn't help that I couldn't see Sandra: I would never normally see her for the last few weeks before a fight. I would talk to her on the phone, but that would be it.

The other thing you'd get in the build-up to a big fight like this would be a procession of people dropping in to see you: a Ray Mancini or a Mickey Duff, saying hello to Terry Lawless, that sort of thing. I remember there was a guy called Edwin Rosario, the former WBC lightweight champion, who was over to fight in London the following week. He was staying at the hotel as well, and we would meet him in the foyer. I remember him saying that he had a message for me from Larry Holmes. Holmes had had as many defences of his heavyweight title as Pedroza had had of his featherweight title, and he was desperate to go one better. 'Hey man,' Rosario told me, 'Larry Holmes is hoping you will kick his ass.' It was well-meaning, good knockabout stuff, but as the days ticked down towards Saturday, it showed there was no escape from the enormity of what I was about to try and achieve.

I never usually had any problems sleeping, but the night before the fight I didn't sleep very well. I was too keyed up with the pressure. It didn't help that I was hungry: my mouth was dry, the room was dry, because I wanted to make sure I was 'drying off', dehydrating away that last pound or two before the weigh-in. If I was heavy, I would dry out two and a half pounds a night, but that close to the fight, I was on the weight and it would have dried out only a pound at most. The weigh-in wasn't until about ten, but I woke up really early, about five-thirty. I tried to get back to sleep again, but just dozed and woke up, dozed and woke up until it was time to get ready for the biggest day of my life.

Chapter 10

Fight Night

The weigh-in for the Pedroza fight took place at the Odeon Cinema in Leicester Square, and was complete chaos. It wasn't far from my hotel on the Edgware Road, but we got stuck in traffic and turned up late. Leicester Square isn't quiet at the best of times, but by the time we got there, a massive crowd was waiting. A huge cheer went up when we arrived, with the crowd chanting, 'McGuigan! McGuigan!' That was to intimidate Pedroza as much as anything, though with nineteen title defences under his belt, it was going to take more than that to faze him.

I was with my friend Sean McGivern and my brother Dermot. When we got there I asked Sean to go and get me a Big Mac. You are dreaming of food just before the weigh-in and that is what I fancied. I wanted it there, so I could eat it as soon as I'd got off the scales. So Sean went off to go to McDonalds, and we went in. We were late, as I said, and as I was walking up the side, Pedroza was already stepping off the scales. Barney was going ballistic: he was saying he hadn't seen him on the scales and wanted him back on. But Pedroza's people were saying, 'No, no, no,' that he'd made the weight and he was not getting back on the scales.

It was a well-worked routine that Pedroza's lot were doing.

When everyone was looking around and wondering what was going on, Pedroza stripped down to his briefs and jumped on the scales. The scales went 'tip tip tip' but before they'd had a chance to settle, his people all cheered and clapped that he'd made the weight, and so everyone in the audience started doing the same. Then they handed Pedroza an empty cup, and he pretended to drink from that. So if he did have to go back on the scales and he was over the weight, then he could claim it was from the drink he'd just had.

Barney was saying that he wanted Pedroza back on the scales, but the WBA inspector, this wrinkled old Panamanian guy, face like the map of South America, was saying that no, he was satisfied that Pedroza had made the weight. Pedroza was off, he clearly didn't want to get back on the scales. I got on the scales and was just under the weight: eight stone, thirteen and three-quarters. Barney, though, was still furious about Pedroza. He grabbed the microphone and told the crowd, 'I am not happy. I am not happy with the British Boxing Board of Control. I am not happy with the WBA inspector. I don't think he made the weight but we are going to go on. It is the first round to them but we will win the most important fight.' The crowd all cheered at that: 'Yeah Barney!' and 'Whoo!' – all that sort of stuff.

I got off the scales and I had a Coke straightaway. What we had done was leave a Coke all night with the top off to get rid of the gas, so you didn't burp when you swallowed it down, but you got all of the sugar. The most important thing was to get fluid down me: there was twelve hours or so to the fight, which was not a lot of time to try and put some weight on. So I had the Coke, drank that down quickly, then swallowed a couple of Lucozades as well. Then I had some water and some soup, and I got to the stage that I couldn't eat the bloody McDonalds. I ate half of the Big Mac and went yuck: I was full.

On the way back from the weigh-in, we went to a chapel. Father

Salvian Maguire was a priest that Barney knew: he'd come to the fight from Belfast, and we said a few prayers. I don't want to make a big deal of that, for me religion is a very personal thing, but it's something I did before all of my big fights. I had done all my training and preparation and I had done that myself, but it was very important to pray that I would win, that I didn't hurt Pedroza in the process, and that I'd come through the fight unscathed. So I prayed for all that. I prayed that I would win not just because it meant a lot to me, but because it was so important for so many people. I wanted to win for them, to give them a celebration, something to cheer about in the middle of everything that was going on. I had to win as much for them as myself – and that is what I prayed for.

I went back to the hotel, had something more to eat and then went for a walk with Sean, Dermot and my brother-in-law Ross, from the Edgware Road down to Hyde Park Corner. I kept it low key: I didn't want to talk to people, have people beeping their horns and stuff, I just wanted to focus on the fight. I then went back to the hotel and tried to get some rest. I didn't sleep as much as I'd have liked to, but lay on the bed with the lights off, trying to think about anything but the fight. But I could never really switch off, whatever I was thinking about, it would always come back to the fight. By about seven I was up and preparing to head to the stadium. I could feel my nerves, for sure, but had a snack, scrambled eggs on toast, I think. It was time to go.

The game plan with Pedroza was to pressurise him and back him up. I wanted to try and jab with him, and just continually keep him under pressure. I wanted to push him back into the corners, and make the ring as small as possible. As I worked my way towards him, I needed to pick up as little damage as possible. Pedroza was a very good straight puncher, a great counterpuncher. He could punch long, long shots, and he could lift your head up with hooks and uppercuts. He'd whack you to the body and beat you round the side of the head. I knew it was going to be extremely difficult walking into that maelstrom without taking some damage in return. But, as the old saying goes, you can't walk through the shower without getting wet.

I wanted to fight at a pace that Pedroza was uncomfortable with. The idea was to make him tired and fatigued, and that would take away his technical advantage. After five or six rounds of keeping the pressure up, I figured his technical advantage would start to wane. With the exception of the Gerald Hayes fight, which lasted ten rounds, Pedroza's half-dozen previous match-ups had all gone the distance. I'd watched the Caba fight and the Hayes one, and I knew that none of these guys could put the sort of pressure on Pedroza that I was able to. That was my advantage.

It always used to annoy me when people said, 'Ah, that McGuigan. He walks into punches.' I didn't do that. I would go in and put pressure on the other guy, and try to make them throw first. I'd make them throw and miss, and then would hit back and make them pay. That was my style. I would get them to the stage where they didn't know when to throw, make them panic. I'd feint, feint, feint: stay on them and keep the pressure up, never let them get their breath back, never let them know where the next punch was coming from. Sure, you'd get caught with the occasional punch, fighting that way, but most of the time my chin was tucked, my head was moving, my hands were up protecting my head and chin.

There's a thin line between slipping a punch and walking into one: it's a fine art and that's what I was good at. I'd slip their shots, let the punch go over my head, and get myself in position to hit them. It took a lot of hard work and dedication to get myself to that level, but over the years I'd learned to be able to see the punches coming, miss them by a whisker, and nail my opponent with a counterpunch. I'd feint to the body and hit to the head, feint to the head and hit to the body. I'd keep doing that, mixing it up until at some point they'd get tired, and when I feinted to the head they'd put their hands up. At that point I'd move in and whack them to the body. That's when you really do the damage, and that is what I wanted to do to Pedroza. I wanted to get him into the position that I could do that to him. But I never quite managed it: I couldn't feint and fool him like I did with the others. He was just too good, too sharp at fighting at close range.

When the opening bell went, I ran out, straight at Pedroza. He circled the ring, semicircle to the right, semicircle to the left, tried to use his long, rangy punches. He was finding his range in those first exchanges, finding his range and snapping shots out. Pedroza was snapping lefts and rights and trying hooks but there wasn't really any power in them, he was just sizing me up and finding his range. Meanwhile, I was walking in to him and putting him under pressure: feinting, snapping jabs at him. It was one-shot-at-a-time stuff, but I was always trying to back him up, keeping on him, on him, on him. It was a gamble what I was doing, I knew that. I was being outboxed and Pedroza won the first few rounds. But that was OK: it was money in the bank as far as I was concerned. I was walking into some shots, but that was the price for being where I wanted to be, keeping myself on him, keeping the pressure up. I was making him work for his rounds, forcing him left, then right, doing miles around the ring.

The corner was happy with how it was going. You're doing good, they told me between rounds. Keep closing the distance, keep using the jab. Make sure your hands are high and don't walk on to his right hands. Walk him down, they encouraged me. Walk him down and apply the pressure: snap the jabs, one-twos when he stops, three shots if he holds his feet. I knew that Pedroza would be peppering me with punches, to try and perplex and bamboozle me. But I never got near that confused stage. I was keeping on him and, all the time, knew I was getting closer and closer.

In the fourth round, Pedroza was still ahead. Then in the fifth, he stayed with me on the inside. He was trying to fend me off and I went left, right, left hook to the body, left hook to the head. And then, because he didn't think I was going to, I went left hook right up his guts. It was bang on the bell, the last shot of the round. I could hear him go 'Uggh!' Even though the noise in the stadium was deafening, I was so close I could hear him breathing, hear his almost primal response. Pedroza didn't panic, but he was definitely hurt and let out a gasp as the bell rang. He jumped up and down on his feet to sort of shake out his system. And I knew that for the first time, I'd properly hurt him.

In the sixth round, I hurt him again. It wasn't for long, only a few seconds, but it was another significant battle to have won. Pedroza had stayed on the inside with me and he tried to pull me down. I moved around and, staying on the inside, sent a right hook round the side … boom! It definitely hurt him. I hit him with a left hook up the stomach and knew I'd hurt him again. At that point, you could see Pedroza thinking, OK, so I can't keep this guy off me. And now I know I'm not strong enough on the inside either. It might only have been a short exchange but, psychologically, it was key.

In the seventh, Pedroza outboxed me. On the commentary, Harry Carpenter was saying, 'McGuigan has not been so effective in this round.' And at that precise moment, I hit Pedroza with a right hand: 'Oh, yes he is! He's got him with a right!' Pedroza was going down and I threw the left hook, just missing him, clipping the side of his head as he went down. Then it was madness. As soon as I hit him and he went down, I turned quickly and ran to the neutral corner. The referee doesn't start the count until you're in that corner, and I knew that a couple of seconds could be the difference, wanted Pedroza to have as little chance to recover as possible.

It was satisfying because I'd been practising that shot

specifically. Gerald Hayes had said to me, that is the shot he is open for, so I knew that once Pedroza tired it was worth a go. I waited for him to put his hand down a little bit, leave his chin open and then went for it. I ran straight to the neutral corner, and the referee, Stanley Christodoulou, picked up the count from the timekeeper: 'One . . . two . . . three . . .' I did what any good pro should do and turned to look at my corner. They should be calming you down, giving you advice – 'throw a left and a right', 'hit him with a big left hook'. But I looked over and they were just leaping up and down, and behind them the crowd were going crazy. The noise in the ground was deafening. I stood there thinking, what punch should I throw now?

The referee got to about six or seven before he was satisfied Pedroza was OK, and allowed the fight to continue. I immediately came charging across, threw this looping right hand at Pedroza ... and missed. It went sailing past his head, and I thought, fuck. I backed Pedroza up to the ropes but he hit me with two sharp left hooks and made it to the end of the round. After that, I knew he was OK, that he wasn't as badly hurt as I'd thought he was. I kind of knew that, to be honest, but the end of the round confirmed it. I went back to the corner and I thought, right then, I've had him once, let's just do it again. I'd won the battle of strength on the inside, had hurt him on the inside and now had knocked him down. Pedroza thought he was outclassing me, but I'd played possum and caught him good. My confidence was up because I knew I could hurt him. I was getting stronger and he was getting weaker. The balance of the fight was beginning to shift – I was marginally ahead, perhaps by one or two points, and it was down to Pedroza to try and get back into the fight.

To give him his dues, Pedroza came out in the eighth round and hit me hard, caught me with a good shot. I remember thinking, fuck, that was hard, but also thinking that he didn't have the same one-punch power that La Porte had. Pedroza was the better

145

fighter: he had a different style and was technically much superior, but he lacked the raw power that La Porte could put into his punches. So although I got hit a lot more, I took some comfort from that. But Pedroza won the round, and brought himself back into the fight. He knew he needed to have a big round, and he delivered.

In the ninth, though, I hurt him again and had him in serious trouble. We were fighting on the inside; Pedroza stayed on the inside and backed me to the ropes. I was leaning in to give myself some room and he was trying to pull me, so I took a step back and pushed him to give myself room to let my punches go. I hit him with a left and then a right hook, hit him on the side of the head. I caught him on the temple and his legs started to wobble. I saw him panicking like a caged lion and I went for it. I ran after him and missed him with the next one: if that had connected, I would have knocked him out. Then I hit him with a left hook, left hook, right hook, right hand, left hook, bang! By this point the bell had gone for end of the round – I couldn't hear it, couldn't hear a bloody thing. The referee stepped in and Del Rio, Pedroza's manager, was going mad – 'The bell! The bell! What the hell are you doing?' – but there was nothing that could be done. The roar of the crowd was so overwhelming, you couldn't hear a thing.

Again I went back to the corner and thought, I've got him. And once more he came back, came back strong and shared the tenth. I put him back under pressure in the eleventh, won that one, won the twelfth as well. The next key moment happened towards the end of the thirteenth. There were about forty-five seconds to go in the round. I threw a long right hand at him and a left hook. He looked vulnerable and his legs sagged again. So I went with another right and a left hook, missed him with both. We were then in a clinch: I pulled my hands back and my arms out. I hit him with another left hook, another right and his legs went again. Out of the corner of my eye, it looked like the ref was about to jump in. I glanced across to see if he was going to stop it. That was a mistake, because next thing I knew, Pedroza had hit me with his right. I fired back at him, fired back again, but Pedroza had recovered. He grabbed and held me, cleared his head and pulled back. I couldn't catch him clean for the remainder of the round.

I kept at him in the fourteenth, but by this point I was thinking, I'm never going to knock this guy out. And then he walked me on to a long right. He was in the corner and I went in with my left hand a bit low. He hit me right on the side of the head. What I remember thinking was that he can't be that tired if he can still hit me that hard. He might have looked lethargic by this point, he didn't seem slotted down and tight, but his technique was so good, and he had all that experience. His poker face never allowed him to show he was tired.

In the final round, I kept working him, just kept working him. He was jabbing and I was slipping them, moving my head and slipping underneath his punches. With about a minute to go I had him again, saw him sort of sagging, and went for it. I didn't let up until the final bell.

That was it. The bell went, and we fell into each other's arms. Pedroza looked at me and simply said, 'You'll be a good champion.'

I knew that I had done well but didn't know quite how well. When you're in the thick of it, in the moment, then you can only think, I've done well here. I thought I had done enough, but wasn't completely sure. There was no doubt from the fans though. From the roaring and the cheering, there was no doubt who they thought had won.

My brother Dermot was always the first one into the ring. He always took every punch with me, every punch. 'You've done it!' he said, and lifted me up on his shoulders. He gave me this hug, and told me he loved me. Eddie Shaw was there, and I gave him a hug too. Barney was there, and suddenly it seemed like the whole crowd was pouring into the ring. There wasn't the security you have now, so there was no way they could clear the ring. Everyone was coming up and saying, 'You've done it! You've won it, you have definitely won it!' And I still wasn't completely certain and was saying, 'Do you think so?' We were meeting and greeting everyone and it felt like forever, that four or five minutes before they announced who had won.

These days they reveal the scores from each individual judge before announcing the winner, to build up the suspense (for the record, Christodoulou scored it 148–138 for me, Fernando Viso 147–140 and Ove Ovesen 149–139). Back then, there was no messing about. The announcer picked up the microphone and declared, 'Ladies and gentlemen . . . by a unanimous decision . . . Barry McGuigan . . .' The roar from the crowd drowned out the rest of it.

The feeling was incredible. Just incredible. When they lifted me up and everything, well, it's difficult even now to really describe it. The sense of elation, of achievement, was completely over-whelming. To have all those people around me cheering and celebrating: my dad and my brother Dermot, my little baby brother who was there as well, my brother-in-law and Sean McGivern. For everyone who helped me get there, the people who had run thousands of miles with me, the sparring partners who had put me through my paces, the coaches and corner men, all those people. For them, for all of them to be part of that moment was just fantastic.

I did three television interviews still taking it all in, still in the ring. I did one with ABC for the Americans, one with Jimmy Magee for RTE and one with Harry Carpenter for the BBC. It was the Carpenter interview where I mentioned Young Ali. I dedicated the win to him, said that it hadn't been an ordinary fighter who beat him that night, but a world champion. It felt surreal saying that, world champion. The mixture of all the mayhem and the memories of Young Ali was too much, and I struggled to hold my emotions back.

By the time we got back to the dressing room, the place had half emptied. The fans were all happy: they were satisfied that they'd seen me win and were off into the night to find another beer. We went into the dressing room, and it was a revolving door of congratulations. Jim Neilly was there from BBC Northern Ireland: Willie John McBride, Mary Peters, Pat Jennings and Dennis Taylor all came in. So many people had turned out for the fight, a real eclectic bunch: J P McManus the stud farm owner was there, Lucian Freud, George Best, Norman Whiteside; the author Irvine Welsh was there, and later wrote about the fight in his novel *Glue*: Frank Bruno, Lloyd Honeyghan, Alan Minter was there doing the television. Someone passed me the phone and it was Garret Fitzgerald, the Irish Taoiseach, offering his congratulations.

I had a shower and went upstairs to the executive suite to meet the press. Sandra was there with Blain: he'd watched the fight being passed around from knee to knee and was so tired. He was moaning about wanting to go to bed, bless him: he wasn't even two. The press were great, they all loved him and thought he was fantastic, but he was so tired we had to go back to the hotel.

We were in the McGuigan coach, and this time the journey was crazy: there were people everywhere. It was very, very slow coming through Shepherd's Bush, along that road from the QPR ground. The fans just surrounded the coach and stopped it, cheering and shouting. Amazing scenes. Eventually we were clear and headed back towards Marble Arch. Word had got out where we were staying and there were more people outside the hotel. Inside, there was a party downstairs and a party upstairs, one on the mezzanine floor and one down below.

I showed my face at both, but by this point I was just so tired, and Sandy was tired and Blain was absolutely exhausted. Sandy was putting Blain to bed and he was being restless, so I went down to say hello to everyone. I knew I couldn't stay long because once I was in, I would never get out of there: everyone was up for the night. I remember Phil Coulter was there, the songwriter, and him saying, 'Barry, Jesus, what a night. Soak it all up, son, enjoy it.' But I'd given so much to get there, given my all for fifteen hard rounds, that I simply had nothing left. I made my excuses and went back up to my wife and my son, neither of whom I'd seen for weeks. I know it sounds ridiculous but I was almost too tired to sleep. I went to bed and tried, tried to get some rest because I knew the madness was only just beginning.

Chapter 11

On Top of the World

I woke up as world champion feeling both great and terrible at the same time. My neck was completely stiff from the fight: my Adam's apple was sore and under my chin was all bruised. My Adam's apple had been punched a lot and it was hard to swallow. There was a sauna in the hotel, so I went down there later that day. There was nobody about, so I did some shadow-boxing, to loosen myself up a bit.

The media stuff started straightaway. There was a press do in the morning: a big conference in the hotel and then we went back up to the hotel room for photographs of us in bed reading the Sunday papers. This will show you how different things were back then: I remember one of the photographers passing his camera to Blain – you play with that, son, he said. A few days later, there was a full-page advert for the camera in the papers, this picture of Blain and the camera taking a photo of me under the headline 'You don't have to be a world champion to use . . .' You think what would happen if someone did that today.

Back then, none of us really knew what to expect. The focus had been so completely on the fight, we hadn't really thought what would happen next. Overnight, we'd become public property.

Sandra had this Katharine Hamnett dress she'd worn for the fight, but had come to the hotel without anything else to wear, and now we had the press to face again. Back at home, we were similarly unprepared. I'd been getting ready for a world title fight, Sandra was pregnant with our second child, had Blain who was under two to look after on her own, and was working as well. When you're dealing with all that, getting the house in perfect condition is the last thing on your mind. But now I was world champion, we were getting calls from back home that people were turning up to look at the house, having a look through the windows and taking photographs.

The other thing we had to get used to was the security. Sandra and I tried to go for a walk round Hyde Park but because there were so many people who wanted to talk to us, and so many security people trying to stop them, it was ridiculous. We'd never experienced anything like it – and couldn't understand how people could live their lives like that. Sandra and I wanted to talk to each other, but with all the security people and everyone, it was like having a ten-way conversation.

We went to Harrods, and that was bedlam too. We were getting followed round, and everyone was expecting us to buy things, but Sandra and I were just thinking how expensive everything was. Sandra bought a pair of John Lennon-type sunglasses that she still has. And we bought some silk for Blain – we used to call it his sleepy stuff because he liked to have it to go to sleep. But that was it: we went back to the hotel suite, which was the only place we could be by ourselves, and get away from it all.

The plan had been to stay in London for a few days and celebrate, but we got a call from Clones to say there'd been a fire at my parents' house. It was the weirdest, most terrible thing. The television had caught fire in the night and their house had burned down. No one had been hurt, thank goodness, but the house was absolutely gutted. So many possessions had gone with it: as well as my parents' things, I lost all my amateur medals, all the videos of my fights. A house can always be rebuilt, but it's those personal things, the ones you can't replace, that make such events really difficult to deal with.

It could have put a dampener on things, but because it was such a crazy weekend, my parents just dealt with it. The elation of my victory cancelled the drama of the fire out. People just went, 'Right, OK,' and got on with things: nothing was going to stop them from celebrating. My parents took it all in their stride in a way that I'm not sure I could have done. Most of their house had burned to the ground and they just carried on. It was strange, though, the timing of it all: to win the world title and lose all my boxing stuff in one night. You can't make that sort of thing up.

After I heard about the fire, I wanted to get back to Clones as soon as possible. So we changed our plans and flew back to Belfast on the Monday morning. The Lord Mayor of Belfast, a guy called John Carson, was there to meet me at the airport, to drive me in his Roller to a civic reception at City Hall. But I'd bought myself this sports car, a red Lotus Excel, and that was there waiting for me at the airport too. I'd been looking forward to that so much, and was so desperate to drive it, that I turned the Lord Mayor down. He was a nice guy, he just said, 'Sure, Barry, no problem. You just follow us in.' So I got in the Lotus and followed the Lord Mayor back to Belfast. We went to the top of Royal Avenue, where the offices of the *Belfast Telegraph* are. I got out the car and got on this float, a truck with a boxing ring on the back, and we continued our way towards City Hall.

The crowd was huge, about 70,000. It was like Loftus Road all over again. People were chanting, 'Barry! Barry!' and the atmosphere was incredible. The truck took forever to get to City Hall. There were just so many people, it was inching its way down the road: if you didn't know the landmarks, you wouldn't have had a clue which street you were on. Everywhere you looked there were people hanging out of windows, climbing up scaffolding to get a good position: people said to me it was like VE-Day all over again. We reached City Hall, where we had this reception: all the dignitaries were there, including Paddy Devlin, who'd helped me. I said hello to so many people. The crowd was still there outside, thousands of them in the street, and I ended up hanging out of a window on the second floor to wave to them. I was cheering them, they were cheering me. Just incredible scenes.

We then drove down to Clones for the next celebration. I was back in the Lotus, and we drove down to the border with a police escort. I had the police to the border, where the Garda special branch were waiting to continue the escort. I knew the border road like the back of my hand, so I said to the guys, you follow me. So I drove and they were driving behind me and I had my new sports car and was taking the mickey: I was flying around and leaving them behind, enjoying myself. Two miles outside of Clones we drove over the back roads so I could get home without going through town – there were thousands of people waiting for us and we'd never get through. I took the Garda down this road round the back of the GAA pitch, and just as I was turning to go out to my house, I scraped the side of my brand-new Lotus. It looked like it was a piece of grass, but it was covering a cement square block and it scraped my pride and joy very badly. I can still hear the noise now.

I didn't have much luck with that Lotus. It had cream seats, and Blain got in the back with one of those black marker pens I'd been using to sign autographs. He said, proudly, 'Look, Daddy!' thinking he was copying me signing photos. Except it wasn't photos he'd been signing, but the brand-new cream seats. If that wasn't enough, he fixed the CD player as well. CD players were the latest thing back then, and my car was one of the first in Northern

Ireland to have one. It stopped working after a couple of days, so I took it back up to Belfast to get it fixed. They had a look and said, 'Somebody has been using it as a money box.' The reason it wasn't working was because Blain had been stuffing the slot with coins and it had blown up.

Back on the Monday, we got back home without anyone realising we'd arrived. So we were able to get back, get sorted out and changed, and then drive up into Clones as if we'd only just got there. Clones was even crazier than Belfast. It was wet but everyone had waited and the Diamond was absolutely packed. It was like Ulster Final day (the culmination of the Ulster Gaelic football competition that takes place in Clones). Tens of thousands of people were there to greet me. The reception was great and everyone wanted to shake my hand. It felt like I'd shaken thousands and thousands of people's hands.

The whole place had been celebrating for days. Because the fight was on the weekend they would have started on the Thursday night, into Friday. Friday was the whole build-up and then on Saturday everybody had left to go to England, so the rest of them had to make up for that. They put big screens up, Sandra's dad's hotel had a television screen up and people watched there. The other hotels would have done the same. They were all staying open, 24 hours. And then there was this great euphoria out in the streets afterwards: people were driving round honking their horns (I remember someone telling me that happened in Belfast, too). There were so many people pouring into the town, camera crews from around the world, people wanting to be part of it, that the locals just put people up in their homes and charged them, then carried on with the celebrations.

It was an amazing feeling again: wonderful to have given everyone who had supported me this moment, to share in my achievement. I wanted to soak it all in, but at the same time I was desperate to see what had happened to my parents' house. We went to have a look at the house, and it was a shock: it was all burned out, a complete mess. The shop at the front was all right, but as soon as you went round the back ... my gym was burned, the kitchen was burned, the living rooms, the bedrooms, the fire had gone through all of them. A bit like the weather, it was the dampener on an otherwise extraordinary day.

A couple of days later, we did the third and final parade, this time in Dublin. We drove down to Swords, which is a little town to the north of the Irish capital. The police picked us up there and they gave us a cavalcade all the way to the top of O'Connell Street. It was great passing all the traffic: everybody pulling over and honking and waving when they realised who it was. We went down to the Mansion House on this bus and it was the maddest parade of the lot. A quarter of a million people had turned out, and there were people as far as the eye could see: they'd move out of the way to let the bus through and then just slot in behind. So it was like we were surrounded by people the whole time. I remember people were throwing toys, too: toys for Blain. Someone had this massive cuddly dog with big floppy ears, and they threw that on to the bus. The trailer and the bus were full of toys by the end of it.

Years later, I met the Irish Ryder Cup golfer Paul McGinley, who has since become a good friend. He was eighteen years old at the time of my victory, and came to watch the parade. He told me that he'd seen the bus and the crowds and thought to himself, I want a bit of that. He worked at his golf and ultimately got his chance, when he sank the winning putt to clinch the Ryder Cup in 2002. 'You did it,' I told him. 'You made it up O'Connell Street.' 'Yes,' Paul replied, 'but it was for the team, it wasn't quite the same as you, champ.'

The whole of that summer was a bit like that. I had a mandatory defence against Bernard Taylor to prepare for, and that would have kept me busy enough on its own. But I had everything that went with being world champion to cope with as well – and I mean everything.

Right from the word go, there were the letters. They arrived by the sackful, two or three sacks of letters a day. I reckon we must have got something like 8,000 or so in the first week alone. There was no organisation or help to deal with it, so Sandra and I did what we could to answer them: we felt that people had taken the effort to write to us, so they deserved a response. It was all hands on deck: the two of us, my Uncle Pete and Auntie Janet, and any other relative or friend that happened to be in the house was also roped in. Janet would open the letters and save the stamps for the blind, and we would sit down and read them. There were the occasional mad ones, a few people writing to ask for money, but the vast majority were just incredibly nice – Hi Barry, really delighted for you, can I have your autograph sort of thing. So we'd reply, write out the address on the envelope by hand and send them back.

Everyone had our address. Everyone had our telephone number. They would just ring up and say they were coming over. There'd be tours coming to our house: you'd wake up in the morning and hear someone outside going, 'And there is the bedroom.' People would come up and knock on the door like you wouldn't believe. People had a neck on them, as we'd say, for anything but soap. They had no qualms whatsoever about coming and ringing the doorbell.

My mum still had the shop on the Diamond, and that was the first port of call for a lot of people. We'd always had a bit of that with my dad's success in the music business when I was growing up. Because of his success as a singer, he was very popular all over the country. He was a very amiable chap, and everybody loved to pop in to the house if they were coming through the town. With the boxing, people would all go to the shop. They'd go to my father-in-law's hotel and have a drink and a chat. Some would get fended off, but plenty of others would find out, or someone would tell them where our house was. And out they would come to say hello.

That's as true with the media as much with the fans. Because of the Ireland situation, my victory was a big story internationally, and we would get journalists and camera crews turning up from all round the world. We were always friendly, never turned anyone away, but again it was hard work: there was no such thing as public relations in Ireland back then, and we were left to deal with it all ourselves. There was no mechanism or filter system: anyone and everyone who turned up got their interview.

I got so many invitations for events, opened so many fêtes and stuff that summer. There was no way I could do them all and find time for my training, but I did my best to accept as many of the requests as possible. There were occasions when I ended up training at ridiculous times to fit it all in: I'd be going into the gym at half-eleven at night and training through to half-one in the morning. Then I would come back home and get up the next day and go off to open a fête in some crazy part of the country. I'd have police guys with me, plain-clothes guys staying in the distance. I'd turn up, shake hands and sign autographs, before jumping into the car, driving home and training into the night again.

There was one event I remember going to near Dublin by helicopter. They flew in to pick Sandra and me up in this little glass bubble. Because everyone in Clones was used to only ever seeing Army helicopters, it got everyone out, flying round the town and landing in front of this crowd at the Starlight Ballroom. On the way down to our function, the headwind was so strong, it would have been quicker to drive. But on the way back, we got home in half the time. When we got to Clones, the helicopter was banking like anything. 'Do you want to see the town?' asked the pilot, doing all these acrobatics to impress the children on the ground. Sandra and I were petrified and happy to make it back to land.

My parents, meanwhile, had moved in next door, to Chapman's, the old chemist's shop that Dad and I had bought the year before. We made a boxing gym out the back there, and that was where I trained. We all helped paint the house, getting our relations in to help with the decorating. So I'd be painting or training or having cups of tea with all these people who were passing through and wanted to say hello.

My boxing success also made me of interest to numerous businesses and companies, all wanting my endorsement for their products. Barney Eastwood's son, Brian, looked after the commercial side of things for a while, and I also had help on some deals from a guy called Tony Clark, and another called Roddy Carr. It was good fun, though the things I got involved in were a strange mixture of stuff.

I remember doing this event for mobile phones. This was the mid-eighties, and the phone was huge, the size of a brick. I was supposed to be talking to Henry Cooper on the other end. He went, 'Hello, Barry,' and I said, 'Hi, Henry, how's it going?' And then the phone went dead. The reception on the phone was diabolical. There were all these journalists and people watching, so I thought I'd better play along and pretend it was all working and I was still talking to Henry. So I was chatting away to myself when the phone starting ringing, and it was obvious I'd been making it up.

There was a Barry McGuigan computer game, which was a huge success at the time. They used me to get the fighting technique right, or as right as they could given the size of computers back then. Like with the mobile phones, technology has moved on a lot. But it looked great at the time and was really popular. It always amazes me how many people remember playing it: people still come up and tell me it was the first computer game that they ever played.

Then there was the food. I had my own flavour of crisps – Barry's Jabs. They were nettle-flavoured: they brought the flavour back recently for an anniversary. Ray Quinn from Donegal revealed to me recently that he owned the company that produced the crisps. I did campaigns for Irish beef in the South and for Monaghan Milk. They'd sponsored me early on, when I was winning the British and European titles, so it was great for them when I beat Pedroza. They renamed the milk 'Champion Milk' after I won the title, and it is still called that today.

One day, this guy appeared at the front door wearing a bowler hat. Bear in mind we were right on the border, and he turned up looking like Winston Churchill. I said to myself, 'Who the hell is this?' and he says, 'Hello, my name is Brian Hitchen, how are you?' Hitchen was then a journalist from the *Daily Star*: he would go on to be editor of the newspaper from 1987 to 1994, before becoming editor of the *Sunday Express*. Awarded the CBE for his services to journalism, he went on to be chairman of Kerry Life and Irish Country Life. He was such a lovely man, and he signed me up to do exclusive articles during my time as champion of the world. It was a long and fruitful relationship with Brian. One of life's gentlemen, his wife Nelly is Irish.

One of the best things about winning the world championship was the opportunity I got to meet all sorts of people. There was this one occasion we were being put up at the St James's Club in London for some event. It was an amazing place: we had a private lift that took us up to our penthouse suite, and it was massive. It was like a big huge apartment. And our bedroom had a Jacuzzi. It was Sandra, Blain and me in that Jacuzzi, twenty-four seven. Anyway, the actor Peter O'Toole was also staying there, and word got to us that he wanted to meet me and say hello.

So Peter O'Toole came upstairs, and it was an absolute pleasure to meet him. He was there with his son Lorcan, who was the same age as Blain, and I went to order some tea. And I came back, and

I'll never forget this, he was sat there with Blain and Lorcan, reading them *Thomas the Tank Engine*. He was so nice with the boys and his voice was just amazing, reading them this story. Not long after that, Blain heard Peter O'Toole on television in a film and without even looking at him he went, 'That's the man that read me *Thomas the Tank Engine*.' And he just picked him out straightaway because he recognised the voice.

To top off a fantastic few months, I finished the year by being voted BBC Sports Personality of the Year, the first boxer to do so since Henry Cooper in 1970. It had been a big year for sport: Dennis Taylor had won the world snooker championship: Steve Cram had broken three world records in nineteen days; Ian Botham had helped England regain the Ashes; Europe had won the Ryder Cup for the first time (before 1979, the competition had been between the US and a GB and Ireland team). Given all of that, it was a hugely proud moment when I found out that I had been voted the winner.

I turned up at the ceremony not knowing the result. People were giving you the wink and the nod, and I knew I had a chance, but still had no idea that I would win the award. I remember I was sat next to Frank Bruno when they read out who'd won: it was Sir Stanley Rous, the former FIFA president, who was reading out the results. He looked liked he was a hundred years old, the poor old man. In third place was Steve Cram, in second Ian Botham, and when he came to announce me as the winner, he got my name wrong, calling me Barry McCochrane. Bruno was laughing away, 'ho ho ho' in his big bass voice. That set me off, and soon everyone else was laughing too. But it was a great honour to have won, to have been voted for in such numbers by the public.

Chapter 12

Defending

When I took the Pedroza fight, we agreed to take on his mandatory challenge within ninety days if I won. That challenger was Bernard Taylor and my first defence took place against him at the King's Hall in Belfast on 28 September 1985. That was no small task: it was asking me to take on someone who was almost as good as Pedroza, but with all the hoopla of being world champion for me to deal with at the same time.

We got in some videos of Taylor fighting, against Marquez (the Mexican I'd sparred with in Chicago) and Pedroza. Taylor looked sensational. Marquez was tough and I had got the better of him the majority of the time. Taylor, though, he had outboxed him completely, boxed the guy's ears off. I watched the video of them, and he just punched the living daylights out of him. I just thought, wow, he made that look easy.

The thing that struck me most of all was Taylor's speed. His speed and reflexes were lightning. He did not look to have any flaws at all. He could drift in and out of punching range and he was immaculate-looking with his combinations: relaxed, fast and sharp. He was hard to hit too: his face was completely unblemished. Taylor had had a staggering amount of amateur fights (489, of which he won 481) and had never been dropped as a pro. No one had put him down. The only fight of his professional career he hadn't won was against Pedroza, and that had been a draw. I watched the videos and thought to myself, my God, I have got a fight on my hands here. It got to the stage where he looked so good on television that I just thought, how am I going to beat this guy? So I stopped watching the videos.

Taylor was the third tough fight I'd had within a year, after La Porte and Pedroza. Everything felt concertinaed in, but I didn't have a problem with the world champion stuff and the training: I've always been good at being able to compartmentalise. I always was very professional and if I needed to turn something down, I would do so, I would disassociate myself from things and say, sorry, I have got to go and train. I am sure some people thought it was rude, and that I was bad-mannered for walking away from things. But what mattered to me was my condition.

Given everything that was going on, it was good to be able to get back into my old routine and get away from it all. I was back in Bangor as before to do my training, working hard and every bit as intensely as before. We'd start off sparring doing four, six, eight rounds – most of the time we would do eight rounds with four different guys, and most of those guys would be bigger than me. We'd put in a flyweight occasionally, just to give me a rest. It would be eight to ten rounds, and then we would build up to fourteen or fifteen rounds, and that was enough for me. Once I had reached that peak I started coming back down again.

I knew that I had to be in shape and had to be quick to beat Taylor. As with Pedroza, we brought in sparring partners who simulated his style: we found a couple of American guys that were quick, fast on their feet and moved around the ring: Bernardo Checa and Humberto Sosa. We started with the English guys as before, who we were using for speed and movement. Then we

brought in the Americans, and built up the sparring rounds to the same intensity as with the Pedroza training.

The sparring was every bit as hard as for Pedroza, if not harder. The thing about being a world champion is that you get lifted and laid. Everybody rolls out the red carpet and you walk into a room and people light up, ask what they can do for you. And then you go in the gym and all your sparring partners want to hit you harder. Because of my title, they were going to try 20 per cent harder and attempt to take my head off. Checa was tough, and well over the weight for a featherweight: it was more like fighting a lightweight. When he did get down to the right weight, he lost all his strength. So it was a good workout for me, but a bit of a false economy for him as a fighter. When Bernardo got his shot at the world title he was stopped in a few rounds because he was shattered at the weight.

We did a sparring session in the Ulster Hall, just to remind me of fighting back inside again. The Pedroza fight had been outside and without the enclosed feel of a big hall. So it was useful to remember that, though at the end of the day, a ring is a ring is a ring. You could be fighting in the middle of Antarctica if you could keep the cool off, you could have it on the top of the ocean, as long as you keep the rain off, and it would be exactly the same. When you have got somebody in there trying to take your head off, you soon pay attention to them and not to your surroundings.

I remember being worried about how mad things were and how mad everything was around me. None of us understood just how big the whole thing would become. Yet it was so important to us that everybody was included and that they all felt part of it. This was a journey for the fans as well as for me. But in the middle of all that excitement and anticipation and belief and hope, I had to do a very serious job, and I had to do it against an exceptional opponent. As the fight closed in, I got to the stage where I thought, this is going to be very difficult, maybe even more difficult than

Pedroza, but you've got to stop worrying about him. Just do it. Just go in there and knock the living daylights out of him.

What I had going for me was, once again, the relentless pressure I could put on an opponent. I watched the fights again and thought, nobody is backing this guy up. They're trying to, but Taylor is able to diffuse them. He will take two or three steps back, turn and step and he will put them back in the middle of the ring. So they were never able to administer the right type of pressure. I knew that I was capable of putting intelligent pressure on him in the way the other fighters couldn't. In the King's Hall, it's a cauldron of deafening noise, he was going to have to deal with that pressure, and the intimidation from the crowd.

After the fight, Taylor blamed the venue for contributing to his defeat. He was from Charlotte in North Carolina, and although he'd boxed all over the States, this fight, his thirty-fifth professional match-up, was the first time that he'd fought abroad. Taylor claimed that the heat and the smokiness of the King's Hall was something he wasn't used to, an excuse that I didn't really buy. Firstly, they must have had that kind of venue in the United States. And secondly, he was from North Carolina, where the heat and humidity can be dreadful. Yes, there can only be a fetid heat in a big arena like the King's Hall, but however many people there are in there, however many television lights, you're still not going to get the same sort of intense heat you get in North Carolina, not a chance. The truth was that Taylor losing was nothing to do with the venue: the heat that he couldn't handle was all coming from me.

Bernard Taylor was extremely confident before the fight. That arrogance and self-belief was all part of his style. He wasn't intimidated by anything or afraid of anyone. He came over about a week before the fight to train, and when he turned up at the weigh-in he was six ounces over. That might sound like nothing, but I was delighted at that. Because he then had to put his sweat gear on with everyone watching, all those staring eyes, and skipped until he worked up a sweat, dried himself off and weighed again. He was still over, so he had to skip and do it again for a second time, before hitting the weight. He'd hardly done anything, it didn't take anything out of him physically, but it was the psychological thing that mattered. Having to do his workout in front of all those people who were going to be screaming for his blood later that night.

The whole weight thing is such an important issue in boxing. It is so easy to get wrong, which was why I would carry my scales with me wherever I'd go. And my own boxers now, they are on the scales before they go to bed, then first thing in the morning when they get up. They have a bite to eat and are on the scales again. We know exactly what they are drying out, what they are putting on and what they are taking off.

It might not sound a big deal, but how you get down to the weight can be a serious risk to your health. If you do it in a hurry – what is known in the business as 'crashing the weight' – you can end up doing yourself a lot of damage. Some fighters will be well over the weight and then try and get it down right at the end – a stone and a half, two stone in a month. You can do it, but in the process of drying out, you're losing fluid in your body, and fluid around your brain. The result is that there is more space between the brain and the skull wall, more movement because there isn't the fluid to cushion it. After the weigh-in, you can try to rehydrate, but that takes at least forty-eight hours: there isn't the time to do it before the fight. So you're stepping into the ring taking a big risk: you get hit with a head shot, and there's a much bigger chance of a tear, because the brain hasn't got that fluid to protect it. And that's how boxers can get brain damage.

That's a world away from Taylor's situation that night – he was just a fraction over, maybe a cup of tea over, perhaps not even that.

As I say, it was the psychological thing for him, that he had to stand in that room for another half-hour. Compare that to how Pedroza and his people had handled the weigh-in before my last fight. I think that could have spooked Taylor a little bit. And if he wasn't spooked then, he certainly was that night.

When Taylor walked into that arena, I reckon it frightened the shit out of him: the noise and the atmosphere was like nothing he'd ever heard. It wasn't hostile in that aggressively partisan way you can get with Latin American crowds: the Irish fans know their boxing and wanted to see a good fight, but at the same time, they weren't going to hold back in showing who they wanted to win. Taylor went out first, and he must have been there in the ring for five or six minutes before I came in. He was dancing around and looking confident, but even so, that atmosphere must have swamped over him. He was nervous; you could tell that by how much quicker he was than normal at the beginning of the fight.

From the first bell, I went straight at him, taking command in the centre of the ring. My hands were high, and I was making sure I wasn't walking on to too many shots, because he could hit hard. Really hard. I realised early on that he was better on his feet than Pedroza. A much better mover, and quicker too. He didn't have the same variety of punches as Pedroza, but he was lightning fast with what he did have, and that was plenty. He'd be on the balls of his feet, throw three or four shots and pull back. I decided that I should throw straight shots in the centre of the ring, and combinations if I got him to the ropes: otherwise, he wouldn't stay around long enough. And when I did hit him with a right hand, a left hook, he would grab me and hold me, stop me, turn me around and push me away.

I did realise when I got close to Taylor that he was strong. He was physically strong. But he would not stay with me. He wouldn't hold his feet. And as a fighter, you know if someone is doing that, then they're not feeling completely confident. It was all about closing him down quickly for me, and I walked into some hefty shots as a result. He did land some good-quality punches on me in those opening rounds: he'd land them and was difficult to catch. So he looked good and I certainly thought he was ahead on points at the beginning.

At the same time, I was hitting him enough to get his respect. Not catching him square but they were glancing off him enough for him to know what I had, to put the fear of God into him. And I was pursuing him relentlessly, continually keeping the pressure up. Although he was spinning around and dancing away, as the fight went on I could see that he was starting to tire. And once he started to tire, I could feel him begin to panic, could feel his panic rising.

Taylor kept moving and moving and it was beginning to take its toll. In the third, fourth, fifth, I got up close and could feel him breathing, hear his panting, and I knew that he didn't like the pressure, that I was really starting to get to him. I would have loved to have had the situation I had with other fighters where they were tired and started exchanging with me, but he wouldn't do that, would just keep springing and bouncing away, taking big breaths at the end of each round. Even when he pulled out of a clinch, I could hear him taking a deep breath. That just made me even more determined to keep on him.

In the sixth, seventh and eighth, I started to hit him. I was only landing a few one-two-three combinations, maybe six in the sixth, then eight, then ten. But they were enough. They were going up in number and in length. Each time, I was able to land one extra punch in the combination. In the eighth, Taylor stuck out a lazy jab near the end of the round and I buried a right hand, a fantastic body punch, right under his heart. Taylor went 'whoosh', like I'd sucked all the air out of him. I gave him a right and a left and the bell went for the end of the round. As I walked back to my corner I went, yes. My gumshield bit, and Harry Carpenter said, 'Look,

McGuigan is smiling!' I wasn't: I was just saying to myself, 'I've got him.'

I went back to the corner. Barney and Eddie were talking to me as usual, there'd be the guy holding the spit bucket or whatever, handing up the water, and I'd spit down. My corner was telling me, OK right, now you are starting to get to him. What you need to do now is to unload a couple of little punches when you get close to him. Just let the shots go. Keep on him, use that jab, bang the right hand into the body, double the left hook up to the head. Stay there when he takes his step back, take a step forward.

So we were talking through all of this, when someone looked over to the other corner and said, 'Hold on, hold on a second. I don't think he's coming out.' It had got to forty-five seconds of the sixty-second break, and Taylor was just sat on the stool and his man was shouting over to the referee, saying he wasn't coming out. There was a bit of confusion at first as to what was going on, but when the crowd realised, and the referee lifted my hand, the place went wild.

I went over and put my arms round Taylor. He didn't really say much, but his little corner man said, 'Yeah, the heat in here was quite hot and Barry was putting a lot of heat on too.' That was telling me the truth. He knew I was going to get Taylor. If he'd come out in the ninth, I might not have knocked him out, but I would have beaten him up. And then in the next round, in the tenth, or the eleventh, his man would have been on the floor. I knew that. Taylor knew that. And that was why he didn't come out.

I was pleased to have won, of course I was, but at the same time I couldn't help feeling a little bit cheated as to how Taylor had capitulated. Because he had outboxed me in those opening rounds, because he was looking good and picking up the points, I really wanted the chance to pay him back for that. I didn't get the chance to do that, and I felt let down as a result. Taylor had sampled a couple of my body shots and thought, good God, this guy is going to really knock shit out of me when I slow down. And he chucked in the towel.

You don't quit in a world title fight. Taylor had come over to try and take my world title and should have gone out on his shield. I don't want to diminish him as a fighter, or take away from what was a fantastic career, but there's no doubt that he was an on-top guy. He liked to be on top and when he was, he was good at dishing it out. It's not fair to say that he couldn't take it, but he certainly didn't like getting the stick. It would have been a bit like me saying after the twelfth round against Steve Cruz, I'm feeling a bit tired and discombobulated here, I think I'll opt out. Taylor certainly didn't show the type of courage Pedroza had displayed. Not a chance. It just shows that winning a world title is more than just having great boxing skills – being a champion is about character as well.

With my mandatory challenge against Bernard Taylor out of the way, I had a bit more space and freedom as to who to fight next: there was nobody specific I had to fight, and no ninety-day deadline to compete by. I had more than enough to keep me occupied and still had all my personal appearances to do, my marketing stuff, and there were various awards coming up, like the BBC Sports Personality of the Year. After fighting and training for three phenomenally hard fights within seven months, plus the defence against Gallouze, the decision was made to wind things down for the rest of the year and have my next fight in early 1986.

I would still keep up my training, make sure I was staying in shape. I would run every day and I would train every day. I would do callisthenics as opposed to weights. It was a daily chore, bang, bang, bang, get into shape, working out, because guys are looking at you. I was always consciously aware of keeping myself sharp for whoever I was going to fight next. That was particularly so because it was around this time I was beginning to find it increasingly difficult to make weight. And maybe it was because I was allowing myself to put on more weight between fights. I would certainly go up a little bit. I love my grub, so I had to work hard not to pile on the pounds.

The fight we settled on was to defend my title against the Argentinian Fernando Sosa at the Royal Dublin Society showground on 15 February. I wanted to box in Dublin because we had this huge support in the South of Ireland as well as the North, and we wanted to go down and put on a show there. It was a way of saying thank you to the fans for the amazing turnout we'd had when I won the world title. I mentioned earlier how big fights had struggled to find an audience in the South, but this time felt different. This time everyone wanted to be there. When I'd fought on the Charlie Nash bill at Dalymount Park back in my first professional fight, the stadium had been all but empty. This time, the tickets sold out in an hour and a half.

I was back in my training schedule and working hard in preparation for the fight over the festive season. On Christmas Day I did a fifteen-mile run. I set off at eight-thirty in the morning and ran over to Lackey Bridge and along unapproved roads up Dernawilt Cross, then up the mountain to Carn Rock. I got back and Sandra had cooked Christmas lunch, and I didn't really feel like eating it after that. She was quite annoyed with me about that, but it was something I had to do.

By January, I was back in Bangor. It was freezing cold and we had these Mexicans over for the sparring, to imitate Sosa. Sosa was strong and powerful, and these guys were tough little balls of strength. This one guy, I flattened him two or three times, but he refused to throw in the towel. He stayed on. Most guys, when you hit them, if you dropped them twice they would normally find an excuse, and get out of camp and go home. But this guy stayed on in there. The Mexicans offered some really tough sparring every single day. Every round that you pounded them, they would come back for more.

The one thing they couldn't deal with was the cold. We gave them the top floor in the house, which was by far the warmest, but that still wasn't enough. The night before they were leaving I decided to go up and say thank you. I went up to the bedroom and knocked at the door and they didn't hear as they were sleeping, so I opened the door and said hello. The Mexicans had their tracksuits on, socks and boots, one of those big green anoraks, and were lying in bed with all that on. I said to them, 'Are you OK?' And they just replied, 'Cold, cold, cold.' They were lovely people, tough as hell but nice with it.

Just over a fortnight before the fight, we got the call that Fernando Sosa had broken his finger. The search went out for a replacement, and we ended up with Danilo Cabrera, a Dominican who had been preparing to fight for the national title. It was great we'd found someone and the fight was going ahead, but Cabrera was a completely different fighter from what I'd been preparing for. Rather than being small and strong and powerful, Cabrera was taller and stringier – he threw longer punches and had an awkward style to deal with.

On top of which, the footage we got hold of to watch him fight was over a year old. The fighter in the videos wasn't really anything to worry about, but the guy who turned up in the ring that night had improved in leaps and bounds. And to add to all that, I'd overcooked it a bit on the weight. At one stage in training I had finished eight stone eleven, so I was almost down to super bantamweight. I had taken off too much. At the weigh-in, I was still under. I was light and a little bit drained as a result, which was not the ideal preparation. Cabrera and his crew could see that I looked gaunt, and went away from the weigh-in all geed up and confident.

The date of the fight had been chosen because Ireland was

playing in a rugby union international against Wales at Lansdowne Road that day. I was staying at the Berkeley Court Hotel, which was right next door. I was trying to get some rest in the afternoon, but the fans were pouring past and word had got out where I was staying, so there was all this chanting and shouting up from below. And then this bloody jazz band struck up. I lifted the mattress off the bed and brought it into the little ensuite bathroom, but I could still hear the noise. I put the water on in the hope that it would lull me to sleep, but no such luck. I took the mattress back into the bedroom, put the pillow over my head and then gave up.

The other thing I remember that afternoon was wanting some beans with scrambled eggs on toast before setting off for the venue: a nice light snack with a good bit of protein and carbohydrate. Sean McGivern had gone down looking for them, and it transpired that because it was such a posh hotel, they didn't actually have any baked beans on the premises. So they'd had to send someone out to buy some, and the nearest shop was a way away. I didn't get the baked beans for another hour, which again was another little niggle.

Coming to the ring it was pretty crazy and noisy as normal, just like the King's Hall. It was like we'd been transported back to Belfast: the noise was deafening and we had a lot of support there and various high-profile people had turned out to watch. The fight started off and immediately you could see the difference between the Danilo Cabrera I'd watched on the tapes and the one I was facing in the ring. There was no doubt that he'd improved as a boxer a lot.

Cabrera was a tough and ambitious fighter. He was durable and could take a shot. I won the early rounds but it was tougher and more competitive than I'd been expecting. He was definitely trying very hard; he would box and fight me. He wasn't afraid to come forward and have a go at me. I was controlling the fight, but even so he would have these spurts of success: I'd block, block, block and then one of his punches would get through. In about the fifth round, he caught me with this jab and his thumb went into my eye. I don't think it was done deliberately, but it started to puff up as a result. They put ice on it in the corner, enswell and everything else (an enswell is a small piece of metal, which is pressed down on the skin to reduce the swelling), but it was still puffing up. It didn't hurt, but it was affecting my vision.

When your eye is swollen, there are only so many times you can get hit before it splits. In the eighth round, Cabrera caught me there again, and I got cut. It started to leak blood and Cabrera saw that and instantly came out of his shell. He walked in and I hit him with a right, a terrific shot. I wobbled him with the right, hit him with the left and boom! Down he went. The crowd went crazy. Cabrera got to his feet again and I pummelled him all round the ring. He was holding on to me and was so strong I was struggling to shove him off. When I did, I started battering him again and the referee jumped in to stop the fight.

Once again, because the noise was deafening, we hadn't heard the bell go, and the referee had stepped in after the round had finished. People were piling into the ring thinking the fight was over, but Cabrera's people were going mad complaining and the referee was conferring to check the time and ordered the fight to go on. Cabrera's people were clever: they milked it for as long as possible to give their man the maximum time to recover. They could see, too, that I'd been cut. Paddy Byrne had got to work on it straightaway, and was working wonders. But even so, Cabrera's people knew that it would only get worse, and that there was a chance the referee might stop the fight.

I don't know what they did to clear Cabrera's head, but he came out for the ninth with renewed vigour. I realised that I'd have to start all over again, get back to grinding him down before I could really go for it once more. I was starting to beat him up again, but he was pumped up because of my cut and wasn't going to give up easily. I was starting to get him, break him down, but he was still throwing some decent punches and he caught me, he hurt me with a good shot in about the tenth.

By the end of the twelfth he was wilting. I beat him up in the thirteenth, but he was young and his powers of recovery were really good. On the fight went into the fourteenth and I beat him from pillar to post. I wobbled him and he was all over the place. I punched him again and his gumshield fell out. He was leaning over and scrabbling on the floor and I looked across at the referee, a guy called Ron Eckert, expecting him to intervene. To my amazement, Eckert just said, 'Box on!' It was a crazy situation. I thought about nudging him in the arse, and making him crawl and fall over. The crowd would have gone hysterical with laughter, but I could have been disqualified for that, and so I resisted. I wasn't unfair, I hit him on the side, and gave the referee another look, as if to say, 'For God's sake,' and this time he stepped in and said it was all over.

The Cabrera fight was a bigger struggle than any of us expected, but I thought I handled him well. I thought the referee should have stopped the fight earlier, should have stopped it in the eighth when Cabrera was all at sea. But he was not authoritative enough: he was a bit inexperienced and he let the fight continue. Cabrera went on to fight Azumah Nelson and lost in ten, which shows he was no slouch. If the referee had stopped the fight in the eighth as he should have done, then that would have been a fairer reflection of my performance.

Even so, I think at that stage I realised for the first time that I was losing a certain amount of strength trying to get to nine stone. Your body fills out as you get older, and I had been fighting as a featherweight since I was nineteen. I was quite tall for the weight: I was big, with a big reach. The older I got, the more getting down to nine stone was beginning to take the edge off me from a strength point of view. That didn't matter so much against a guy like Cabrera, but once I went up against someone who could match me punch for punch, that lack of strength might just make all the difference.

Chapter 13

Las Vegas

After winning the title in London, and defences in Belfast and Dublin, the next goal was to take the show to the United States. I wanted to try and make it over there. I wanted to try and break the big time and be as successful over there as I had become over here. I'd had the coverage on the American networks, so they already knew who I was, and what I was about. They knew the kind of support I had, and although transatlantic flights weren't as cheap or as quick back then, they knew there were people who would pay to fly over and follow me. There were various places we could have fought – the east coast, with the Irish connection, was one option – but this was the time when Las Vegas was acquiring its reputation as the boxing capital of the world: Larry Holmes had fought here on numerous occasions, including his 1980 contest with Muhammad Ali: the Thomas Hearns fights with Sugar Ray Leonard, Roberto Duran and Marvin Hagler all took place here.

Leonard, Hearns, Hagler and Duran were a quartet of great fighters whose battles dominated the boxing landscape in the 1980s. For me, it was Sugar Ray Leonard who was the most complete box/fighter. He was the most adaptable and the best all-rounder there was: he could box, he could fight, he could turn on the gas and was as brave as they come. I also thought his conduct outside the ring was exemplary – he was a real example for boxers in how to behave. I've been fortunate to get to know him over the years – we have done speaking engagements together and both took part in the television show *The Contender Challenge* where I coached a UK team to take on Leonard's American boxers.

Not that Sugar Ray Leonard had it all his own way, by any means. Marvin Hagler didn't have the nickname 'Marvellous' for nothing. He was one of the greatest middleweights ever, no doubt about that. He was a phenomenal fighter – very focused and everything he did was carefully thought out. He carried with him a palpable sense of animosity towards his opponents and was a tough, tough opponent. Hagler was ultra-professional in every-thing he did, but I'm glad to say that the single-mindedness he took into the ring has not extended out of it: both Marvin and his wife Kay are good company, and we always have a great time when we see them.

Thomas Hearns was another contemporary fighter who I was glad I never had to face. I always admired his big long levers, and the way that he could hit an opponent from distance. Roberto Duran, as I have already mentioned, was someone who I watched growing up, and will always admire. I loved his style of fighting: the way he made himself so difficult for an opponent to hit; the way he could come at his opponent from any number of different angles. He had courage, too: to come back after the second Sugar Ray Leonard contest – the infamous 'No Mas' fight – was very much the mark of the man.

There haven't been many fighters over the years better than Sugar Ray Leonard and his rivals. But if you ask me who I think the greatest fighter of all time is, I'd have to say Sugar Ray Robinson. In a remarkable career that spanned over two and a half decades, Robinson fought 200 professional fights, and won 173 of them. He won the middleweight title on five different occasions, a remarkable achievement, and was also the world welterweight champion for four years. All in all, he faced eighteen fighters who were world champions at everything from lightweight to light heavyweight, and defeated fourteen of them. Sugar Ray Leonard and Muhammad Ali were unbelievable fighters, but Sugar Ray Robinson, and the way he fought, paved the way for their subsequent careers. Robinson brought a style of fighting to boxing that hadn't been seen before – a style that both Ali and Leonard looked at and copied, leading to their own remarkable success.

The Vegas fight was set for Caesar's Palace on 23 June 1986. My opponent, as it should have been before he pulled out of the previous fight, was once again announced as the Argentinian Fernando Sosa. The fight was part of what was called the 'Triple Hitter', with three big names on the card: as well as myself, Tommy Hearns and Roberto Duran were also to fight that night. Hearns was defending his WBC light-middleweight title against Mark Medal, while Roberto Duran was lined up against Robbie Sims, the younger half-brother of Marvin Hagler.

Part of the deal for the fight was to do a promotional tour of the United States. That took place in May, and the promoters worked us hard. Hearns, Duran and myself were flown all over the US, visiting nine different cities in just eight days: New York, Boston, Miami, Chicago, St Louis, San Francisco, San Diego, Las Vegas and Los Angeles. It was a lot of work and physically tiring, all that flying, but it needed to be done.

It was all a bit surreal, to be honest, flying around with Tommy and Roberto. They were great characters to be around: incredible guys, great fun. Tommy was a card player, and played poker as we flew around. It was the Caesar's Palace jet and we had a great croupier, a pretty blonde girl who took a shine to Tommy. Roberto was a smashing guy, too. He didn't speak any English, only Spanish, but he was a lovely, welcoming guy. It was amazing to think that this was the same guy I used to watch on those grainy Betamax tapes back in the seventies, when I was growing up and getting into my boxing. And now here I was, on the same bill, with the same billing as him. I remember they made us do this cringeworthy advert in Las Vegas, the three of us wearing top hats and tuxedos and carrying canes. But it was great fun to hang out with them.

The promotional schedule was packed, but I trained when I could. The one that sticks in the memory was when we were in Las Vegas, and Duran and I were driven out into the desert at six in the morning for a run by the trainer Miguel Diaz. There was this long road which went about fifteen miles straight up into the mountains, a nice steady climb. Duran had this group of about ten to fifteen people with him. He didn't really like to run. It was more about weight management for him: he was doing it to sweat and burn off the calories, and you don't need to go too fast for that.

I liked to run fast, so I set off ahead, with these two young boxers, Spanish Americans, who were also good runners. The guy who was organising the run had picked them because he knew that I went at a decent pace: he was determined that these lads would beat me. I'm what they call a 'half wheeler' in cycling when I run – that's what they call cyclists who always like to be half a wheel ahead of everyone else. So I was belting along, trying to stay ahead of them, and they were keeping up with me, chatting and asking me questions. It wasn't until the last mile that I was able to crack them, and make it to the car first. So I made it to the car and then ran back down to find Duran, who was still jogging his way up, about a mile and a half back along the road.

After the tour, I went back to Bangor, the usual camp. We trained and sparred there for a couple of weeks or so, and then flew back out to the States, this time to Palm Springs. My American base was in the Desert Hotel there, which we'd chosen to try and acclimatise to the heat. And we'd only been there a few days when, for the second time, we got a call to say Sosa was pulling out of the fight. The first occasion he'd broken his finger, this time he had problems with his eyes.

There was less than a month to go before the fight at this stage, and once again the search went out for a replacement. Jose Marmolejo was one possibility, the Panamanian who I'd sparred with before the Pedroza fight; the others were Antonio Esparragoza, Antonio Rivera and the young Texan fighter, Steve Cruz. It worried me a bit that all the fighters had fought and lived in hot temperatures: Marmolejo was from Panama, Esparragoza, Venezuela, and Rivera, Puerto Rico. Cruz lived in San Antonio, which is a similar temperature to Las Vegas, so he had this Tex-Mex background. But we went for him because we thought he was probably a little green: he'd been stopped in the first round by the Mexican Lenny Valdez. So we thought he was the best bet.

The weigh-in for the fight was at Caesar's Palace, in one of the big auditoriums out the back. It was on this wooden stage, where everybody was sort of lifted up because the arena was quite full with people: fans who'd flown over, fans from boxing generally, and other Vegas visitors (among the celebrities who came to see the fight were Annie Lennox, Dave Stewart, and Bob Geldof and Paula Yates, who'd got married in Vegas a couple of days before). I'd arrived about an hour early, and was actually about six ounces under the weight. So I had a little bit of orange juice to drink: not much, just a bit. All the preliminary fighters had already weighed in by the time I got back to the scales and, as I say, the scales were on this wooden platform and not solid ground. An hour or so earlier, they'd given my weight at six ounces under. All I'd had was a little swig of orange juice, hardly anything at all, and now they were saying I was three or four ounces over.

I protested, and said that the scales must be wrong, that they needed to be recalibrated. Then Cruz gets on, and he is over as well, even though he'd been under an hour or so before as well. Because all the other guys had jumped on and off and it was a cushiony sort of stage, the scales had gone out, and needed recalibrating. We had to wait while they did that, and then weigh in again. This time, both Cruz and I were under the weight.

The heat was obviously going to be an issue. The fight was scheduled for six o'clock and it was 110 degrees. I remember we were able to pick our corner, and we chose the one that the sunlight was not shining directly into. Cruz had this Mexican guy who worked his corner, he also had this big lump the size of a table. So he stood there between rounds, blocking the sun off his fighter. So there'd be respite for sixty seconds between rounds but otherwise you were in the full glare the whole time. I think the sun was behind a cloud for about three rounds, but that was it. Otherwise, it was frying-pan stuff out there.

I started the fight off reasonably sharp, thinking, I've got to get this guy out of here. But Cruz was quick and on the ball in response. He wasn't going to be caught cold as he had been against Lenny Valdez. This was his big chance, and he was definitely ready for this one. I was trying to stay on him, keep my hands high, keep my work rate up, and for the first few rounds it was going well. I was jabbing him back, moving OK and getting my hands back most of the time. I was double-jabbing him back to the ropes and hitting him with the right hand.

Right back at the beginning of my professional career, I'd fought Jean Marc Renard in my fourth fight at the Ulster Hall and he'd floored me with his trademark left-hook counter. Cruz had a good counter left hook too, and in the tenth he caught me with one, exactly as Renard had, and with exactly the same result. He caught me on the temple and I went down. I remember looking over and saying, 'I'm OK, I'm fine,' and I got to my feet again. But my legs were a little unsteady: it makes you disorientated getting hit on the

A hero's welcome to my home town,
Clones, after the Pedroza fight.
Ray McManus / SPORTSFILE

Preparing for a photo shoot
before winning the 1985 BBC
Sports Personality of the Year.
Action Images / Sporting Pictures / Dave Callow

The remarkable welcome home after winning the world title: Belfast's Royal
Avenue, 1985. Stanley Matchett / Mirrorpix.com

Defending my title against Danilo Cabrera, at the Royal Dublin Showground, February 1986. Ray McManus / Sportsfile.com

Getting knocked down by Steve Cruz in Las Vegas, June 1986 (note Bob Geldof and Paula Yates in the crowd). Action Images / Sporting Pictures / Nick Kidd

Looking out of dead man's eyes:
Chris Smith's picture was voted
Sporting Photo of the Decade.
Chris Smith / Getty Images

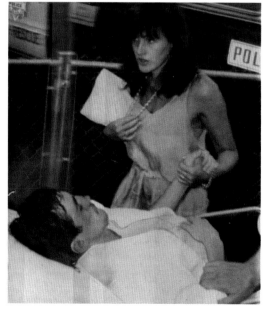

Sandra accompanies me to the
hospital after the Cruz fight.
Frank Barrett / Daily Star

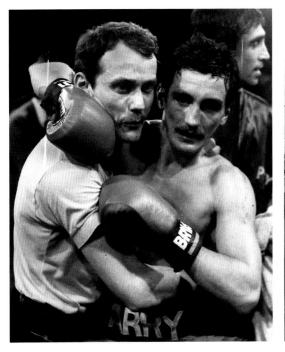

Dermot and me after stopping Tomas Da Cruz at Kenilworth Road, 1988. Jack Kay / Daily Express

In my dressing room after fighting Julio Miranda, December 1988: the moment I wondered if the magic had disappeared.

Lawrence Lustig / Daily Star

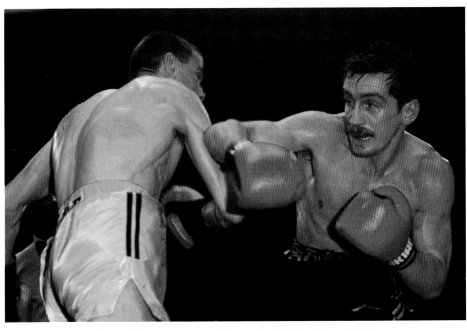

Exchanging punches with Jim McDonnell: my final fight, May 1989. Action Images

Above: Daddy's girl: at home with my daughter Danika, aged 5, in 1991.
Lawrence Lustig / Daily Star

With Sandra and the kids after receiving my MBE in 1994.
David Spurders / Express Newspapers

Practising a combination of punches in the ring with Daniel Day-Lewis during the making of *The Boxer* in 1997. Frank Connor / Universal Pictures

With the 'Greatest', Muhammad Ali, in 2000.

My induction speech at the International Boxing Hall of Fame, 2005: the icing on the cake of my boxing career.

Working the corner with my son, Shane, at the Ulster Senior semi-finals, 2008.

Jonathan Porter / Presseye.com

With Sandra at the Laureus World Sports Awards in Abu Dhabi, 2010. I'm proud to be an ambassador for Laureus, which helps young people around the world.
Gareth Cattermole / Getty Images Sport

At home in Kent with another one of my boxers, Floyd.
Paul Hackett / Sunday Times

temple and it took thirty or forty seconds for my legs to come back, to get my equilibrium again.

I came right back at him. I won the eleventh, even the twelfth and thirteenth. I was bringing it back, but at the same time could feel how tired, how sapped I was. But I was determined to stay in the fight, and somehow found the strength to do so. The fourteenth round, though, that one really emptied the tank. I came back to the corner and I was absolutely wrecked: I had nothing inside me after that. There's a famous picture of this guy, a Panamanian guy who was helping out in my corner, pulling my ear and biting it – apparently that clears your head or something. You see the picture and I'm just staring. I look completely out of it. I don't know if that was the dehydration or what it was, I'm not a medical guy. I just know I was pretty hollow. I still had my determination, but as I went out for the last round, that was about all I had left.

I went out for the fifteenth round and I was still ahead: all I had to do was draw the last round and I'd have retained my title. I didn't know that at the time, though I knew it must have been close. But though I could see the punches coming, I just couldn't get out of the way. He hit me with a couple of rights, and I was trying to hold it together, moved back and I was down. I looked at the corner and I went, 'I'm OK.' I got up and of course he came right in and was spraying punches at me. I ran around the ring again and he was pushing me around the ring and suddenly, I was on the deck again. I wasn't actually knocked down by the force of the punch the second time, it was actually just pushing. But if you are knocked down three times in a round the fight is over anyway. So I realised when I got up, I was like, 'Got to stay on my feet this time.' And so I held on as much as I could and threw a few punches back, but it was never going to be enough, it was just damage limitation.

The scores were as close as they could have been: Medardo

Villalobos gave it Cruz 143–139; Guy Jutras had it 142–141 and Angel Tovar 143–142. It was those two knockdowns that lost me the fight: if I'd only gone down the once, then I would have drawn the fight and retained my title. Or if I hadn't been docked a point for hitting low during the fight, I wouldn't have lost. That had been a borderline decision – it hadn't been intentional, my hand had slipped. Whereas Cruz had caught me deliberately low, hit me right up the bollocks and got away with it. But all of that is a load of what ifs. To be honest, I had finished so badly, I wouldn't have wanted to win that way. To be knocked down in the last round was a defeat as far as I was concerned.

When I got back to the dressing room, I was beginning to feel a bit disorientated. I think that was a combination of being caught so many times and of the dehydration. I certainly hadn't drunk much during the fight, hardly anything for the first six or seven rounds, but you can't really in boxing. You can't drink copious amounts of water, because you'd get a bloated belly.

It was a whole mixture of emotions. I was dealing with the defeat, with the disappointment and thinking, oh shit, it has gone. I was in tears that I'd lost my title. So I was feeling that and disorientated and the paramedics were beginning to get a bit worried about me. I asked someone a question that I'd already asked them, and the medics were concerned that something was wrong. And at that point they decided they should take me to hospital. They wrapped me in tinfoil, like you do the runners at the end of a marathon, and off we went. Sandra came with me, and had to give the hospital her credit card to pay. She gave them the wrong one and it was rejected. It felt like I'd only just lost the title, and already people didn't want to know.

They gave me a brain scan and I joked about that later: I said they had to go back for another one because they couldn't find one the first time. They put me on an intravenous drip and I had to stay in overnight. It was a strange night, but I did sleep, woke and slept again throughout. The next day I just wanted to get out. I had to have another brain scan, and then I was allowed to go.

My main thought at this stage was, how do I handle the shame of losing? That's a strong word, but it was how I felt at losing my title. I was worried how the press would be, how the people at home would react. I really felt that I had let people down: all those people who had supported me, pinned their hopes on me, the ones who'd spent their money to come over and watch the fight. I knew how much winning the title had meant to people, and was worried that losing would create a similarly strong response. As it worked out, the fans were brilliant. I had so many nice letters and support from people. Back in Clones, they held a big reception for me even though I'd lost, which I was hugely touched by. But as hard as people tried, it was still difficult to get away from the huge disappointment of defeat. And the Cruz fight wasn't just the end of the biggest year of my career: it was just the beginning of one of the worst years of my life.

Chapter 14

Dad

For such a non-fight, the night that I beat Farid Gallouze to retain my European title turned out to be a hugely significant one in my life. As I've already described, as I was beating Gallouze in two rounds, the deal was being done with Eusebio Pedroza to give me a shot at his featherweight crown. But something else also happened that night that was to put even getting a world title fight into perspective.

Prior to the Gallouze fight, my dad had been out in America, doing a residency at Dirty Nellie's in the Bronx. It was a while away from home – four weeks, six weeks, something like that – but it was decent money, so he would go over and do these stints. But he always wanted to see me box, so he'd come back on the day of the fight to watch me take on Gallouze. The fight had been out at Wembley, and we were driving back to our hotel in west London when I saw this figure on the side of the road. We couldn't have been far away, perhaps just 100 yards or so from the hotel, and I saw my dad. He was walking and – this was the bit I couldn't believe – he was heading into a pub.

My father hadn't had a drink for years. For years. I immediately thought, oh my God, what is going on here? Sandy was saying, 'Look, calm down,' but I needed to know what was happening.

I said to the driver, 'Let me out, please. Could you pull up there?' and Sandy was going, 'Please don't get into trouble with him.'

I said, 'I am just going to ask him what he is doing.'

'Leave him alone,' Sandy suggested, 'he will come back to the hotel.' But I couldn't.

'I am going to ask him what he is doing,' I repeated.

The car pulled over and I said to Sandy, 'Just go on up to the hotel and I will be down in five minutes.' So I jumped out of the car and walked into the bar. The place was packed and everyone was looking at me: I had just been on *Sportsnight*, and so everyone had been watching and recognised who I was. Anyway, I walked in quickly and spotted Dad straightaway. He was having a whisky. I went up to him and went, 'Dad'. And he said, 'What are you doing here?'

I replied, 'More importantly, what are you doing here? And what is that?' I asked, pointing at the whisky. And he just went, 'I have got some bad news. I don't want to tell you about it. I am having a drink.'

I told him, 'Dad. You can't drink,' but he wasn't to be budged. 'Go back to the hotel,' he said. 'I'm having this one drink and I will come back and explain.' By this point, because the fight had just been on the TV, everyone was looking. I didn't want a scene, so I said to him, 'OK, Dad, just one drink,' and he replied, 'I promise you. I'll be back in five minutes.'

I went back to the hotel and, true to his word, five minutes later Dad came up. And he told me how he had been playing at Dirty Nellie's as normal, when halfway through the performance, he had collapsed on stage. He'd been taken to hospital, where they ran a load of tests on him. The results came back, and the doctor said to him that he'd got a rare blood disease, a type of cancer. The doctor said, 'I'm sorry to tell you, Mr McGuigan, but you probably have about two years to live.'

I didn't believe that. How could they know that, I said. How could they make that type of prediction? I told my father that it must have been nonsense, that he had to stop thinking about it. And that worked: it pacified him and calmed him down. But I was to be proved wrong and the doctor tragically correct: two years and three months after the Gallouze fight, my father was to pass away.

Coming home from Vegas felt like it went on for ever. It was a long journey and everyone was tired. There was a big reception when I got back to Clones, which was lovely, to show me that they were every bit as supportive as when I was winning. The town all turned out, but it was half the audience of when I won the title.

Everywhere I went, you couldn't get away from the fact that I'd lost. I didn't want to go anywhere else because that was where our home was, but you knew it was on everybody's mind: that's what it is like living in a small town. The fight was what everyone was talking about, and wanted to talk to you about when they saw you. People were always nice and friendly, the people of Clones are great people, but I just wanted to get away from it all and that was impossible. It just wasn't that easy, you know.

When I look back on it, I realise too how difficult this period must have been for my family. We were all really close, and I realise now how much it must have affected them all. What was being said to my younger brother at school? You know how hateful kids can be. What was being said to my mum? There would have been those who wouldn't have much supported me, the hard-line Republicans who would have revelled in my problems. In a way, because I had all these other things on my plate, what people were saying was the least of my problems. My family didn't have that luxury, and so it affected them. Certainly, it had a big impact on my brother Dermot. I think it affected him tremendously because he lived his life vicariously through me. There'd be people he had a drink with who'd be joshing him about it, but Dermot would have been taking it personally: my loss was his loss. It all had a big effect on him.

And what happened straightaway after the fight was the falling-out with my manager Barney Eastwood. I don't want to go into all that here, it isn't really the time or the place. There's more than enough that has been written about it, if that's what you're interested in: certainly, there was plenty of coverage at the time, which I had to try and cope with. The situation quickly became a legal one, and culminated in a court case in Belfast the following May.

I was incredibly lucky to have a solicitor called Eamon McEvoy on my side. McEvoy didn't just work on the case, but became a great friend as well. We spent a lot of time at his house, with his wife Sheila and their four lovely kids, and that was a tremendous support to me. I was spending a lot of time going back and forth between Clones and Belfast, and it was nice to have that breathing space, with everything that was going on. I really was concerned about what would happen with the court case and how it would affect me, but Eamon was always tremendously reassuring. Don't worry about it, it will be fine, he would tell me. Even if the worst comes to the worst, it'll be fine.

What I would say about Barney Eastwood is that when our relationship worked, it worked extremely well. He had a lot of strengths as a promoter and a manager. His organisational skills were brilliant, and he had a bunch of guys around him who were really good at what they did. He knew the game, he knew boxing, and was exceptionally good at building a team. One such example of his knowledge of the game was in using his contacts to bring over the Panamanian and South American sparring partners for the big fights. That played an important part in my preparation, no doubt about it.

At the beginning, I got on very well with him. Initially we were very close: I liked his company and I think he liked mine. There's no doubt despite everything that happened he is a remarkable character, with incredible energy. And he's very intelligent too: he was very good at reading people, could talk to anyone for five or ten minutes and work them out. He made a big effort with the media, got the boxing journalists on board from both sides of the border. That was a smart thing to do, made them feel like they were part of it, part of the journey. He also shared my vision of peace and harmony regarding the politics we were submerged in. So it was disappointing the way it ended, but there's nothing to be gained in dwelling on that. I'd rather remember the good times, when the partnership was successful, and leave it at that.

It's important, too, to keep all the Barney Eastwood stuff in perspective. Although that was the story that was prominent in the press at the time, the thing that was making the headlines, in actual fact there were other things going on that mattered far more to me than the legal stuff. Barney Eastwood was just business: it was the terrible, tragic personal issues I had to cope with that really made the year such a painful one. For me, family always comes first and when something happens to someone you love and care about deeply, those are the things that really keep you awake at night. When you are dealing with your baby daughter almost dying and your dad being diagnosed with cancer, who said this or said that doesn't seem quite so important.

When my sisters, my identical twin sisters Rachel and Rebecca, were young they used to get febrile convulsions all the time. It would frighten the life out of you: they would go into fits and, my God, it was petrifying. I don't know whether my daughter Danika inherited that, whether there was some family trait, but in the summer after the Cruz fight, she started fitting too. She was only eight months old at the time, and it was very, very scary.

The first time it happened was in September 1986 and I was in Belfast, commentating on the Lloyd Honeyghan – Donald Curry fight, which was taking place in Atlantic City. I was working for ITV via Ulster TV in Belfast: the television centre is in Havelock House there. The call came through while we were on air that Nika was gravely ill, but no one told me until after the programme had finished. I would have been furious about that, if I'd had any time to be so, but I was only interested in getting down to Monaghan Hospital, where she'd been taken, as quickly as I could.

I jumped in the car and drove like a lunatic from Belfast down to Monaghan Hospital, praying that she was OK. I remember coming to Middletown, the border checkpoint and, because I was so concerned, just flying down the road. Normally there are red lights, and they stop you and ask, 'What have you got in the car, let us see your licence and have a look in the boot.' But they knew my car, and as I drove up, nobody came out, there was this green light and I drove straight through. And when that happened, I thought they must know something. She must be dead.

I drove on down, and as I drove up to the hospital there was this ambulance coming out and Sandy was sat in the front seat. She saw me and jumped out, got in the car with me and I swung the car round and followed the ambulance with Nika in, away from Monaghan to the Lady of Lourdes Hospital in Drogheda, which was a far bigger, more comprehensive hospital. I kept saying, 'How is she? How is she?' Sandy just said, 'I don't know.'

She told me how Danika's heart had stopped twice on the way to the hospital, and she'd had to take over the driving while the general practitioner had resuscitated her. They had been fighting the whole way down the road to keep her alive. And when they went into Monaghan Hospital she was very, very blue but they'd got her going again and decided to take her to Drogheda. So we followed the ambulance, and just as we got the other side of a place called Ardee, they put a sign up in the back, written on an

A4 piece of paper. That was the moment we knew Nika was going to be all right. The sign they were holding up, it just said, 'She's OK'.

The next time it happened, I was away in London, modelling some sports training gear called Olympic Gold. Sandy was staying at Rossnowlagh, at my mother-in-law's caravan, this beautiful place on the coast of Donegal. Sandy was visiting a place just down the road called Ballyshannon and was walking along pushing the buggy with her mother, when suddenly Nika started foaming at the mouth again and fitting. Sandra ran into the nearest doctor's surgery, and I remember her telling me the doctor had the cheek to say, 'Calm down.' Sandra was saying, 'She's fitting, she almost passed away a couple of months ago. She needs help immediately.'

The doctor said, 'I haven't got any stesolids, you'll need some valium.' Sandra said, 'For the child?' and he replied, 'No, for you!' When I think of the cheek that he had, this guy, I was so cross with him. Anyway, the chemist was across the road, and Sandra got what Nika needed there, and she was then rushed to Sligo General Hospital. I was in London while all this was happening, and cut short what I was doing as soon as I heard: it's a horrible feeling, waiting at the airport to get home, knowing there's nothing you can do.

While all this was going on, the last thing I wanted to do was go anywhere near a gym. I couldn't even think about it. Looking back, that was probably a mistake – getting back into training was probably the best thing I could have done, to get back into a routine and try and take my mind off things.

The fact was, I wanted a break. I had a complete break and didn't train at all for quite a long time. In fact, I don't think I trained until the end of the year. The reason I did was because I was asked to do a run for the Simon Community in Dublin and

I ran a ten-kilometre race in Phoenix Park. I wasn't really fit at all and I remember near the end of the race that Michael Carruth, who later went on to win Ireland's first ever boxing gold medal at the Barcelona Olympics, passed me with about 600 metres to go. I hadn't trained and I wasn't as fit, and though I tried to keep up with him, I just watched him pull away from me. That was the first training I'd done for about six months, and it was hard for me to take how out of shape I had become.

But with everything else going on, I just couldn't consider going back into training. With Dad and Nika and all of that, I was so down, I didn't want to do anything. He was such an intricate part of everything I had done, my dad. He'd built the gym, he'd bought the gear, he had travelled with me and driven me everywhere as a kid. So when he was sick it felt like I couldn't box, because he wouldn't be involved. We did not want to leave him behind, emotionally or psychologically, we didn't want him to think he wasn't part of it any more. And so I stayed away from the gym.

Towards the end of 1986, my dad got ill, really ill. A couple of months out from Christmas, he was wearing a white vest and having a shave when he said, 'Look, my tummy is swollen on the side.' He was in the bathroom, which at the time was right next to the kitchen, while the house was being rebuilt after the fire. I will never forget it: 'Barry,' he called out, and I went in and he showed me. I saw it and told him he should get it checked out immediately. Dad was joking about, saying, 'Oh, it's probably cancer,' and I said, 'Don't say that, Dad, please.' He went to see the doctor and it was OK for a while, but then he started getting terrific pains, really bad ones, and we knew that something wasn't right.

This was around Christmas time or just after, and Dad went in and this time they diagnosed that he definitely had something. He asked a lot of questions, and the doctor was straight with him about the situation. Dad asked, 'How bad is it?' The doctor said,

'Well, it is bad. You've got a tumour in your stomach, I believe, as a result of lymphatic cancer, and that is it.' My dad asked, 'How bad is that?' and the doctor said, 'You'll be lucky if you get better.'

When my dad heard that, he gave up. That's it, he thought, this is it. He had another series of tests, then went down to St Vincent's Hospital in Dublin. Ironically, the hospital was near to the RTE studios, where he used to go all the time to sing on TV shows.

Dad was in there for nine weeks, before he died in June. He never got home. They operated on him the day before the court case with Barney Eastwood at the beginning of May. I was driving back and forth from Belfast to Dublin, trying to deal with both and struggling to cope with either. When they opened Dad up, the tumour was the size of a cornflakes box. These days, I think they would have done it differently, and would probably have tried to shrink it. With the techniques they've got today, I think he'd have had a better chance of survival. But who knows: certainly by the time they opened it up, the tumour had probably got too big to do anything about.

It was a desperately sad time. My son Jake's birth in June was an isolated highlight. We took him down for Dad to see him, but because he was in intensive care by this point, they would not let the baby in. So we took Polaroids in the car, and took those in to show Dad. He was very, very sick at this stage. It was just the most horrible time. It could not have been worse. I remember the day I knew Dad was going to die. He wasn't allowed to eat and he was standing by the side of the bed: he was so skinny, looked very sick and was just very sad. I couldn't wait to get out of the hospital. I was with my mother and I cried like I had never cried before. We were in a café near the hospital and as I was sobbing, Mum was telling me to stop. But I couldn't, because at that point I knew all my hoping that Dad would get better was not going to work. I knew the man that meant so much to me, my father that I loved so much, was going to die.

My dad was fifty-two years old when he died. Way, way, way too young, and something we have a terrible track record for in the family: Dad's brother Seamus was fifty-four when he died; his other brother Kevin was fifty-three, and his daughter Joan fifty-three. It is one of the cruellest things, losing your father so young. And my brother Daniel was only ten. I was the one who had to tell him: 'Daniel, your dad isn't going to get better'. The look on his face is something that I will never forget.

When I think about my dad now, I remember him as just the loveliest guy: funny, witty, cultured, intelligent. He was a very giving, very kind fellow, and fantastically talented too. He could play five musical instruments and had the most amazing voice, one of the best singing voices Ireland has ever heard. He could go from falsetto straight through to bass, had the greatest control. He was a great dad and we were always so proud of him. He was always very good to me and was a great example for the way you should live your life: being a friend to people, being good, loyal and honourable.

Chapter 15

Return to the Ring

It was only after my father had died that I decided to get back in the ring. I wanted to do it for him. I wanted to see if there was something left, to find out whether I still had that drive and ambition, whether I could climb back up to the top of the tree again.

I made the decision to sign up with Frank Warren. I liked him and I met him a few times. We shook hands and we talked and I met his wife Susan and Ernie Fossey, his friend and assistant. Warren was young: he was only nine years older than me (and coincidentally with the same birthday) and was very good company. He met with Eamon McEvoy, who liked him too, and I thought, this is the guy I want to go with. I liked what Warren was doing with his boxers, people like Keith Wallace and Terry Marsh, who were getting good opportunities. Warren had a decent relationship with ITV, which was no bad thing, and when he made the offer, it seemed too good a package to turn down.

The other major decision I made in the months following my dad's death was to move to England. After all the events of the previous year, I needed to get away. It was an incredibly difficult decision: I love my country dearly, but the flip side of being in a close community is that sometimes everything can feel a little too close. Because everyone knew who I was, there was never the opportunity to get away from everything that had happened. The past was ever present, and it left me feeling nailed down, made it more difficult to move on. I didn't want to train in that atmosphere.

I had been doing things over in England by this point anyway, and I was always taken aback by how friendly and supportive people were. Everywhere I went everybody knew me and was lovely to me, and I just thought, wow, this is a surprise. I decided there were two ways of doing this. I could live in England during the week, do my training with Frank and everything, and go home at the weekends. But I knew my marriage wouldn't have survived, and that was the most important thing in my life. Then there were my kids: I had three of them by this point and didn't want to spend so long away from them.

I had been messing about, doing a bit of tin-top racing with a guy called Chris Taylor and a team called Grey Wolf. I had gone over to England and done a few races with him. Chris was an estate agent and he bought some nice houses and vetted houses and said there was a great house in the village that he lived in, Great Brickhill in Buckinghamshire. It was the time of the property boom, and it seemed like a decent investment. So I bought it, and we moved in, in November 1987.

As I say, it was a hard decision to make. We had always been a close-knit family, and we were moving away from all that, all that support. For the first time, I was properly independent. That was a big challenge for me. My brother was not there every day and I couldn't pop up the road and pick him up and go training with him, as I was used to. So he had to be flown back and forth, which took some getting used to. And as tough as it was for me, it was tough for my family too. But it had to be done: it was time to get on with my life, to start over and move on.

*

I'd had a long time out of boxing, almost two years, and it took a while to get back into it. I had to build myself back up: I started with the bag work and pad work. I did lots of running, sprinting and skipping and circuit training to get my fitness back. Then I started sparring: I remember I was getting headaches for about three weeks when the sparring began. I had to get used to getting hit again, getting my body used to being hit again. It was good to be back in the ring. I actually felt as if I'd slipped back into the groove fairly early on. It was the match sharpness that took a bit longer to return, that I really had to fight to regain.

Frank recommended I work with a guy called Jimmy Tibbs. He was fantastic: we got on like a house on fire and I loved his company, loved training with him. I'd go to the Vauxhall Motors ABC gym in Luton and do some training there: it was a proper old-type gym, with a wooden floor, big ring, roped-off area. All the gear was there and the showers and saunas. The facilities were fantastic. I broke it back in slowly and then started to spar with a guy called Mo Hussein, who was the Commonwealth lightweight champion. He was very good and he was tough and he would come forward and, like me, he never liked to step backwards. So we had fantastic heavy-duty sparring sessions: we'd go five or six rounds, knocking bells out of each other.

We'd move around for the sparring, go down to West Ham or to the St Pancras gym. It didn't really matter where you were as long as the sparring was good. There was a guy called Paul Day who was a light welterweight from Welwyn Garden City. A very nice guy, tall and upright, and a good sparring partner as well. We got people down from the Phil Martin gym in Manchester to spar with, had sessions with Carl Crook, Gary Jacobs, Najib Daho and Natty Dowell. There was another boxer from Luton, John Ashton, whose brother Renard was a British international amateur boxer. I sparred extensively with him, and we became good friends.

The sparring was excellent, but it did feel strange being back. It felt odd not having my brother there all of the time. Jimmy was great about that – he'd do the pads with me but when Dermot was over, he didn't have a problem with Dermot getting in and doing a bit on the pads with me as well. As a coach myself now, I've learned that you can almost see more watching from a distance because you see where the guy's feet are. When you are actually holding the pads you are only concentrating on what is coming at you in punching range: you can't look at the boxer's feet, his balance and his shape. Jimmy was smart enough to know that, and so was happy to step back and let Dermot work with me.

My comeback fight was against Nicky Perez, at Alexandra Palace on 20 April 1988. The idea was to have a couple of fights, shake the ring rust off before thinking about a title challenge. Even so, Perez was certainly no slouch. He was a typical Mexican kid, long-haired and tough, a decent box-fighter. He was an experienced pro and the North American champion: he might not have been world level, but he wasn't far below and was definitely a decent opponent, a classy journeyman.

It felt great to be back. Alexandra Palace was a great venue and it was a good bill for the punters: Nigel Benn was boxing for the Commonwealth title that night as well. There was a decent atmosphere, and a lot of people came over from Ireland to watch the fight: not as many as for Pedroza, but a sizeable contingent. I remember Dave Stewart from the Eurythmics being there, plus Bob Geldof and the *EastEnders* actor Nick Berry, who was huge at the time.

It's always been my style to stop guys. It's never been about outpointing people: my aim is always to take them out. I was quite pumped for the fight, as you might imagine, and went for Perez right from the start. I could feel the ring rust, and that I was a bit untidy, but I was still catching him, no trouble. Perez knew from pretty early on that I wasn't going to stop until I knocked him out. I had him down twice, and the referee stopped the fight in the fourth. It was a decent night's work and it felt good to be back. But at the same time, I came away knowing my sharpness wasn't quite there yet, that there was still work to be done.

Particularly as my next opponent was a notch up in class. Tomaz da Cruz from Brazil was the WBC number four and had only lost twice in thirty-two fights, one of those to Julio Cesar Chavez for the world title. Everything about the fight, in fact, went up a gear. We chose Kenilworth Road, the Luton Town football ground, as the venue, and pulled in an audience of 14,000: again, it was a great atmosphere, a lot of support. The fight was shown on ITV, and American TV were back on board as well. So the momentum was beginning to build again, everything was on track for another tilt at the world title.

Back in training I felt as though I was making progress, definitely. I was coming back to myself, was getting it again. I was sparring really well, and was doing eight rounds of sparring – I just felt I didn't need to do those fifteen rounds any more – but I was doing eight rounds with guys who were light welterweights, bigger than me and stronger. I sparred with a guy called Tony Pep, a six-foot-tall Canadian, super featherweight and a class act – one of those fighters who is better in the gym than the ring. I did a lot of work with him: he gave me hard workouts and could hit really hard. He was a Tommy Hearns-type fighter: he could dish it out and take it. Many years later, Pep fought Ricky Hatton: Hatton stopped him with his body shots, but Pep, by this time, was fighting out of his natural weight category, at light welterweight. So he was a class act, good both to push myself and to measure my progress against.

I could feel things were coming together again. I was working really hard, running and pushing myself in the gym, doing weights and getting stronger. My weight was coming back down, too. In the lay-off, I'd gone up to ten, ten and a half stone. But I knew that was because I was eating rubbish and sweets and stuff, which was always my predilection, having cake or sherry trifle or whatever. I disciplined myself, put myself on a regimented diet again and the weight came off. Both the Perez and Da Cruz fights were made at nine stone four, which was comfortable. I wasn't having to squeeze myself to get those extra ounces off, and lose that strength in the process.

I sparred with other fighters apart from Pep – Benjie Marquez and Tony Ekubia, for example – but Pep's style was the one that got me ready for Da Cruz. Da Cruz was the sort of fighter who could handle a punch, could take a lot of stick. I knew that against Julio Cesar Chavez he had taken a pounding but hadn't gone down. I went into the fight thinking, well, if I can get rid of him quicker than Chavez had, then that will look impressive. I set about him from the off, beat him from pillar to post, never let him get into the fight. I took a round longer than Chavez to finish him off, but I dominated the fight: Da Cruz never won a round and, as with the Nicky Perez fight, the referee stepped in to stop it in the fourth. It was a good performance, definitely better than against Perez, and I was pleased to feel that my sharpness was starting to return.

After beating Da Cruz, I felt I was getting near to a world title shot. I'd despatched two fighters, both in four rounds, and felt my sharpness starting to return. I knew that there were complicating factors with each of the possible super-featherweight title fights: with Azumah Nelson, money was an issue; Tony Lopez wouldn't leave his native Sacramento; Brian Mitchell, meanwhile, was from South Africa. This was the height of apartheid and, what was more, I knew I had a bit of a fan in the shape of Nelson Mandela. Mandela had always had an interest in boxing and had been an amateur heavyweight in his youth. Stanley Christodoulou, who refereed my fight with Eusebio Pedroza, was in contact with Mandela and told me Mandela had followed the fight from his prison cell – he'd listened to the fight live on the World Service and then watched it on television a week later. Stanley told me that Mandela had been interested in my political stance, and had peppered him with questions about me. When Mandela was released from prison, Stanley said I should have gone out to meet him. It would have been fantastic to have done so, and it is one of my biggest regrets that I have never taken that opportunity up.

At this stage, fighting Azumah Nelson, Tony Lopez or Brian Mitchell felt like something for the future. I still needed a couple more fights to find out if I was really ready. I felt I needed to get my head down, ensure that the organising bodies were recognising and ranking me. I needed to show them that I had intent, and that I wanted to box for the title. I wanted to shake that last little bit of ring-rustiness off, and get myself in a position where they had no choice but to sit up and take notice. We had the TV, we had decent audiences, and as long as I was doing that and making some noise, eventually someone would return to the negotiating table and have a discussion. It was a bit difficult being in that position, but I knew that was the way it worked. And in a way, it suited me: I was concerned about getting completely rid of the ring-rustiness, and having a couple more fights before a title challenge could only help that.

The fight we took was against Julio Miranda in December 1988. It was meant to take place on the Isle of Dogs, but ended up at Pickett's Lock in north London. The fight was shown on ITV, and pulled in an audience of just under twelve million – the sort of numbers promoters would kill for today. Miranda was the Argentine champion, and was a difficult, durable fighter: he'd only been beaten once in his previous thirty-four fights. He was a typical Argentine fighter – not a great puncher, but a good all-rounder. Their biggest redeeming feature is their toughness, and that they could take a lot of stick. They always had decent levels of fitness and could take you the distance, but most of the time you could take them on and beat them on points.

For all the talk about wanting to impress the organising bodies, the Miranda fight was not a good performance. I still beat the guy: I got rid of him and there weren't many people who did that. But I struggled a bit and didn't look good in despatching him. I don't know how much of that was a psychological thing. I don't know whether because it wasn't a fight of great importance I wasn't as switched on as I should have been. But I was acutely aware that I was having difficulty with a guy I would normally have beaten comfortably. I remember having him down in the third, badly hurt and out on his feet, and I couldn't finish him off. I had always been a great finisher but I couldn't put the guy away. And that worried me.

I remember thinking that in my previous incarnation he would not have lasted through the third round, but he did and towards the end of the round, it got worse. There was a clash of heads, which I don't think was deliberate, it was just gamesmanship, you know: you drop your head in there and if you can get away with it, you get away with it. But in the bang of heads, I was cut above both eyes. When Miranda saw that, he came out of his shell. He kept sticking the jab up at me, snapping the jab up, hitting the cuts and tearing them open. And they just got worse and worse.

I had never bled before and suddenly I had become a bleeder. It was horrible: the blood was coming into my eyes, and I couldn't see him. I was blinkered and he was winging punches at me and I was thinking, fucking hell, this fella is getting better. It took a couple of rounds before my cuts man Ernie Fossey was able to stem the blood. Miranda hit me with some decent shots and hurt me. He didn't hurt me badly but I remember thinking, ow, because it was a good shot. Then late in the seventh I put him down with a really good right-hander. I picked up where I left off in the eighth. I turned it on and caught him, wobbled him and stopped him.

Part of me thought, well, maybe that was just a bad day at the office. Everyone has them – I'd had one earlier in my career against Charm Chiteule, and that too had been a struggle, a difficult fight. But at the same time, I knew that Chiteule was better than this guy, and that I should have been able to get rid of him. The truth was that I didn't finish him the way I used to. I'd picked up some collateral damage, and overall it was a poor performance.

I remember sitting in my dressing room after the fight and thinking, whoa, what happened there? I sat there and mulled over the fight. There is a picture of me and Sandy sitting there, and she has got her hand on my shoulder and I am looking concerned. I remember it all too well, sitting in the dressing room and thinking, shit, that didn't go right. That didn't go the way it should have gone.

What I felt was that the little bit of magic had gone. That spark of intuition, something that you can't get through hours and hours of training, that instinctive bit of magic had disappeared. All of the other elements about your boxing you can build but not that innate sharpness, knowing when an opponent is in trouble and being able to take advantage, to hit him with the right sort of shots, step inside and nail him. I didn't understand where it had gone or why it had gone, but it just didn't seem to be there. That little bit of magic wasn't there any more.

In a funny kind of way, the fact that I hadn't performed well against Miranda improved my chances of getting a world title shot. If you look too good, then the champions get worried about facing you in case they lose. But put in a mixed performance and suddenly people are thinking, 'Well, yes, we will give him a shot then.' Suddenly, people are making noises about being willing to travel over to you, rather than you having to travel to them.

Promoters watch a performance like mine against Miranda, start feeling confident that their man can win, and are suddenly happy to talk.

But before we could get into negotiations for that, Barry Hearn made a really good offer to fight Jim McDonnell in Manchester. What actually happened was that I was in Jersey, staying for a few days with Billy Walker, the legendary sixties heavyweight. Barry Hearn had been in discussion with the Manchester promoter Jack Trickett, who had done some stuff together with Billy. So Hearn was talking to Trickett and Trickett mentioned that I was staying with Billy. So Hearn said, 'Why don't you tell him that I want this fight and I am willing to give him good money to take it?'

The situation was that my deal with Frank Warren had been for three fights. The Hearn offer was great money, he was confident he could get the fight as a final eliminator and it all seemed too good to turn down. Jim McDonnell, I thought, is a guy I can beat. And in doing so, I will get a shot at the world title. The fight was the official final eliminator for the WBC super-featherweight title, with the winner guaranteed a match-up with Azumah Nelson.

So I said yes, and the date was set for 31 May 1989 at the G-Mex Centre in Manchester, with a supporting bill that included Jess Harding, Peter English, Carl Crook, Najib Daho, Mark Reefer and Joey Jacobs. The headline on the posters was 'Nowhere To Run, Nowhere To Hide'. Under my photo was my nickname, The Clones Cyclone, and under McDonnell's was his: the Assassin. Little did I know when I agreed to the fight that his moniker was to prove so prescient, or that the fight would turn out to be so significant. I went into it thinking it was going to be a stepping stone to the next major challenge in my career. But as it turned out, it was to be a full stop instead.

Chapter 16

The Final Bell

Jim McDonnell was a tough opponent, no doubt about it. This was a fighter who'd gone the distance with Brian Mitchell, and was someone that Azumah Nelson would take twelve rounds to finish off. He was a quick mover, hard to pin down and had some decent counterpunches. As quick as he was with his hands, it was the speed of his feet that was the real problem. McDonnell would never hold his position for long: he liked to jab and move away. As soon as you tried to close him down, he'd be off again.

The challenge for a fighter of my style was to try and make McDonnell trade with me. The way to do that was to tire your opponent out. I was one of those guys that would have chased and chased and chased, and as the fight went on, would eventually have worn him down. That's what you do: you can't plant your feet and hit your punches with any real power when you're moving about. You have to walk them down, hold your feet and punch with authority. The longer the fight went on, the greater would have been my chances of winning.

All that, though, was academic, because early in the second round I got a cut above the eye. I walked in and McDonnell threw a long left hook. He was stretching for it, and caught me with the heel of his hand. We were wearing these Bryan gloves, and they are hard in the palm side of the glove: they have no padding there, so it was the heel of his hand right on the bone above my right eye. You know, I didn't even move to get out of the way or block him. It wasn't even a particularly hard punch, but I felt it immediately: it was like someone had hit me with a piece of hard wood, smack on the eye. It felt like someone had cracked me there, and it just opened up.

I got back to the corner at the end of the round, and I remember Ernie Fossey's reaction. 'Holy fuck,' he said. Ernie was a great cuts man, one of the best in the business, so I knew if he was saying 'Holy fuck' that this was serious. Normally, he'd be as cool as you like, wouldn't give anything away so as not to worry you. But this cut was so bad, he couldn't help himself reacting. From his expression, the look in his eyes, I knew that I was in trouble. Ernie had all the proper stuff, you know, the adrenalin and everything, and did what he could to patch it up. If anyone could have sorted that cut, I knew it would have been him. He told me, 'Don't worry, it'll be fine,' but I think that both he and I knew that it wouldn't be.

McDonnell was cute. He knew he just had to keep out of the way, and sooner or later the referee would stop the fight. I ran after him, was chasing as he moved around the ring. I was trying to stay on top of him, but he was too quick, too fresh that early in the fight. The referee, Mickey Vann, had always been a bit neurotic about cuts in my opinion, and at the start of the fourth, he was saying, 'This is a very bad cut.' I said, 'No, give me a chance, give me a chance.' But McDonnell caught me with a couple of shots and the cut opened up again. That was it: the referee just jumped in to stop it.

My immediate reaction was to be furious with Mickey Vann. I swore at him, said, 'For fuck's sake, this is crazy, this is stupid.'

So I was swearing at Vann while McDonnell's corner were jumping and screaming, leaping up and down and all that. It was a big surprise he'd won: no way had they expected him to beat me. But to be fair to Mickey Vann, he'd been absolutely right to stop the fight. When I got back to the dressing room and looked in the mirror, I just went, 'Jesus Christ'. It was a dreadful cut, a really nasty one: it needed seven stitches to sew it up. I went in to see Mickey Vann and apologised for what I'd said.

It was the second fight in succession that I'd been badly cut. It was as though I'd had as many cuts in my comeback fights as in the first part of my career put together. One of the reasons for that could have been to do with the question of scar tissue. This builds up over the course of a boxing career, and is more apparent the older a fighter gets. It's particularly noticeable with journeymen: they've had so many nicks and hacks over the years, that the skin becomes 'welty'-looking and rough around the eyes. The reason for this is the adrenalin that is used to prevent the cut from bleeding. This creates a sort of caking underneath the flesh. Although this can be removed with an operation, most boxers don't have the time, and instead you end up with a build-up of scar tissue.

Of course, no two boxers are the same. Some people have more pronounced cheekbones than others: some are more vulnerable than others as a result, though not always. Some fighters would bleed more easily than others. Henry Cooper was so susceptible to being cut that it was said you could blow on him and he bled. But I'd never really had any of that. I'd got cut badly in the Cabrera fight, got a nick on my eye in the Chiteule fight, but otherwise nothing to write home about. Not really, not until the end.

So the scar tissue builds up and you become more vulnerable. Even then, you don't know what sort of punch is going to do it. You don't know when it is going to happen. So yes, my skin was starting to get more fragile, but I could have gone another six fights without getting cut. You just don't know.

I'd been back in my dressing room for about ten minutes or so when I made the decision to retire. I looked in the mirror and I just thought, it's time to stop. I'm not going to box any more. Too many things had changed with the move to England: my dad was no longer there, my family weren't around me any more. I harked back to the thought I'd had after the Miranda fight – that the magic had gone. I'd achieved everything I'd wanted to achieve in my career. I couldn't see the reason to continue.

I'd trained every bit as hard for the later fights. I trained really hard, did all the work in the gym, ran on the roads. I'd done every bit as much as I had for those earlier fights, and maybe that was the problem. Maybe I had burned myself out with some of the stuff for those other fights. Maybe I had left a lot of my best work in the gym. I had put so much effort into everything, sparred a lot, done loads and loads of sparring and maybe that had caught up with me. Boxing is a young man's sport and maybe it was time to let the young guys through.

It was after the Miranda fight that I'd had my doubts as to whether or not I could produce the form that won me the world title. If I carried on, was I just going to struggle and become a journeyman for others? I didn't have the mentality for that: I wanted to go out at the top and I was near enough to do that. I hadn't disgraced myself, I had come back and I had really put the time and effort into it. I had worked really hard but that little edge had gone. Boxing is a business where you make quick decisions: you make sensible calculated decisions but you make them at the right time. It is not a sport to be hanging around in. I had been involved in that tragic fight with Young Ali, and I had seen a lot of guys get hurt in the business. I had responsibilities – I now had four young kids. To carry on when you knew you didn't have that edge would have been a foolish and possibly a dangerous thing to do.

Carlos Palomino, the seventies welterweight champion, once famously said how fighters were always the last to know when it was time to go, but he was determined to be the first. Those were my sentiments, exactly. I was only twenty-eight years old, which was still young, really. But it's not so much to do with age: it is the amount of punches you take that determines how old you are. I'd had thirty-five professional fights and, mentally, I was tired of it all. I was in a different place in my life: things had moved on and the love affair I'd always had with boxing was beginning to wane. I'd sort of fallen out of love with the sport. So I thought to myself, now is the time to bow out. So I followed Palomino's lead, and made the decision to retire.

Eamon McEvoy, my solicitor, close friend and confidant was there, and I remember saying to him, 'Eamon, I think I am going to throw in the towel.' Eamon said to me, 'If you are going to do it, do it. Don't muck around.'

I remember Frank Warren being taken aback when I told him, but no one tried to dissuade me or change my mind. I wasn't the sort of character to make that decision lightly: they knew that I meant it. We had this impromptu press conference in the hallway at the bottom of the stairs, and I stood on this rubbish bin and told everyone that I had an announcement to make. There were gasps from some people, and I'm sure some of the journalists thought, give it two months and he'll be back in the ring. But I never contemplated getting back in the ring again.

Actually, that's not quite true. There was a moment in October 1993 when I did consider it. I was doing the ITV broadcast for the second Benn–Eubank fight at Old Trafford. Because the fight was a draw, they had a follow-up programme the next day in London to discuss it. I was in the studio waiting for everyone to arrive when Don King showed up and worked on me for about an hour.

'Come on,' he said, 'I'll put you on in America and we'll have them little leprechauns and we will have people playing the harp and fiddle and, man, I'll make you millions. I'm telling you, I'll make you millions, man. I'm telling you.' I remember him skilfully massaging my ego and it was all nice and complimentary to hear all that. King gave me half an hour to think about it, but all I needed was about five minutes. I said, 'No, Don. I am not interested, but thank you.' He gave me all the 'you are making a big mistake' stuff, but I knew I didn't want to go back. And that was the only time it came up.

It's difficult to describe how I felt about retiring. It didn't feel a release or relief or anything like that: it was less about looking back, and more about thinking, this is the start of another chapter. I was only twenty-eight and had just given up the one thing I was really good at. I had a wife and four children and needed to work out quickly what I was going to do in terms of providing for them. So that was the priority, rather than reflecting back on what had or hadn't been.

The immediate answer for me was media work. I had done bits and bobs of commentary for various people, for ITV and the BBC and RTE in Ireland, and that seemed the obvious way to go. I met a guy called Bev Walker, he was an agent, and he looked after Sharon Davis, Emlyn Hughes and Sean Kerly, the hockey player who won Olympic gold in Seoul. He told me not to worry, and that he could get me plenty of stuff. Then I started straightaway with Jim Rosenthal and a boxing programme called *Seconds Out* on ITV. That was on during the week and myself and Rosenthal presented it. I was the colour commentator, doing the studio analysis as opposed to blow-by-blow ringside. It was great to work with Jim, who is both a consummate professional and a really nice person: he has been a great friend of mine over the years.

I loved doing the TV work. Really loved it. I had to travel and that was great too, I got to go all over the place. I went to America and struck up a relationship with a really good friend of mine called Mat Tinley, who was in charge of a cable station called Prime Ticket. Prime Ticket had been started by a guy called Bill Daniels, and had been there first, before HBO or Showtime or any of the others. He was the guy who started it all. Mat Tinley was his grandson, and funnily enough, I got to meet him through Bono, the U2 lead singer. I have been a huge fan of U2 through the years. Their music and success have been a source of inspiration to me. Bono has one of the most inimitable voices in pop music and they all are such good people. Mat was also a massive U2 fan, and he'd met Bono at some do or other, and they'd got talking and Mat said he was looking for commentators. I'd met Bono loads of times, and so he said, 'Why don't you give Barry a call?' So that was fantastic. They teamed me up with a guy called Rich Marotta: a great commentator, and fantastic to work with.

So I worked for Prime, I had the stuff on ITV, did some work for the BBC, Eurosport, and worked with Barry Hearn on Screen Sport. I was inundated with work. The fights were coming around thick and fast and I was doing as many as I could handle. It was fantastic. I remember doing the first Tyson–Bruno fight for Sky in 1989, which was the start of their whole pay-per-view system. Mike Tyson is someone I've always felt affinity towards, because of the link with my dad. The fact that Dad had been to see him train and was raving about him from an early age meant that I always followed his career closely. For me, if Tyson could have found a way to control his self-destructive side, then he could have been the greatest heavyweight champion of all time. At his peak, his speed was something else, and proof that size isn't everything in the heaviest division: his game was all about pace and power, a style that was a throwback to the likes of Henry Armstrong (a bigger version, obviously) with a touch of Joe Frazier in there too.

When Tyson fought Bruno, I felt he had a crucial psychological edge even before the first bell had sounded. In the early 1980s, Tyson had once been brought in as a sparring partner for Bruno: he so dominated the session that Terry Lawless didn't use him any more. I think that experience was in the back of both their minds, and left a big dent in Frank as to whether or not he could beat him. You could never fault Frank Bruno in terms of courage, but I never found him the most fluid of fighters to watch. There was something a bit mechanical about his style, though there was no doubting either his commitment or the strength of his punches; when Bruno connected, he really connected. I remember seeing him fight James 'Bonecrusher' Smith in 1984, and watching him get knocked out in the tenth round. I felt even then that there was something vulnerable about the way Frank fought: it was a fragility that Tyson at his peak ruthlessly exploited.

In the mid-nineties, Frank Warren signed an exclusive deal with Sky Sports and I also signed a deal to work with them. Sky wanted me to work in the studio, and I was teamed up with a guy called Paul Dempsey. He is of Irish stock but reared in Leicester, and we were, if you like, the face of Sky boxing. Dempsey was the polished presenter and I was the colour. It was great: I worked for Sky until 2005. They were absolutely fantastic to me: they gave me a wonderful opportunity and I was lucky to have a great working relationship with the head of sport, Vic Wakeling.

We covered a load of fights, and all the big names of the era. Ricky Hatton is a boxer who I've always had a lot of time for. I really liked his style of fighting: his relentless attacking body punches were something I could relate to! I noticed his potential early on, and followed his career closely. I remember that when it was announced that he would be fighting Kostya Tszyu for the IBF light-welterweight title not many people gave him a chance. I wasn't so sure about that; the match-up reminded me of when I was up against Pedroza. I knew that Hatton was a far better fighter than he was being given credit for, and to many people's surprise, I predicted that he would win.

It wasn't just Hatton's style in the ring that reminded me of my own boxing career. The way that he is easily approachable was reminiscent of how I tried to deal with my own boxing success. I went up and watched him train at the Betta Bodies gym in Manchester, and both the feel and the way he approached his training also felt quite familiar. I watched him spar with the same sort of intensity that I used to put into my own sessions, and enjoyed the good, bubbly atmosphere in the gym. The reassuring influence of Ricky's father was another important influence that I could relate to.

Joe Calzaghe, by contrast, was less one of the lads and more his own man. Which isn't to say that he wasn't a terrific fighter, of course he was, but it is only human to like the boxers who fight in the same way as you did – that's why I always felt warm towards Ricky Hatton. Calzaghe was blessed with fantastically quick hands: he was very adaptable and had the power to knock opponents out. The fact he held the world title for as long as he did and remained unbeaten throughout his career was a remarkable achievement, and marks him down as one of the greatest British fighters.

Nigel Benn and Chris Eubank were two other wonderful fighters, though very different in their styles. Eubank had a terrific chin, and a very good right hand. From a character point of view, he is an interesting person, if somewhat eccentric! He liked me, and was always very generous in his comments about my own fighting career. I did get the sense that he wanted to impress, and felt that sometimes he would 'perform' in front of me. As good a fighter as Eubank was, he did have the capacity to switch off in the ring: by contrast, Nigel Benn was relentless. One got the sense that he genuinely wanted to hurt people. There was no messing about with him, and I admired that. It was the same sort of attitude that

Marvin Hagler brought to the ring. Despite Eubank's efforts to impress me, and Benn's more sullen, sometimes truculent demeanour out of the ring, out of the two fighters, I always felt that it was Benn who had the edge. Of course, Steve Collins, the Celtic warrior, beat both of them at the end of their careers. Steve was a tremendously tough fighter who could mix it with anybody. Earlier in his career, when he was based in Boston, he gave the great Mike McCallum, the 'Bodysnatcher', a tough fight. Steve won both the middleweight and supermiddleweight world titles and got out of the game at the right time.

Prince Naseem was another fighter whose style I really liked. He certainly wasn't short on confidence as a fighter: I remember him claiming he could knock me out! Naseem had the sort of bold-as-brass approach that you either loved or hated. I always found him a bit of a funny mixture as a fighter: he had this reckless, gung-ho attitude that seemed to ooze confidence; but though he gave the impression he wasn't nervous, I often wondered whether his arrogance was a masking of just that, a way for him to hide his real concerns.

Lennox Lewis I knew was the real deal from the moment I first saw him. I have to say that the way he boxed never really did it for me. I felt he was far too safe as a fighter, and it sometimes seemed as though he would wait for ever before putting his foot on the gas. But there's no doubt he was one of the better heavyweight champions, even if the fact he has been knocked out twice damaged his overall reputation. What I have always particularly admired about Lennox is how he managed his affairs outside the ring. He decided to do his own thing and promote himself, rather than sign up with anyone: he had his own little team sorting stuff out, and I really admire him for doing that.

While I'm talking about fighters, I should also say a few words about Amir Khan. I think he's a great kid, with a decent personality and a sense of humility to how he goes about things.

He's a fast, aggressive and brave fighter and I think he has done really well. Long before he was knocked out by Breidis Prescott, I felt he should be being coached by someone like Freddie Roach. Amir has quick hands and feet and Roach is the sort of trainer who can do things with guys that are fast. The more time Amir spends with Roach, the better I think he will get. He has the potential to do really well in the States and I hope he gets the success all his hard work deserves.

I've always liked doing the TV stuff. It was a nice life in the sense that I was doing something that I really enjoyed, so it didn't feel like a job at all. So I did the TV and the personal appearances and the after-dinner speaking. And I had my newspaper column too. I'd done that since I'd signed up with the *Daily Star* in the mid-eighties. I signed for Brian Hitchen, and when he moved to the *Express* I went with him. I did about seven years with the *Express* and the *Star* and then I moved to the *Daily Mirror*. I have been writing for the *Mirror* for twelve years now. Dare I say it, it's one of the better weekly boxing columns. I write about things that are important in boxing and people like to hear my opinion. We have a big readership. I remember seeing Richard Wallace, the editor of the *Daily Mirror*, at the Pride of Britain awards in 2009. He said, 'Barry, I want to tell you that your column is absolutely brilliant.' I was thrilled to hear that, it was great to know that people value what I've got to say.

We moved down to Kent at the end of the 1980s to a beautiful house in the countryside, where we've lived ever since. We've loved Kent from the moment we arrived, and still do. It was a great place to bring up our children, and although it is a large house, it's not too big and feels like a real 'lived in' house. It has been the perfect family home.

I quit boxing at the right time. I achieved what I wanted to achieve, I'd done well for myself, and got out without ever having been badly injured or anything like that. I was lucky, too, that there was something else I was good at, that I could go on and do all right for myself in the years after. I know how lucky I am to have been able to do that, and that, sadly, for so many boxers the opposite is the case. Their career comes to an end and their world falls apart: it's the classic 'rags to riches to rags' story, and you see it in boxing time and time again.

The reason that some boxers take up the sport is a way to escape from problems in their personal life. The problem is that once their career is over, they soon realise that those same problems are there, and that boxing wasn't the answer they had hoped it might be. You look at the biographies of fighters, and so many come from disjointed backgrounds and hard-bitten tough areas: so many haven't benefited from love and unconditional support when they were growing up. I know how fortunate I've been to have always had that family support to fall back on.

For any fighter finishing their career, readjusting to the real world is a difficult thing to do, and many boxers find it hard to cope. The thing that has been getting them out of bed in the morning has been taken away from them, and many of them are left asking, 'What do I do now?' This is true of all retiring sportsmen, but I believe there is something unique about boxing that exacerbates the difficulty of this transition. I have often thought it noticeable how little psychological help boxers get: medical help is readily available, and they can't get you to the doctor quickly enough if anything happens in the ring. But the mental toll that the sport takes is somewhat overlooked, and this can store up problems for when a fighter's career is over.

If you lose in a team sport, you have all the other guys to share the loss with you. Boxing is not the only individual sport, but none of the others are quite so brutal. If you lose a running race, it is not so devastating. There is something unique about boxing that puts you up on such an egotistical and emotional high that separates it from every other sport. In boxing, you still have guys with you, people who might live and travel with you. But however supportive your team might be, at the end of the day they're not the ones who actually take the punches. They don't go through the pain that a boxer suffers: the sore heads, the aching joints and muscles, the difficulty of making weight and the months of dieting.

One of the things that I find difficult when I hear about ex-boxers struggling to get by is that any fighter who has been even half successful must have the wherewithal to make a go of things. To be a successful boxer requires more than just raw talent: it requires physical effort, hard work and discipline. If these former fighters could show just a fraction of the drive they displayed during their boxing career, then who knows what else they could achieve?

I wanted to do something about this, and so in 1993, I helped set up the Professional Boxers Association with Nicky Piper and Colin McMillan. The idea of the scheme was to begin by focusing on contemporary fighters: we wanted to offer them counselling and psychological support from early on in their career, so they didn't end up following the same trajectory as so many fighters before them. If we could get these young fighters thinking about their future while they were still in the sport, then they would be far better prepared for when it was time to hang up their gloves. We wanted to set these young fighters off on the right track, and then turn our attention to helping the old fighters.

When a fighter finished boxing and asked, 'What do I do now?' I wanted to show them just how many careers there were that their boxing skills could lead on to. One option was to study for a sports-science degree or a foundation course. They could utilise the general knowledge they had accrued about nutrition, strength and conditioning, cardiovascular training and weight training and the skills of boxing: one possibility would be to become an ABA coach. A fighter could use the training they have done to take a personal fitness course. Ten weeks later, they can have gained their qualification and be in a position to charge £35 or £40 an hour. Bit by bit, an alternative career can begin to form and take shape.

But all of this can only happen when fighters have the incentive to get up and do it themselves. The problem with ex-fighters is that they feel so bad about themselves, they think, ah, this is it, it's all over and done with. So many of them are short-sighted, so many of them didn't focus their attention on planning ahead. But you only have to look at the success some ex-boxers have had to know that it doesn't have to be that way. Jim Watt, for example, I've known since I was sixteen or seventeen. He had a great career and took up commentary: he and Reggie Gutteridge formed a great partnership. He has done well for himself: he is bright and intelligent and was always a model example to me. Another guy that I really admired in Ireland is a fellow called Mick Dowling. He never turned professional but Mick was an outstanding amateur. He won eight national titles and is a well-spoken guy. He's got great dignity, has a great family, has been smart with his money and invested. Nicky Piper, too, is another success story. He had the intelligence to use all the contacts that he had. And Piper has plenty of intelligence: he has an IQ of 153, a pro boxer who became a member of Mensa.

I worked hard to make a go of the Professional Boxers Association, but the project never got the sort of financial support it needed to be a success. We had great help from the GMB union up in Wakefield, but recruiting members proved to be more difficult than we'd hoped. As much as I was prepared to give the organisation my time and energy to get things going, what we really needed was more money, a stronger structure and better office facilities from which to work.

What we also needed was a stronger response from the fighters themselves. As passionate as I was about helping them, that can only happen if fighters are receptive to what you're suggesting. If not, then the danger is that you can come across as a bit hectoring and that can put people off. It was a frustrating experience for me: we were trying to set up a support system for these ex-fighters, and as much as so many of them needed that help, a lot of them just didn't want to know. All in all, I ended up putting fifteen years into the organisation, at which point I decided that I'd taken things as far as I could. There was only so much I could give to people who weren't interested, particularly when I had plenty of personal problems of my own to deal with.

Chapter 17

Dermot

There have been a number of occasions in my life where something good has happened, only to be balanced out by something negative. So the night we did the deal to fight for the world title was the night I learned that my father might have cancer. The night I won the world title, my parents' house burned down. In 1994, I received the MBE, but the same year, my brother Dermot took his own life.

I'd actually accepted the MBE at the third time of being offered that honour. The first time I'd been offered it was in 1985, after I'd won the world title. We got a letter through the post from the Palace. I turned it down for the sake of my family. I was living in Clones, right on the border; the last place in the South before you get to the North, and vice versa. Clones is a Republican town, and there were plenty of other Republican pockets of support not so far away. So to accept the award – the Member of the Order of the British Empire – was asking for trouble for both me and my family. There's no way I could have put them at risk. It would have been a dangerous thing to do. I declined: a decision that the Palace understood.

The following year, after I had lost the title, the Palace wrote again, this time offering me the OBE. It was a fabulous gesture again, but nothing had really changed – it was still the height of the Troubles, and I didn't want to make myself a target. So I went back to them and explained the situation, and they were very understanding. And I thought that was that, to be honest. I had my break and came back, got into commentary and the Professional Boxers Association. And then, after I'd set that up, I got another letter, offering me the MBE again. This time, I'd been living in England for several years. The Troubles were still going on but by the mid-nineties it wasn't as intense and violent as it had been: things were beginning to move politically, leading to the IRA calling a ceasefire in August 1994. So the situation felt different.

I knew, too, that I was incredibly lucky to have been offered it again: normally, they offer it to you once, and that is it. I was touched that they did that. So I said yes, and went to the Palace to collect it. There were loads of people there collecting awards: Prince Charles was handing them out as the Queen was away. It was a wonderful day, and nice to be honoured for 'services to boxing'. It was great to be recognised for what I was trying to do with the Professional Boxers Association.

But while that moment in the sun was great, my memories of that year are completely overshadowed by what happened with Dermot. Dermot and I had always been very close growing up: I had five sisters and two brothers, but Dermot was the closest in age to me, a year and a bit older, and we did everything together. We shared the same bedroom, we got into boxing together, and Dermot was good, let me tell you. He had a longer reach than me, and was naturally skilful. He was a very decent boxer and was my main sparring partner when I was at my gym in Clones: we sparred hundreds of rounds. As I progressed through the ranks, he was with me every step of the way, doing the pad work, training with me when he could. He would always be the first into the ring after the fight. Dermot was a very fine athlete himself and also an excellent golfer: he held the course record on the old course at Clones Golf Club.

When I lost the world title, I know it would have hit Dermot hard. He would never have said anything, he was the sort of guy who would internalise things, but I know it was difficult for him. He was a tough guy and so nobody mucked him around. But he would have been conscious of what people would have been saying, and that would have been hard for him. When I moved away, I know that would have been difficult for him to deal with as well. I know I missed him, and that it was the same the other way round, that I wasn't there to support him. I wasn't there any more to give him that emotional support in the same way.

Dermot split up with this girl he'd been seeing and he took it really hard. He was crazy about her, and found it a real problem to deal with. He took to the bottle, which is something he'd never done, and I was really worried about him. I brought him over to Canterbury to my home and took him to St Martin's Hospital in Canterbury to try and sort him out. I knew the drinking wasn't a long-term problem, but I wanted to get him off it. He stayed in there for the best part of a week or so, and they said he was all right, gave him some medication and let him come out.

Dermot came to stay after he'd been in St Martin's, and lived with us for a while. He was on this medication, but for all intents and purposes he seemed better again. He'd stay up late at night, I remember that, but otherwise he seemed OK. I told him that he would be fine. He was a very charming, nice, loveable guy, and I told him there were loads of girls out there who would have a lot of time for him.

It was 1994. I don't know if it was a harbinger of what was to come, but it was around May time when he was staying with us, and the thing I remember most was watching the San Marino Grand Prix together, the one where Ayrton Senna was killed. We had a big settee in the kitchen and we watched it in there, we watched this tragedy unfold in front of us. I am a petrolhead anyway, have always liked my cars, but had also had the fortune to meet Senna a couple of years before. I took part in this 'Petit Prix' charity race before the Grand Prix at Silverstone in 1992. There was me and Jeremy Clarkson, Nick Mason, Pamela Stephenson, Jason Donovan and twenty-four others, all in these little CRX Hondas. I'd been at the track doing some tests the week before, and Ron Dennis introduced me to Senna. I met him and he was just a real nice guy. He was Brazilian but spoke excellent English. And in terms of driving, he was truly a genius behind the wheel.

The 1994 San Marino Grand Prix was a terrible weekend for Formula One. The driver Roland Ratzenberger had been killed in the qualifying sessions. The race itself was stopped almost immediately after another serious accident involving J J Lehto and Pedro Lamy. After the restart, Senna was leading Michael Schumacher, who was breathing down his neck at the time. It was said later that the steering rack or something had snapped because he had quite big feet and they had to readjust where they put their feet. There were all sorts of reasons but I don't know what was under pressure or what happened from a technical point of view. Senna was doing 200mph when the steering rack cracked, or whatever it was went wrong, and he went sliding across the gravel track and hit the little wall.

I remember watching him go off and saying, 'Oh my God, he's dead. He's definitely dead.' It was the way he went off and also because I saw Sid Watkins out there. I knew Sid through the British Brain and Spine Foundation, who we'd been involved with because of the number of boxers who have neurosurgery. I'd met him through that, and he was such a lovely guy, and when I saw him running towards Senna's car, I just knew that things were really bad. What with watching it happen and having met Senna and everything, I was gutted, really gutted. Dermot and I both got quite upset about it. I was really down about it, and Dermot was quite emotional too. 'Stop it, Barry,' he said, 'there is nothing you can do about it.'

Looking back on it now, those words are just so poignant. So poignant. We put Dermot on the plane because he wanted to go back home again. My friend Fergus Lavery picked him up at Belfast Airport and drove him to Clones. Dermot went out to meet his ex, to try and patch things up. But things didn't work out. He went straight to the off-licence and bought a bottle of vodka, or a couple of bottles of vodka, and went to my mum's and went to bed. Into the bedroom and just didn't come out for three or four days. Mum rang me up and said, 'Barry, he's in a bad way again.' He decided he would move in to Chapman's, which was next door to my mother's shop, where my parents had stayed when we had the fire. Dermot went to stay in there and it was there that he ended his life.

Dermot was prescribed antidepressants and had been seeing a psychiatrist, who told my mother that Dermot was 'para-suicidal'. In other words, he'd talk about taking his life but not actually do anything about it. But he didn't just talk about it: sadly, my brother hanged himself ten days later.

I miss my brother. He was such a great man, and I would love to still have him here. I would love for my brother to still be alive, for my dad to be alive, to be able to see my kids and how they have come on, to have those relationships with them as a loving uncle and a caring grandfather. It's devastating for all my family. It has taken so long to come to terms with Dermot's suicide. I don't know if we will ever get over it. The really sad thing is I see some of the girls now who Dermot used to go out with and some of them are separated and on their own. It just makes you think – things could have worked out fine and he could have been happily married with his own family. But Dermot was so distraught, he couldn't see that.

When someone you love so much takes their own life, I can't begin to explain how difficult it is to deal with. I don't think you can ever get over something like that, not really. The heartbreaking thing is, so many people end their lives that way every year. And the vast majority of them are men, it's always young men. I don't know what that's about or why that is, but I do know the incredible pain for the families it leaves behind. Dermot was such a serious guy, with so much going on underneath. It can be hard sometimes to talk to those people, and to get those people to talk to you. I only wish that there had been a way I could have helped Dermot more: if anyone could have done it, I know I would have been the one who could have talked him down off the box that fateful day. I know that because he left only me and my mother a letter. To know that and to have to live with the fact that I'll never see him again is agonising.

At the end of 1994, I met the actor Daniel Day-Lewis. I met him with the director Jim Sheridan, who I knew well already: I had worked with Jim on a book, *Leave the Fighting to McGuigan*, in the mid-1980s. Jim said to me that he wanted to do a boxing movie, and he wanted me to be involved. We met up at the end of 1994 and then in early 1995 I brought Daniel to the Nigel Benn – Gerald McClellan fight at the New London Arena. It was the first pro fight Daniel had ever been to. We went to the fight and I was working with Jim Rosenthal: Dan was sitting ringside, and what a first fight to see. Incredible, incredible fight. It ended up tragically: McClellan was very badly injured. Benn was down in the first round twice and I still don't know to this day how he made the count. McClellan knocked him completely out of the ring and Gary Newbon, who was working for ITV, actually helped to push him back into the ring. The count was fourteen seconds at least. To get through that and then to stop McClellan was a phenomenal effort.

McClellan was blinking, even five rounds into the fight he was blinking, so he had some sort of damage. It was only after it when he lapsed into unconsciousness that we knew how bad it was. Which for me brought back Young Ali and all those horrible memories again. However, Daniel sampled how amazing it was and he loved the atmosphere. So the boxing film was on, and I agreed to train him for the role.

Daniel is a great guy, a lovely man: brilliantly talented and very hard-working. Christ Almighty, what a hard worker. I love people who are passionate about what they do and are meticulous in their preparation, but Daniel was something else. Once he went for a role, he completely absorbed himself in it. He was making the movie *The Crucible* in America at the time: they had built a set like the old New England-type houses with little old Tudor windows, and inside one of them they built him a boxing gym. He had a punchbag or a couple of punchbags and everything else so he could actually do his workout every day. And when he got time off, he would head back to London and I would train him at the Fitzroy Lodge gym in London. We got him sparring in the Crumlin gym in Dublin, he sparred with the Greek Olympic team. He sparred everywhere and he was so good. He really got so good.

To give you some indication of that, the principal photography for the film started in early 1997 and Daniel had just turned forty years old. So he was in his late thirties, start of his forties, as we trained, and I got him sparring a guy called Geoff McCreesh, who was the British welterweight champion. McCreesh had knocked out a guy called Kevin Lueshing to win his title: Lueshing had previously fought for the world title against the great Puerto Rican Felix Trinidad, and knocked the champion down, almost caused an upset. McCreesh was good, that is my point: a tough, tough guy and he sparred extensively with Daniel for about six months. He probably sparred easy on Daniel to begin with, to be honest, but as time went on, Daniel got better and began giving Geoff a bit of trouble. By the end they were doing eight rounds together, and I swear you couldn't separate them. There was nothing between them.

The only time Daniel had ever done any boxing before that was for the making of the film *In the Name of the Father*. There was a scene in that he'd had to do a bit of training for. There was a guy that Jim Sheridan knew very well, a Belfast flyweight from the late sixties, early seventies, called Micky Tohill. And he'd said to Daniel, 'Why don't you come and do a bit of training?' That's how he started. He'd got a bit of a taste for it and then with me it became much more intense. I said to Daniel, in order to get really good for this role, we are going to have to train and spar you a lot. Because if I don't get you to spar you won't look natural in the ring and it will all look stilted. And he just worked like a demon. My God. Never seen anybody train so hard.

I got in a guy called Damien Denny who was a former Irish international boxer: a very good boxer and had almost reached British title standard as a pro. During the preparation for the movie I met Damien and did some work with him as well. He was a bit overweight and I said to him, you get a couple of stone off you and we will try and get you a part in the movie. He started training like hell, dropped the weight and was one of Daniel's main opponents in the actual movie. There was another guy called Clayton Stewart, he was one of the opponents as well. So it was Damien Denny and Clayton Stewart who were Daniel's opponents in the movie, which ended up being called *The Boxer*.

I helped train Daniel, and I spent a lot of time talking to Jim Sheridan too. The plot of *The Boxer* wasn't based on my life, but Jim certainly used things that happened to me as background in creating his story; there were things that happened that he used as inspiration, and from there he went on and created his own wonderful narrative. He's a great storyteller, Jim Sheridan, and sharp as anything on the politics: he was so accurate in his observations, in catching what was happening at the time.

One bit from my life that Jim did use was the Young Ali fight. He completely mirror-imaged the setting but changed the finish. Clayton Stewart played the Ali equivalent, and Daniel Day-Lewis was beating him up very badly and the referee couldn't see it. He took an enormous amount of punishment, and then in the fifth or sixth round – bang! – the Day-Lewis character knocked him down and he just could hardly get up. The referee is in there saying, 'Come on, box on.' And Dan goes, 'What do you want me to do, kill the guy?' He says, 'Box on.' So Dan puts his hands up and the ref says, 'Box on, I am telling you.' Dan says, 'No, I am not doing this.' So he hits him a few more times and he goes, 'Stop the fight, referee.' He says, 'No.' So Dan turns and walks out. The referee shouts after him, 'You are disqualified.' And he lifts the other guy's hand up who is helpless. It was different from what happened to me, but the setting was uncanny: they recreated the Great Room from the Grovesnor Hotel, and my God, the detail in the set was unbelievable. It was like being back there, and that was quite a weird experience.

The other thing I did on the film was to choreograph all the fight scenes. I worked out all the choreographed moves, put in some half-hits and misses, made them actually spar and made it look real. It looked authentic, which I was really pleased about. We would start with them sparring, properly sparring, and then we would move into the routine we'd worked out. There would be a pattern of moves where Daniel would, say, slip a jab underneath, left hook to the body, right hook, slip underneath it again, left hook to the head and right hand, left hook, right hand. We would do that over and over again. Slow motion, fast, and you would always do the sparring as you moved into it. And it was great. It worked out really well.

*

The filming of *The Boxer* went on from the beginning of March through to the middle of July that year. I was doing the film in Dublin and flying back and forth to commentate on fights for Sky, then coming back to see the family at weekends. And then, just a couple of days from the end of the filming, my life flipped again. Once more, just as something was going well, I had the rug pulled out from under me.

We were doing a scene in the Ardmore Studios in Bray. It was the Grovesnor House scene and I was on the set when somebody came in and said, 'Barry, come quickly.' And I had to go to the phone in the studio office to take the call. I ran out of the set to the office and I could hear our doctor on the phone. He said, 'Look, I have very bad news for you, Barry.' I could hear Sandy weeping in the background as he said, 'Your daughter Danika has got leukaemia.'

I left immediately, drove straight to the airport, got on the plane, flew into London, then went straight to St Bart's Hospital. And that was it. It was the end of the filming for me: I spent six weeks on the floor by the hospital bed, keeping my fingers crossed and praying that she would get better. Danika got home, and she'd had a Hickman line put in, but then she got infected again and had to go back in for another operation to put the line in again. This time she stopped breathing on the operating table. She actually died on the table and they had to resuscitate her and get the operation finished.

Danika was only eleven years old. She'd had febrile convulsions as a baby as I'd mentioned earlier, had got through that and was a brilliant kid, as bright and buoyant as you could hope for, and now this. It was shocking stuff. They did a lumbar puncture after two weeks and, thankfully, they told us she'd responded well to the initial treatment. I know how incredibly lucky we were: out of the eleven kids on Danika's ward, seven of them died. Seven: an absolute tragedy. The kids would be in there, and they knew what was going on. The doctors would say that someone had been transferred to another hospital or that their treatment was over, but Danika and the others knew what was happening. After a while, they just stopped asking the questions or talking about them.

By the grace of God, Danika came through. We took her home and looked after her. Our other kids were great: it must have been hard for them because we were so focused on Nika, we had to be so careful about cleanliness and making sure she didn't catch anything. But they loved her and were all worried about her, and were hugely supportive. So many people got in touch and wrote to us, telling us they were praying for her and that sort of thing. Again, I can't begin to explain how touched I was. It was so touching to know people were thinking about us in the middle of this terrible, terrible crisis.

Towards the end of the year, as Danika was getting better, Daniel Day-Lewis called and said, 'Barry, I have looked at the footage of the boxing scenes here and I am not happy with it. I know it's not a great time for you, but could you come over to New York and do some editing?' By that point, Danika was on the mend, so I flew over to Manhattan and spent a week in the editing suite, sifting through the footage of the boxing scenes. I went through the boxing scenes one by one, pieced them together from a fighter's perspective. It was a lot of work – there were ten shots of every sequence of punches, and we were locked in the suite that whole week, morning, noon and night. At the end of it, Daniel said he was delighted with the result. You could see he was thrilled with the finished product. *The Boxer* was nominated for three Golden Globes: for Best Picture, Actor and Director.

So I was heavily involved in the editing of the film. It was a lot of work but I thoroughly enjoyed the experience. I'd love to get involved in another film project at some stage in future. I got my name in the credits, which I was chuffed about. And right at the end, you have to keep watching to see it, the film is dedicated to Jim's dad, to my dad, and to my brother Dermot. As you can imagine, that meant an awful lot to me.

Chapter 18

Giving Back

If somebody had told me in the 1980s that Gerry Adams would shake hands with Ian Paisley or Peter Robinson I would have said, put that man in a white suit and lock him up in a padded cell. Swear to God I would. What has happened in Northern Ireland in recent years has been nothing short of remarkable. Things have come on further than I ever thought I would see happen. It is a different place now, no doubt about it. I think there's still further to go on the journey, but the relative peace of the last decade is a world away from the country I knew when I was growing up.

The way I feel about Northern Ireland is the way I feel about my brother Dermot. I get upset that I don't think about him enough these days. It upsets me because it means I have forgotten about him. For Northern Ireland, for all the people caught up in the Troubles, who had their lives and families torn apart, I feel the same. I used to feel so angry with the terrorists, with the IRA and UVF. And when I think about some of the atrocities that occurred, well, it's hard to comprehend, even now. What on earth did this look like to people overseas?

The balancing act that is needed in Northern Ireland is to never forget the people who have suffered, but to try to put the past to one side as well, to move forward and move on. For the peace, tranquillity and acceptance to disseminate right down through the generations, will take years to totally take root. And as much as the situation is about two communities learning to get along, I believe that meaningful change will only come from within families themselves. What parents tell their children ultimately matters much more than what the politicians say.

Northern Ireland needs to move beyond the 'us and them' syndrome that has dominated it for so many years. I know that it's no easy thing to do: these attitudes are entrenched by so many years of violence and terror. To bring your children up with a different set of values to those of the community you live in is undoubtedly difficult. But only by people being brave enough to go against the grain can these engrained attitudes be overturned. Only by teaching the next generation to see both sides of the story can real respect flourish between the two communities.

For me, the future of Northern Ireland starts with schooling young people. I've been an advocate of integrated education since the early 1980s, having a single system of schools rather than separate Protestant and Catholic establishments. I first showed my support back in 1985, when I opened Hazelwood College in Belfast with John Carson, the then Lord Mayor. For me, these schools have been one of the biggest success stories in Northern Ireland. Integrated schools started out with no support, the government made it difficult for them to get up and running. The schools had to sustain themselves for years; they had to prove that there was an abundance of parents who wanted to send their children there.

It was a huge risk with their children's education, for these parents to take their son or daughter out of a state school that had a good record, and put them in a new school that didn't have a reputation. Some of the schools didn't even have any buildings:

there were makeshift colleges, with kids being taught in Portacabins; there were even some parents who remortagaged their houses to finance the whole thing. The courage of those people getting the scheme off the ground is incredible.

Now there's a great opportunity for it all to change. In autumn 2010, Peter Robinson, the First Minister, came out and said that education in Northern Ireland is a benign form of apartheid. That was a line that those of us supporting integrated schools had been using for years. Because that is exactly what the school system in Northern Ireland is: you're segregated at four years old, taught in a Catholic or Protestant school, and only come together at university. By which point that separation mentality, for so many people, is already engrained.

If Northern Ireland wants a shared future, a proper shared future, it has to start with the schools. It could never have happened while the Troubles were going on. But now, we have had thirteen, fourteen years of relative peace, and now is the time to change. It might be one of the few silver linings of the current economic situation: because of the state of the finances, maybe people are questioning the cost of funding two separate school systems. And maybe that will be the catalyst to make the change. But it has to be done properly and carefully and the government has to use the tried and proven successful methods of the Integrated Education Fund.

Some people might say to me, you're not living there any more, you're not in the middle of it, you don't really understand. But I do understand: anybody with common sense could appreciate my position. The reality is that if you really want people to understand each other and to have lasting friendships for the rest of their lives, you have to go to school together. And respect each other. And understand that there are two beliefs. There may be two different types of loyalty, if you want, but effectively we are exactly the same. Just because you are Orange or you are Green doesn't matter. Life is too short to have that type of hatred and animosity. I've seen how that is a short step from violence, and it's just not worth it, it just isn't.

I am very proud of my home town, Clones. I have got property there and always love to go back, though I don't know whether I will ever go home to live. It would be great to move back to Ireland one day, but if I did, it would be nearer one of the big cities – to Dublin or Belfast, perhaps. Maybe when things slow down a bit, I might consider going back, but I've no intention of that happening any time soon. I want to be busy all the time and I don't ever want to retire. I might slow down but I am not going to retire. That is the ambition. That is what my future is, but whether I eventually go back or not, Ireland and Northern Ireland are very, very important to me. And I will always try to help in as many ways as I can to create harmony, and to promote all the good things about it, and show the rest of the world what a great place it is.

It hasn't only been schools in Northern Ireland that I have taken an interest in over the years. After my involvement in the Professional Boxers Association came to an end, it didn't stop my desire to put something back into boxing, to use boxing for the better. I decided to refocus my energies on colleges, to start putting my time into kids who are still in education and who I can influence. I wanted to get kids to stay on in education, and use their interest in boxing as a way to encourage that. I realised that boxing could be a catalyst to interest otherwise disenfranchised young people, get them back into college and improve their job prospects.

There is a section of the young population in the UK who are classified as 'NEET': these are people between the ages of sixteen and twenty-four who are not in employment, education or training. The 'NEET' kids number just under 200,000 in the 16–18 age group; that's about one in ten teenagers of that age. For the entire 16–24 age range that NEET relates to, the total number is just under a million people. That's a big, big problem. These are people who have dropped out of school and have disengaged with the system. With little or no qualifications, their chances of getting a job are limited. Some get involved in crime because they have nothing else to do. It's a terrible situation, and a personal tragedy for the individuals involved.

My belief is that boxing can be a way to re-engage these NEET kids in a way that traditional education or training cannot. That's because boxing has a unique place in people's perceptions. It is something that is respected by all kids whether they are middle-class kids or working-class kids. They all have respect for boxing. If we can use that respect to try and re-engage kids in fitness and health and get them back into education, then it can give them a fresh start and a better chance in life.

In 2009, I launched the first of my Barry McGuigan Boxing Academies. The idea behind the scheme is to work with colleges to provide access to boxing expertise and related services for 16–19-year-olds, so that the combination of education and boxing activities creates sustainable changes in each of their lifestyles. The key is that you need skill and discipline to be successful in boxing: I want to show the students that if they can apply the same sort of drive towards their academic studies as well, then they can also fulfil their educational potential. By doing so, this widens their future educational, training and employment options. At the same time, the scheme helps young people to take responsibility for their future by raising their self-esteem, health awareness and self-motivation.

There are now four academies around the country, in Leicester, East Berkshire, Bristol and Stockport, with interest for another four in various parts of the country. There are fifteen to twenty boxers enrolled at each, both boys and girls, who get quality training by ABA Level 3 coaches. They get about nine hours of boxing a week, and do this in tandem with whatever course they are studying for; a diverse range of vocational courses from sports science to social care, plumbing to plastering. At the end of the scheme, the students are in a position where they can move on to higher or further education if they want: if they want to go into work, then they've got qualifications to go out and impress a prospective employer with.

Having got the academies up and running, as well as the teenagers signed up to do the courses, we then also use the facilities to entice the NEET kids back into the system. We get these kids into the boxing unit and get them training: they can do fifteen or sixteen hours a week. Although it is boxing-based, we throw in other stuff as well, a bit of basketball or football, for example, to keep things fresh and interesting. Getting these kids in there and getting them excited is the way to reignite their interest in education. The aim is to show these kids how flexible and varied modern education is, and what the benefits from studying can be: not just for their job prospects, but also for themselves, as people. We did a trial scheme in Leicester: out of the ten kids who started, eight of them finished, and four ended up returning to full-time education.

I am also patron of the Advanced Apprenticeship in Sporting Excellence, or the AASE, for boxing. The AASE is a national scheme for elite athletes that allows them to train for their chosen sport and at the same time work towards a sports-science or foundation degree. The scheme has already had a number of notable successes: the most prominent being the swimmer, Rebecca Adlington, who won double gold at the Beijing Olympics.

I became involved in the scheme after being contacted by Kevin Hamblin, the principal at Filton College in Bristol. Filton College is home of the Bristol Academy of Sport, with academies in everything from basketball to cricket, fencing to taekwondo. Hamblin was keen to add boxing to his roster, and align it to my boxing academies. The problem was that boxing wasn't included in the AASE scheme. The amateur boxing people had tried and failed to get it included: they hadn't been able to come up with a structure that satisfied the educational demands of the scheme. So I went with Kevin to meet Skills Active, the overseeing body. We had to get educational people in to devise a system which dovetailed a proper educational plan into a boxing training programme. I was delighted when Skills Active accepted our proposal: it meant that boxing was now part of the AASE.

I was thrilled to be able to help set that up and I'm delighted to be the patron of the scheme. I don't get any money out of it or anything else but I get great satisfaction knowing that I helped to push that through. When the scheme faced its funding being cut, I went to see Hugh Robertson, who happens to be both the Olympic Minister and my local MP. I implored him to ensure that AASE for the ABA wasn't dropped. I said, 'Look, all these other sports are helped but boxing is being hard hit. Yet boxing delivered more medals per pound than any other sport at the last Olympics bar cycling. And not only that, but many of the kids come from economically deprived backgrounds.' I said, 'We desperately need this, Hugh, please don't let us down!' And they decided to keep the funding, which is great news.

One of the great things about my boxing career has been the many and varied opportunities it has opened up as a result. Doing *The Boxer* with Daniel Day-Lewis and Jim Sheridan, getting involved so intimately in the making of a film, was a wonderful experience. And that was just one of many projects I've been offered over the years. I couldn't tell you the number of reality TV programmes I've been asked to go on. *I'm A Celebrity* I've been offered a couple of times. *Dancing on Ice* and *Strictly Come Dancing*, I've turned those down, too; I've got two left feet and would just have been awful.

The one that did interest me, and which I ended up doing in 2007, was *Hell's Kitchen*. I think it interested me because it was a chance to learn a skill. I've never really done any cooking at home: Sandra is such a great cook and a good organiser that I've never really had to. All I could do was the basics, and I mean the basics. I thought to myself, you know what, I'll give this one a go, and learn how to do it from a master.

I made sure I did a little bit of preparation before I went on. My sister Laura was the catering manager at Kew Gardens, so I asked her if I could spend a couple of days in the kitchen. So I went in there and the guys were brilliant. They showed me the basics: how to cut and dice, how to peel vegetables quickly, handle meat, skin a chicken, that sort of thing. All very basic stuff, but at least I knew I could go on without making a fool of myself. And I certainly needed that. The camera crew came down to the house to shoot some footage for the programme. I made them a scrambled egg and managed to make a right hash of it. I burned the butter and the scrambled eggs were all brown. And the camera crew didn't say anything, just 'Lovely, yes that's lovely'. And then they played it on the opening programme, to show how bad I was at cooking.

It was the usual mixture of celebrities who took part: the other contestants that were on that series were Rosie Boycott, Paul Young, Jim Davidson, Adele Silva, Anneka Rice, Brian Dowling, Kelly LeBrock, Abigail Clancy and Lee Ryan. A right mix of characters, and we all lived together for the duration of the show. It was Marco Pierre White who was in charge, and I have to say, I instantly took a liking to the guy. He just had a sort of edge to him, you know. He is one of those guys that is such a professional. He had that drive, that determination to do things until he got them right, and that was an attitude I understood, that I'd always taken with my boxing.

We were divided into teams, red and blue, and we were

competing against each other. It was hard work and long days, and it could get monotonous with loads and loads of peeling and preparation. But that suited me because I am a grafter anyway and I'll stick at things and I am physically strong. I spent all my time in there doing chin-ups and sit-ups and squats and press-ups, just to keep going. It was a routine every day, so I just got up and I did my thing, stuck to the task and tried to have a good time with everybody. I was fine with that because I'd always had the discipline with my training. Some of the celebrities in there, they weren't used to working hard, and it didn't take long for them to get tired and for the cracks to show.

The producers knew that, so they would keep piling the pressure on. They were working you hard, and then there was Marco to deal with as well, because it was very much his kitchen, very much his way or the highway. He would teach you to do something, and then make you do it ten times, and I learned quite quickly that he would only let you make so many mistakes, because he would not suffer fools for long. I realised that this guy needs you to pay attention to him. I watched him working and listened very carefully, and talked to him and tried to understand him. Because I really wanted to learn and I actually did learn a lot of stuff and I got quite good. I think, too, that it helped that I knew so little about cooking. I was a clean slate for him, and he could teach me his way of doing things, without anything else getting in the way.

It was actually a great experience and it was good discipline. I was proud of myself that I was able to keep my cool the whole way through, because loads of things could have put you off. It was great to meet and spend time with all these people. Rosie Boycott was fantastic, she was great. She was ejected almost at the beginning, which I was very disappointed about because I loved her company. Abigail Clancy was stunning to look at and a sweetheart to boot, really sound and down to earth. Paul Young was a top guy, Kelly LeBrock was great fun too, and still looked amazing as well.

I ended up being the mediator between all those that were fighting and Jim Davidson seemed to be fighting with everybody. The funny thing is, I loved his company. I sat there every night roaring with laughter at him when he told jokes. I love old-fashioned jokes and I am not sensitive about Irish jokes or whatever else and he is a funny man. But he said some stuff to Brian Dowling that he shouldn't have and Brian took offence. I remember saying to him, 'Look, Jim, you really don't need to be as rude as you are to people. You didn't need to be so hurtful to him.' Jim asked, 'How do you know?' because I wasn't actually there at the time. 'All I am saying is he was very upset . . .' I said, 'if you can't control your temper you should see somebody about it.' So he got up and walked out. He didn't speak to me. And there were so many complaints about what he'd said that Marco had to ask him to leave. It was a shame because he was a great character.

At the end of it all, it was between me and Adele Silva, the *Emmerdale* actress. It wasn't a cooking contest, and I knew that. If the show had been about who was the best cook, I would have come last. But it was a popularity contest, and whether it was because I'd kept my head down and got on with things, whether it was because of the mediation thing and getting on with people or whatever, people picked up the phone and voted for me, and I won. And that was a good feeling. It was nice to know that people actually liked me and liked my personality.

The funniest thing was that a few days after I'd finished the programme, I was invited to this event at the Roundhouse in north London. It was a charity thing and I was there on behalf of ITV. Sandra and I had got there a bit early, so we pulled up at the side of the road and went into this little restaurant to get a cup of coffee before the event started. As I walked in, this little young fellow was in there with his parents – he was about ten I would say. As I walked in, the boy saw me and recognised me. 'Oh my God, Mum!' he said. 'There's that famous chef, Barry McGuigan!'

Chapter 19

The Next Chapter

In 2005, I was inducted into the International Boxing Hall of Fame, a huge honour. I'd already been inducted into the World Boxing Hall of Fame in Los Angeles in 2000, but the International Boxing Hall of the Fame is the big one. I think it is only four fighters a year they induct, and then there are posthumous awards for fighters who have passed away and additional awards for referees, judges, managers and writers. In 2005, the boxing inductees were myself, Bobby Chacon, Terry Norris and an Italian guy called Duilio Loi. The writer Bert Sugar was inducted as was, posthumously, Harry Mullan, who had been the editor of *Boxing News* for so many years and a personal friend of mine.

The ceremony itself is held in a place called Canastota in upstate New York. There is a stadium there and a place where you get inducted, and the Days Inn, where all the inductees have to stay. It's based in Canastota in honour of Carmen Basilio, who was from there, and who in 1957 beat Sugar Ray Robinson for the world middleweight title, in one of the most famous fights in the history of boxing: Basilio won a split-decision verdict after fifteen thrilling rounds: the following year Robinson won his title back after another split decision – both contests were voted by *Ring* magazine as their fight of the year.

The International Boxing Hall of Fame only began in 1990, but it's a huge deal now. The induction ceremony is part of a weekend-long festival, and the population of the town quadruples, with boxing fans from all over the world coming to watch. There's a parade in open-top cars and they have Hollywood people down for that: the year I was there, Ryan O'Neal was the Grand Marshal. There are memorabilia fairs, and boxing matches and training sessions to go to as well as the ceremony itself. So it is a great event, and I was honoured to be part of it. To be included in that list, that family of great fighters and hugely popular fight people, was the icing on the cake of my career. It was nice to have that recognition of everything I had achieved.

I had always taken a back seat when it came to my own children and boxing. I never wanted to push it or promote it, but let them come to it naturally, make the decision themselves if they wanted to go down that route. They had to show an interest in it, because unless you are passionate about it, boxing is not a sport to be doing. And that was what my youngest son Shane did. He showed an interest and when he was sixteen he came to me and said, Dad, I would like to have a go at boxing.

I have spoken to so many parents over the years on this issue, people coming up to me and saying that their son would like to take up boxing; what should they do? I've always encouraged them and said, yes, absolutely, let him box. It doesn't matter where he is from, what background he is from, he will learn something out of it. He may learn that it is not for him but he will enjoy it. He will enjoy the discipline, the training, he will enjoy the camaraderie in the gym. He will learn how to defend himself and, what is more, he can vent his spleen and get rid of his anger in a positive way and he won't want to take it out on somebody on the street. Even so, when Shane said he wanted to box, I've got to be honest and say that my initial thought was, I'm not sure I want him to do it. I told him to go away and think about it, which he did. He went off for a couple of weeks and he didn't change his mind. He came back and said, you know, Dad, I really do want to do it.

Shane's mind was made up, and I wasn't going to change it. Which left two options. I could let him go to the local club, down to the Aylesham club which we had become members of, to be trained. But I was worried they would be queuing up round the block to decapitate him, because of his surname. Alternatively, I thought, I could train him myself through the club. And so that is what I did: I went and got myself a proper ABA coaching licence. I had to go off for four weekends and do the courses, get my assistant coach badge, and then the full one. I got my badges and started to train Shane. We trained down at the Aylesham club and got him a couple of contests. It was difficult to begin with: we went to so many tournaments and the number of times people would pull out: they'd see Shane's surname and decide they didn't want to fight.

I remember one of the first fights we got him, against a guy called Mark McKiernan, who went on to win the London ABAs at light heavyweight. Shane is a light middleweight, a junior middleweight, so he was giving away quite a bit of weight. The fight was in Crawley, at one of the hotels down by the airport, and it was only Shane's second fight – McKiernan had fought at least fifteen – but I could see he was good. He had a couple of technical deficiencies, but I had trained him really hard, and Shane looked good. His body punches were great and he could bang really hard: he fought like a pro because I trained him like a pro. I was sitting on the sidelines shouting my head off, and in the third round Shane knocked McKiernan out with a body shot. It was a great performance.

So I could see from the start that Shane had potential. I remember Steve Collins was there that night, and he was all, 'Who is this guy?' He didn't know he was my son. In the next fight, Shane didn't have it all his own way: his opponent was older and more experienced, and there was more to deal with. But Shane still did well: Ricky Hatton was there that night and was impressed with him, thought his upper-body movement was very good. Then we went to Dublin to fight this guy who was very experienced and Shane knocked him out in the first round.

About this time I met a guy called Lee Pullen who was a GB coach and he lived in Kent, albeit Romney Marsh. I was always conscious that I was training Shane like a pro and I needed someone really good to coach him in the amateur style. Lee is one of the best ABA coaches I have ever met. What's more, he's one of the most fantastic human beings you could hope to meet. He's a gentleman and Shane and I have so much to thank him for, for all his help in training Shane.

We entered the Novice Championships, which is open to anyone who has had less than ten fights. Shane won the Southern Counties section easily, and we went up to Coventry for the last sixteen. His opponent was this guy called Curtis Valentine, who'd had eight fights and won seven by a knockout. Before that, he'd had about forty kick-boxing bouts. So he was a good fighter and very experienced, but Shane took the punches and gave him a hammering. We went up to Newbiggin near Newcastle for the quarterfinals, where Shane beat this guy called James Maxwell, who was Shane Neary's son. In the semis, he took on this army boxer, a guy by the name of Hepplewhite. He was talented, long and rangy with a very good style, but Shane was still too good for him, and knocked him out in the second.

I was enjoying being involved. I was loving the coaching and the journey, living the life with him and travelling down that route. I got a sense of what it must have been like for Dad and my family when I had been fighting all those years before. So Shane was through to the final, which took place down at the naval dock in Portsmouth, against a guy called Knighton from the Raleigh club in Essex. The guy was quite good on his feet, but Shane closed him down in the second and was all over him in the third. I thought Shane had beaten him clearly enough, but when they announced he had won, the crowd booed him. They booed him because of who he was: they thought he'd got the result because he was my son. Which was, of course, complete rubbish.

The next year, I entered Shane for the Ulster Seniors. He had still only had about sixteen bouts or so at this stage. He won his way through to the semi-finals, where he fought a guy called James Ferron from the Holy Family club. Ferron had won a handful of All-Ireland juvenile titles and Four Nations titles, and was a far more experienced fighter: very quick, very flashy. He had quick hands and got a load of shots in, in the first round, but Shane buried a couple of left hooks into his body and took the steam out of him. In the second round, Shane knocked him down with a right hand. The guy got up, but was completely gone, so the referee stopped the fight. In the final, Shane beat a guy called Eamon Macauley. It was another close decision, but Shane got it, and once again the crowd booed. Once again, I felt that was desperately unfair on him.

It was heartbreaking to hear that reaction as a father, particularly as I knew exactly how hard Shane had been working to win the title. He had trained so hard, twice or three times a day. He'd have one day's rest a week and that would be it. He'd watched his food meticulously and was a really good kid. So to hear people booing him when he'd put all that effort in was very frustrating. Shane was really good about it: he took it on the chin and said, onwards and upwards. So we went down for the Irish Under-21s in October/November 2008: Shane had four fights and won the title at 71kg. I was just so proud of him to have done that.

In early 2009, Shane took a contest against a navy guy down in Hastings. He was a little bull of a guy, he came running in and firing punches non-stop. The ring was about twelve or fourteen feet square – very small. Shane was firing back and I thought he hurt him a few times to the body but the rounds were short and it was over too quickly. I thought he deserved to win it but the other kid got it. We then bypassed the English ABA to go instead for the Ulster Seniors again in 2009. Shane was up against this guy called Niall McGinley from Omagh in the semi-finals. He beat this guy all over the place, completely hammered him. But somehow the decision went against him.

I'd been there myself, of course, back in my own amateur days. At the European Juniors against Yuri Gladychev, and at the Moscow Olympics against Wilfred Kabunda, I'd had to deal with bad decisions going against me. After Shane lost the decision against McGinley, he did a half-hour on the pads with Lee Pullen just to finish, just to get it out of the system. We were going to do some training over the summer, do a couple of camps, but Shane said, 'Dad, I'm giving it a break now.' I could completely understand where he was coming from: I'd done the same myself after Moscow.

After that, Shane became a personal trainer. He did a Level 3 Premier course and he got 100 per cent: not many of them get that. He is now working in a high-end gym in Chelsea called KX. Peter Douben, who owns the club, has been very good to him: he sponsored Shane during the last couple of years of his amateur boxing, allowing him to train properly, which he was very grateful for. He loves what he is doing now, and is still madly interested in the boxing, especially the nutrition and strength and condition training. But whether he will get back into the ring or not, I don't know.

I'm proud of Shane: I'm proud of all my children. They've all chosen such different careers: my eldest son Blain is a musician;

Nika is an actress. Jake is a scratch golfer, and spent some time out in Florida playing over there. He came back and finished his business degree, and did an internship with IMG, the sports agency. He's now working with me on my academies and my promotions. They've all done well for themselves and I couldn't be a prouder father.

Looking after Shane set something off in me. Getting back into that everyday routine and doing the training, I really liked that feeling. I got a lot out of watching Shane learning, doing things that Lee and I had taught him. I could see that although boxing is a tough old business, when people listened to you and put the effort in, you could actually be quite successful. Working with Shane really got me thinking about helping other guys, managing and training and looking after them.

The first guy I signed was a kid that went through the Novice Championships with Shane called Troy James, a super featherweight from Coventry. I took on a guy called Chris Keane, who won the ABA heavyweight title in 2009. I also signed Carl Frampton, who is this incredibly talented kid from Belfast. I think Carl is world class. At the time of writing, he's had eight fights, eight unbeatens and five stoppages. In December 2010 he beat Gavin Reid in two rounds to win the Celtic title.

The first show that I put on was in Belfast. I went back to Belfast because that is where I started, that is where my fan base is. It's also where Frampton is from and it was an outstanding success. We got a great crowd at the Ulster Hall, a lot of excitement, and Carl performed absolutely brilliantly. He was taking on Yuri Voronin, a three-times European title challenger, and he just wiped the floor with him. Carl dropped him twice and battered the living daylights out of him. The referee had to stop the fight, otherwise Carl would have flattened him. He gave a great performance, and the two other guys won on the undercard too.

We had six fights in total, six great fights, and everybody was thrilled.

I was delighted at how well the evening went, both inside and outside the ring. Given the current economic situation, especially over in Ireland, I couldn't have picked a more difficult time to set out as a promoter. But there's nothing I like better than a challenge, and we just knuckled down and got on with it. We had a great response from people for what we were trying to do: the Board of Control, the City Hall and the media have all been hugely supportive of our efforts. Setanta came on board to do the television coverage, which was a great boost. They've signed up to show a number of fights and I think it's a fantastic deal all round: I can bring them great fights and an amazing atmosphere: they can give my young boxers the sort of exposure that will kick-start their careers.

I have to tell you, the noise and the atmosphere of the hall brought it all back for me. I got the old butterflies in the stomach I used to get, was really living it with my fighters. I think the fact that Carl Frampton is from Belfast makes it slightly closer between me and him, the fact that I have been down the road that he has been down and been involved with the guys that he has been involved with. He's almost become part of the family: he comes down to my house to train, and is good friends with Jake and Shane. Shane has helped him a lot with the nutrition and everything: he's a genius at drawing up these diet sheets and sorting out the strength and condition training.

It's certainly not a quiet life I've chosen for myself. I've got the media work to keep me busy. I've been writing my weekly column for the *Daily Mirror* for twelve years now and still love it. I collaborate with the very talented Kevin Garside, who's a lovely man and who I've been working with for several years. Then there are the TV commentaries: I'm back working with Sky now and the new head of boxing Adam Smith is a dear friend of mine. Adam has taken over the reins and apart from being a top presenter, he is a great man: passionate, hard-working, loves his boxing and has an encyclopaedic knowledge of the game. He has a great team of talented people around him who work extremely hard and I look forward to working with them extensively in the future. And I've also got the academies to take care of.

I love to be busy and I love to be active, and I like to have a number of irons in the fire. I'd love for the promoting to really take off. I would like to promote and manage a stable of fighters and bring guys through to become champions, British, European and ultimately world champions. I'd love to build that stable and have my own brand of gyms, and have the academies where I give kids an opportunity to realise their dream and to stay in education. I have got Shane, who has tremendous knowledge on the sport, and Jake has a business degree and I would like the two of them to be involved with me, because they know the business intricately. And obviously Blain has his own thing and Nika has her own thing.

We'll see. After all, who knows how things will turn out? One thing I've learned over the years is that things change. I don't even know where I'll be living in ten years' time. We've lived in the same house for twenty-one years now, and it's been a lovely place, and the kids have great memories here. But it is important not to get too emotionally attached to property: it's only bricks and mortar. So maybe it's time to move closer into London, or further down into the countryside: it'll depend how the promoting goes, how much time I'll need to spend in the capital. But life is great and I just hope it keeps going. I hope I have good health and all my family have good health. We continue to be happy and to do what we enjoy doing and make a living at it. You can't really ask for much more than that.

If you're a young person thinking about going into boxing, or are a parent whose child is interested in boxing, my advice would be to go for it. Amateur boxing is very safe. Kids are competing in the same age bracket, in the same weight category: you cannot box anybody who is more than a kilo and a half heavier than you, unless the parties have agreed, so that is three pounds difference maximum, and there are age limits as well. The majority of competition gloves are well-padded, close-cell foam, injected moulding so that most of the padding is at the front. Occasionally there are accidents when gloves are a bit worn or whatever, but everybody wears a head guard and you never get more than one standing count. More than one standing count in a round means the fight is over.

Have a go for all the reasons I have mentioned before: it teaches kids discipline, self-respect, respect for others, goal-setting, getting a chance to get fit, learning about nutrition, what is good for you and what is bad for you. There's the chance to travel and get all excited about something, have something to look forward to. For many kids who are not straight-A students, life can feel confusing and unfulfilled and they don't know what to do. Taking part in boxing can be an answer to all that, it really can.

Boxing is good for you. It is really good for you. You'll find out whether or not it is for you and, if nothing else, it will give you an interest in the sport. You can't box until you are twelve years old, but even if you are younger, you can learn the basics: they will train you first in stance and guard, footwork, how to deliver a straight punch, how to deliver a hook, how to put combinations together, how to move forward and back. Only then will you get into touch sparring, and then you get into open sparring. And they will always spar you with someone of similar weight. And it is great fun, too. Great fun for these kids, and they get so excited about going up against competition. It doesn't work for everybody, but it is always good to have a go at it. I would definitely recommend it for anybody.

I really hope that in the years ahead, boxing continues to

blossom and get better. And safer too. We need to find a way to have more clarity in the sport, more simplicity and less clutter. There are loads of different titles and organisations – junior champions and champions emeritus and what have you – and it has got to be sorted out. That is going to take time because it means cutting people out who are at the moment earning money. Sorting all that out is not going to be easy.

But it needs to be done. Boxing needs to sort this out to stop the rot, to get the sport back to where it belongs. There's competition now from the Ultimate Fighting Championship and mixed martial arts, whatever you want to call it. And that's attracting fans who would otherwise be interested in boxing. I don't think UFC involves the same level of skill as boxing. It takes an awful lot of skill to be good at boxing, and phenomenal dedication. That's because you are only able to strike with your upper body, not your legs. Your legs are there to get you into position to punch and get you out of position defensively and to enable you to hit with power. For me, boxing at its best is the greatest skill of all: it is an art.

A guy can throw a punch and miss your chin by two millimetres and nothing happens. Or he can throw a punch with that tiny fraction of a difference and knock you out. That is why people talk about the art of boxing. You can call it brutal if you want, for sure, but don't tell me that it isn't art. You see Sugar Ray Robinson box, and watch the level of skill involved. You get someone like Muhammad Ali who is six foot three and sixteen stone, being able to move as gracefully as he did around the ring. You look at his speed and coordination, dexterity and fluidity, you look at the way he could ride a punch, and if that isn't art, I don't know what is.

Boxing may be brutal. There may be blood and bruising and hurt and pain, but that is part of the art too. It remains for me the greatest sport in the world, no question about it. The skills you need to succeed, there are only certain guys who can do it to the highest level. But that almost makes it more endearing: that there are only a few that can actually reach the very top, and do so with grace and dignity and class. For a while, I was fortunate enough to be among them, and no one can ever take that away from me. Boxing has inspired my life, and if my story can inspire others to follow me into the ring, then that makes all my achievements even more worthwhile.

Acknowledgements

My thanks go to everyone who helped me get this book together: David Phillips for his ongoing help and support, along with all at James Grant; Ed Faulkner and his team at Virgin and Random House for their help and encouragement; Tom Bromley for his patience, hard work and understanding; Duncan Raban and the photo editors at the *Daily Star* for helping me to find the photographs I needed.

There are several unsung heroes to whom I am extremely grateful:Eamon McAvoy and his family; also Michael Lavery and Donnell Deeny's unconditional support made a huge difference to my professional and personal life during a difficult time. I'd also like to mention Paul Dunkley and David Hammond, who were too modest to let me mention them elsewhere. During my career I had passionate and fanatic supporters who travelled long and far both to see me box and to welcome me home: thank you.

Last but by no means least, to the McGuigan and Mealiff families, who have been a rock bed of support right from the beginning. You took the punches with me and sometimes even for me and for that I can never thank you enough. The fight goes on – by my estimation we're just entering round eight – and I'm lucky to have you in my corner.

Index